WHAT ME BEFELL

WORKS BY THE SAME AUTHOR

IN ENGLISH

A Literary History of the English People from the Origins to the Civil War, 3 vols.

English Wayfaring Life in the Middle Ages (XIVth Century).

English Novel in the time of Shakespeare.

A French Ambassador at the Court of Charles II (Count Cominges).

Piers Plowman, a contribution to the History of English Mysticism.

English Essays from a French Pen.

The Romance of a King's Life (James II of Scotland).

Shakespeare in France under the Ancient Régime.

With Americans of Past and Present Days.

The School for Ambassadors and other Essays.

IN FRENCH

Les Sports et Jeux d'Exercice dans l'Ancienne France.

Histoire abrégée de la Littérature Anglaise.

Ronsard (in the series "Les Grands Ecrivains Français").

Instructions aux Ambassadeurs de France en Angleterre (1648–1690).

Le Sentiment Américain pendant la Guerre.

IN LATIN

De Josepho Exoniensi vel Iscano.

Jusserand

WHAT ME BEFELL

The Reminiscences of

J. J. JUSSERAND

WITH ILLUSTRATIONS

> " Bot now, how trowe ye? suich a fantasye
> Fell me to mynd, that ay me thoght the bell
> Said to me ' Tell on, man, quwhat the befell.' "
> *The Kingis Quair.*

BOSTON AND NEW YORK

HOUGHTON MIFFLIN COMPANY

1933

PRINTED IN GREAT BRITAIN

TABLE OF CONTENTS

I

Saint-Haon-le-Châtel
Le Bachelard—Lyons

VI

AT THE COLLÈGE DE FRANCE
TURC—"LES GRANDS ECRIVAINS FRANÇAIS"
1885–1887

VII

LONDON ONCE MORE
1887–1890

VICTORIAN ENGLAND

VIII

PARIS ONCE MORE
1890–1898

LIST OF ILLUSTRATIONS

FOREWORD

THESE Reminiscences are offered to the reader unfinished, for, as the author was telling "what him befell," the call of Death came, and it has been deemed better to present them as they were left, rather than add anything to what the author himself had written.

INTRODUCTION

"THERE are seldom any events befalling... which concern
no more than a single person." So said an English writer
of nearly two centuries ago when life upon the earth was
not as interdependent as it is now. Those events which
befell M. Jules Jusserand were of concern to many — to
thousands, even hundreds of thousands, on both sides of
the Atlantic. Indeed, so intimately did events in America
touch his life and those of his life touch others, and so
much was he at home in what came to be his second land,
that it has been said of him: "Whichever way he crosses
the Atlantic, he is going home."

No envoy from the other side and of other native speech
was more at home in America or more widely beloved and
honored by our people than was he in his day here. There
was such charm and distinction in all that he did and said
that even when he did the most practical things and discussed the most prosaic subjects, a certain *élan* showed
itself — a glow of unusual intellectual ardor. One could
say of him what a countryman of his said of another,
"*Même quand l'oiseau marche on sent qu'il a des ailes.*" Often
he gave proof that he had the wings of eloquence.

Coming at thirty-seven to the United States, he found a
congenial spirit in the young President of that day,
Theodore Roosevelt. Their minds found fields of common
interest. The Ambassador, who had written books on
poetry, mysticism, wayfaring, English literature and criticism in general, and on ethnology, politics, and athletics
in particular, found a man in the Presidency who could
travel with him to the verges of the known. He discovered
also a match at one of the ancient games of which he had
written in his latest book, and also an American who could
walk long distances with him. With an exceptional back-

ground of study and in the enjoyment of such companionship, he easily acquired an understanding of the best in
American life.

When he retired in 1924, after twenty-two years of successful service, Mr. Root said of him that "no finer states-
manship, no more judicious diplomacy, no wiser sympathy
has ever taken part in the great affairs of the world." His
long and distinguished career embraced the period of the
Great War, with the years of our neutrality, our ultimate
part in the struggle, and the terrible aftermath of the
triumph. Through it all he maintained an attitude of
great dignity, patience, and intelligence, greatly assisted
by his wife, a representative of our highest American type.
It was not only France's but America's good fortune that
these twain were here in the days of international tension
and world conflict.

But there was back of his coming to America a period of
training, experience, and official acquaintance, extending
literally from England to Japan and from Russia to Tunis,
which equipped him to be at home anywhere in the world
and to have converse on equal terms with the greatest
minds of any land. The chapters which tell of his three
periods in London, culminating in the years when the
Victorian period "still shone in all its lustre," give to the
reader fresh and delightful associations with the statesmen,
the artists, the men of letters of that time. Another chapter
lets one share the intimacies of the gatherings of the
"thinkers, poets, historians, grammarians" in Paris who
habitually came "in the best dispositions" to the home of
one of the group. There one found what was "uppermost
in men's minds."

But still farther back are the exquisite chapters which
give a picture of French family life — simple, thrifty,
beautiful and moving in its sweet relations. One can better
understand French character after reading the last letter
of the father to the son. One scene can no more be forgotten than Millet's "Angelus":

After supper, evening prayers were said by our mother who, as well as our father, knelt on the floor, we with the institutrice back of them and the servants back of us.

It invites the remark that "those who believe that puritanism exists only in Protestant families have no idea of what it can be in a Catholic one."

M. Jusserand tells of his last visit to a great English historian who in the parting said, "Jusserand, I want you so much to ——" but could not finish the sentence. The wish of every reader of this charming work which ends so abruptly — the pen literally fell from his hand while at work upon it but a few days before his death — must be, "Oh, Monsieur Jusserand, I want you so much to finish it."

But we have in supplement his last words to America spoken across the sea which could never separate him from us — his "farewell forever," as he called his message:

The sands in the hour-glass are running low; I must take leave, probably forever. May peace, prosperity, happy homes be the meed of your energy, good sense and kind hearts. When we judge each other we are not bound to applaud all that the other does, nor even to avoid expressing our blame when there is cause; but blame must not be peppered with sarcasm and irony; the tone should be that of the affectionate reproach to a loved brother.... Remember this also, and be well persuaded of its truth: the future is not in the hands of Fate, but in ours.

He never ceased to be "the admirable Ambassador." He was in reality in constant friendly ambassadorial service between America and Europe to the end of his days — till death itself him befell.

JOHN H. FINLEY

CHAPTER I

On a spur of red granite, fronting the "Monts de la Madeleine" and overlooking the valley of the Loire, stands the small walled city of Saint-Haon-le-Châtel, *Sancti Abundi Castrum* in mediæval Latin. It was included in the territory of the Forez, made famous, as the Arcady of France, by the most popular of all the long-winded romances of the seventeenth century, *l'Astrée* of Honoré d'Urfé. The Forez, with its capital, in early days Feurs (Forum segusianorum) and later Montbrison, was ruled by its counts, one of whom, Renaud, had granted the inhabitants of Saint-Haon, in the thirteenth century, the right to fortify their place and had favoured them with a penal code, minutely foreseeing, with proper punishment, all the misbehaviours they might be guilty of: murder, arson, striking with a club or sword, causing blood to flow or not to flow; "if a man or a woman is caught in adultery, he or she will pay sixty sols," the sols going not to the wronged husband or wife, but to the count; the same for all misdeeds; the worse behaved the inhabitants, the better filled the count's coffers.

At the extinction of the second dynasty of its counts, Saint-Haon and the rest of the Forez passed, in the fourteenth century, by the marriage of the last heiress, into the ducal house of Bourbon, frequently at feud with the royal branch of the family. In the "Guerre de la Praguerie," so called on account of its similitude to the recent rebellion in Bohemia, Charles duc de Bourbon and other dukes and grandees, persuaded the young Dauphin, aged seventeen, to rise against his father

B

King Charles VII: as that Dauphin was the future
Louis XI they had no trouble, given his temper, in
persuading him. So there was civil war; the King came
in person in 1440 and laid siege to the fortresses of the
duc de Bourbon, among which Saint-Haon. After a
vigorous defence, still remembered by the inhabitants,
and embellished by legend, the place was stormed by the
royal army. The existence of a spring still in use, called
Fondange (the fount of the Angel), had been revealed,
it is said, to the inhabitants by an angel during the
siege. Given its site, however, it must have been of
more help to the besiegers than to the besieged; that
angel was obviously royalist.

Though broken down here and there, the walls still
surround the city, and ten or twelve towers, more or less
complete, remain, as well as the principal gate, which
has preserved, and a very rare curiosity they are, its
ogival doors of thick oak, studded with square-headed
protruding iron nails. What distinguished a town from
a village in those days, was not that the group of houses
should be especially large, but that it should possess a
continuous wall. When Louis XIV, who considered
that he had reason to complain of the people there,
ordered the walls of Orange to be demolished, the
citizens bitterly remonstrated for two reasons: their
place would cease to be a city, and the wolves could not
be kept out.

Numerous houses of the fifteenth or sixteenth centuries
are still in existence at Saint-Haon, some with protruding
upper floors, some embellished with towers and sculptured
stone mantels. The church was begun in the twelfth
century; a large door opposite the entrance leads through
the church to the old, now abandoned, cemetery, and is
surmounted by a grim inscription: One of the dead
of times gone addresses the new-comer, and the living
who accompany him, saying, "Where thou passest I
have passed; where I have passed thou shalt pass; like

thee I have been of the living; like me thou shalt be of the dead."

Westward of Saint-Haon rise mountains covered with forests, most of them belonging to the State, some small patches, to us; in front spreads the fertile valley of the Loire, bounded on the horizon by the hills of the Beaujolais which, according to the season, the weather, the hour of the day, assume a variety of hues, dark or pale green, dark or pale blue, pink in the sun, blue in the shade. A number of rivulets flow from the heights through wheat-fields, meadows and vineyards; they move on, now leisurely, now at a quicker pace, singing among the pebbles, outlined in their undulating course by trees and underbrush that take on in the distance the greenish-blue tints of the trees in old tapestries. The red roofs of villages or of numerous isolated farms brighten the landscape.

The Forez is near Auvergne; both were thickly populated by Celts in pre-Roman times. Some celtic traditions still survive, such as the reverence in which is held the very rare mistletoe growing on oaks, so important in druidic times. I remember a farmer of ours calling on my father and showing him with pride a branch of oak with the mistletoe still upon it. Such mistletoe was supposed to possess certain mysterious healing powers.

The year was divided for us into three parts: the chief one was spent in Saint-Haon, where we had our principal house, large, plain, strongly built, with an old-fashioned walled-in garden, clipped yew trees, a "bosquet" abundantly frequented by singing birds, a " clos " for fruit trees and vegetables, a " salle d'ombrage " lower down, and a pigeon-house. The view over the plain and the ridge of tall hills closing the horizon was lovely.

The family consisted of my father, mother, maternal grandfather, four children (two boys and two girls) and " Mademoiselle " the institutrice. Three of the children had been born in Lyons, in 1855, 1856 and 1857, I being the eldest; the youngest daughter was born at Saint-Haon ; the day of her baptism in the old church, one of the earliest of my childhood remembrances, was for the village a day of general festivity; the cortège seemed to our young eyes magnificent; sugared almonds and bright new sous were, according to custom, thrown by the handful from the windows of our house to the young people of the little city; the sous had been secured direct from the mint by my father so that they shone like gold and were not long allowed to lie idle on the ground.

My father, born in Lyons on " the first of the complementary days, year VII of the French Republic, one and indivisible," had studied at the *Lycée* and I consider as one of the treasures of my library, two little calf-bound volumes, *Le Cook de la Jeunesse*, an abbreviated account of the famous navigator's journey, bestowed on " ingenuum adolescentem Julium Jusserand " as a first prize for general " excellency." He practised law part of his life, until the death of his own father having left him well off, as " well off " was understood in those days; he centred his activities on the upbringing of his children and the management of his property, devoting, however, a considerable part of his time to reading. He never wrote a line for print, nor filled nor desired any function of any sort; his natural wit, absolute disinterestedness, his envying nobody, the sanity of his views and advice, won him the respect of all.

With his kindliness, however, he, and my mother too, had the austere ideal as to behaviour usual then in French families. My mother, of handsome features and great musical talents, was especially conspicuous for her firm will and her strict notion of duty. For her too the bringing up of her children was the chief object of her thoughts; mundane amusements were to her of no interest. We were early taught that there were two ways of doing things, great or small as they might be, the right way and the wrong way. Do not allow yourself, we were

told, to neglect the right way even in what may appear
indifferent; it would blunt your readiness to act
properly, as a matter of course, on occasions of more
importance. The tenets of morals and religion, the respect
and obedience due to parents and teachers, the importance
of availing oneself to the utmost of any occasion to learn,
were impressed on us so deeply as to be above cavil or
discussion. After supper, evening prayers were said
by our mother, who, as well as our father, knelt on
the floor, we, with the institutrice, back of them and the
servants back of us. Those who believe that puritanism
exists only in Protestant families have no idea of what
it can be in a Catholic one.

Withal great freedom was granted us; our parents
felt convinced that we would not take undue advantage
of it; firearms were early put in our hands; we were
allowed to roam our mountains freely, either by ourselves
or with the little peasants living on our property. We
walked great distances, sometimes as much as sixty
kilometres in a day, we climbed rocks, swam rivers:
for the body too must learn and develop; we did not
suspect how useful these "accomplishments" would
prove to one of us who was, long long afterwards, to be
Ambassador to America and join the President of the
United States in his rambles.

When we were older we were allowed to establish a
chemical laboratory on the ground floor of the pigeon-
house, but it is doubtful whether Mademoiselle or our
parents would have approved of our experiments if
they had known of them. For these tended to nothing
less than making gunpowder and gun-cotton. We had,
like Dr. Faustus, our books and retorts; the sisters would
heat the retorts; then the day for experimenting arrived;
we put some of our concoction in a great-grandfather's
flint-lock pistol discovered in a garret, attached the
deadly instrument to a tree of the "salle d'ombrage,"
pulled the trigger with a cord,—and behold! had the

humiliation of seeing our powder issue in bright sparks
from the priming-pan, while the load remained asleep in
the pistol. No accident happened, however, only the
pigeons in the room above were somewhat incommoded
by the fumes. The sole practical use our powder was
put to was to augment the unpretentious fireworks we
usually displayed on our mother's fête day, to which
display was sometimes added the performance of a play
composed, occasionally in verse, by Mademoiselle.

One item in our education would have pleased Ben
Franklin: we were taught to use as much as possible
our left hand, not to the extent of writing with it, but to
that of carrying heavy loads and playing billiards.
Franklin, as is well known, has for the subject of one of
his " Bagatelles " as he called them: " A complaint
of the left hand ": for the unjust preference accorded to
the right one.

The use of playthings was discouraged; we were
expected to shift for ourselves and find sports or means
of amusement without such help. When toys were
given us by friends of the family they were carefully
packed away in a cupboard where grand-nephews and
grand-nieces have since discovered them. Not many,
I am afraid, long survived the discovery.

On Sundays, the chief people of the place dined at our
house; dinner was still, at that time, the midday meal.
There came the justice of the peace, an old retired officer
with ruddy cheeks and white mustachio, making him
look like a Confederate captain; the school teacher
whose son was to die later in Cambodia, " far from
France, striving to win minds and hearts to her," as
reads the inscription on his tomb; the notary, a very
different person from what the word implies in America,
being the confidential business adviser of the local people,
the recorder of the deeds concerning their property
and their families. With them the parish priest and his
assistant. The latter, in our childhood, was Abbé

Mondel, an optimistic ever-smiling ecclesiastic, never losing his good humour in spite of persistent bad luck or inborn clumsiness; if he would sit, his cassock was sure to push back his chair and he would sit on the floor; when he wanted to catch a train he would arrive not many minutes, but just one, after the train had gone; when he risked a quotation he could never remember more than the first half. His duties, however, were faithfully performed. When, after many years of humble achievements, he retired to a home for aged priests, he wrote me a long letter so beautiful and touching that I would print it in full if it had not been lost in my many removals. In it he explained his views of life, his sense of duty and lack of ambition: and late, I found that we had lived unawares side by side with a saint.

His successor, Abbé Planche, was of a different sort; very pale, with a long, thin, hooked nose, a wide mouth and thin lips, a man of few words and many dreams, he gave all the hours not strictly needed by his religious functions, for which he was ever late, to mechanisms and inventions. At a time when such an art was a rarity, he was an excellent amateur photographer. His principal invention was an alarm clock, better justifying such a name than many others, for at the appointed time the mechanism fired a pistol; the firing lit a match and the match lit a candle. This invention was patented, a useless precaution, for no one tried to steal it, and it turned out that the public did not care to be awakened by a pistol shot.

At these meals, the children, as it was for them a sort of tuition, were allowed to come, just as usual. They were instructed to listen, but to speak only if a question was put to them, in which case they must try to answer in a proper tone, without boldness or shyness, a difficult equilibrium which they were expected to observe. When dessert was served they were given leave to go out; and out they went, climbed trees, girls included, in the "bosquet" and ate their cakes in what Ronsard called the "haute maison des oiseaux bocagers."

After the meal, the company played billiards, smoking and talking of the last events in Saint-Haon or in the world; and they were offered a beverage considered very elegant, because it was uncommon in this wine country, namely beer, of which we were allowed to have a sip, but only mixed with water, for no one knew whether this strange liquid was good for children.

Autumn was spent at Le Bachelard, a very modest old house, some two miles distant, in the midst of the little hamlet formed by the homes, stables, barns and cellars of the peasant families working on the property. The ceilings are supported in ancient fashion by apparent oak beams; the chief curiosity consists in a wall-paper of large dimensions dating back to the time of the Directoire, and representing pastoral and other scenes in the midst of the imaginary Greek ruins then so much the fashion. When, years and years later, I was sent to Poland at the time of the Bolshevist onslaught, I would go alone, of evenings, to the Lazienki park, and there meditate on how France could best help that country in her direst need. I was there in congenial surroundings, for I had found to my surprise, realized in stone by the last Polish king, Stanislas-Augustus, those same fancy Greek ruins, broken columns, bridges, statues and fountains, pictured on the wall-paper at Le Bachelard.

Almost every day, moreover, whatever the season or the weather, with us or without us, our parents drove to the Bachelard, returning at dusk when the angelus bells of the neighbouring village of Renaison could be heard, now melancholy, now merry, one of their favourite chimes of the latter sort being the tune of the Roi Dagobert, not a very religious one, in spite of Saint Eloi playing a part in the song. At the Bachelard grew for us the necessaries of life. The property is not a very large one, but its products are varied, including wheat, wine, meat, eggs and poultry, milk and cheese, fruit, nuts and chestnuts in abundance, wood for the fire, granite for constructions or repairs, walnut oil for the salad (to our taste most excellent), colza oil for the peasant's lamps, exactly similar in shape to the Roman ones, but of iron instead of terra-cotta, and with an iron hook which allows them to be hung to any wooden post. Little money was needed to live decently on such an estate. I remember the *granger* who culti-vated the mountain part of the property, saying once with pride (and some exaggeration) to my father : " I buy only salt and iron."

All the peasants on that land, *granger* included, were, and still are, *métayers*, which means that, besides they, their crops, and their cattle (a fixed number of which were supplied to them by us) being housed, their remuneration consisted in half the products of the land. Such products, at least the solid ones, were brought before a wooden *galerie*, opening on the court-yard and on which my parents usually sat. The *métayer* made two heaps, and it was his interest to make them equal, for we had the right to select either. According to customs established time out of mind, they rendered also certain services such as fetching wood in the mountain for our use in winter, or stone (blue granite) when we built, or carrying to the Loire canal, by which it would be conveyed to Paris, the year's vintage, and it was quite a sight to see, on an autumn morning, the procession of carts, loaded with casks, following, at the slow pace of the oxen or cows, the alley which leads through the property to the high-road.

There was also what was called the Easter omelet. On Easter morning each "métayer" brought to Saint-Haon a fixed number of chickens, eggs, cheeses, pounds of butter; the entrance hall was filled with them; cacklings arose from the baskets. Most of these supplies were taken the next day to market by our man-servant and sold.

No machinery was used; corn was threshed with the flail. Before the threshing began, the workers vied with each other who could throw his flail furthest. The one who was last in the contest had to take the worst place at the flaying, where he would receive most dust in his face; and the one who had succeeded best would, before the work began, stand up and shout to the four points of the compass: " It is So-and-so who is the pig."

Six families lived on the estate; there never was any serious trouble; if by chance a contention arose between some of them, our parents were allowed in their patriarchal way to settle it. If an event of any importance happened in our family, either happy or sad, a marriage or burial, they took part in it; they were of the family.

Most of them saved enough to buy some small piece of land and a house in which, when age should come, to quietly spend their last years. With them, as with most French people, the love of mother earth was inborn. When the Great War came, one of them who had already joined his regiment, secured a twenty-four-hours permit for some important business. When night came and there was moonlight, he thought of a field that he had left half ploughed. He went to the stable, hitched his cows to a plough and, clad in the red trousers that our soldiers unfortunately still wore in those early days of the conflict, he set to work under the moon, an unusual sight and fit to tempt an artist's brush. At the first rays of the sun the ploughing was finished, and he returned to the front to defend the land on which he and his fellow-peasants were born.

The first thing done when we came to settle at the Bachelard, and autumnal fogs and rains began to threaten, was to put every member of the family in *sabots* (wooden shoes), a kind of foot-wear to which one becomes easily accustomed: none better to ward off the cold. The question was of importance with the primitive means of heating then in use and with a *chattière* (cat-hole) open in every door, including the front one opening on the courtyard, in order to allow Mr. Puss to freely go a-hunting.

It was for us children a season of climbing; among thorns and brambles we reached with particular glee the *Grand Roc*, from which there was an extensive view over the plain, and whose cavities and strange stone corridors gave it the appearance of a mediæval fortress. A great deal of merry hide and seek took place in the intricacies of the granite. The *Grand Roc* was so beloved that when my health began to break, fearing that I might not long be able to visit it, I went up once more, and remembering so many happy hours spent there, feeling that I was perhaps parting with a friend, I bent down and kissed the rugged stone good-bye.

The crops came in one by one, cereals, potatoes, apples, peaches, beans, nuts and almonds, chestnuts, and, most important of all, wine. We remained at the Bachelard until after the All Hallow fair, the principal cattle fair of the region, and until after the sale of most of those crops. Patiently we waited for the merchants, who came or did not come, so that we often had to prolong our stay.

In mediæval times, masters and servants ate their meals in the same hall; with the growing refinement of manners, more seclusion was relished, and masters retired into their " withdrawing-rooms," the present-day drawing-room. Some trace of the older customs remained at the Bachelard: the servants ate in the kitchen at a large oaken board, near the tall-mantled chimney where a complicated machinery, long out of use, had in time past turned a spit of considerable magnitude. We ate in the room with the beautiful wall-paper, but a glass door between the two places allowed the masters to see the servants and the servants to see the masters.

The long autumn evenings were devoted to the pre-

paration of the journey to Lyons, where the winter
was always spent. There too the Bachelard had partly
to feed us; in view of the voyage, nuts and dry beans
were selected, apples were wrapped one by one in paper
and large square baskets were filled with them. Butter,
melted and salted for safe preservation, dry cheese,
potatoes, wine, nut-oil, hams and other goods were
also made ready and sent to Lyons one hundred kilometres away, not by that new-fangled, expensive device,
the railway, but by the road, in care of a *roulier* (carrier),
who brought the provisions to our door. Once or twice
during the winter a servant came with a new supply,
some chickens and other commodities.

The rapid increase of the family (three children in
three years, a fourth a little later) had caused it to leave
its inadequate apartment, Rue des Marronniers, near the
Place Bellecour, and move to the Place Napoléon, a
square in the centre of which was a statue of the
Emperor, represented with his hand on his heart, uttering
the words attributed to him on his return from Elba:
" Lyonnais, je vous aime." At the revolution of 1870,
as the Lyonnese had ceased to love any Napoleon, the
statue was broken to pieces.

My father had once seen the original of that image.
When the return from Elba took place, being then a lad
of fifteen, he had witnessed an impressive scene on the
Place Bellecour, and had returned home carrying two un-
forgettable memories: he had seen the great Emperor
and had lost his umbrella.

The Place Napoléon, with its trees, stone benches,
some plots of grass and flowers, was for us a delightful
playground. " Mademoiselle " accompanied us, and
our parents could see from their windows on the second
floor what we were doing. When it was raining, and
rain is a frequent calamity in Lyons, we adjourned to
the near-by principal railway station of the city; its
vast hall afforded a convenient and sheltered place for

us to run after our balls, roll our hoops or play hide-and-seek: neither travellers nor officials in those kindly days ever objected.

The family later moved to a corner house of the Quai d'Occident and Rue de la Reine, the latter re-baptised Rue Franklin in 1870 as better befitting a republic. Our apartment overlooked the Saône river, on which a number of small steamers went up and down stream, and some bigger ones, called *Gladiateurs*, plied between Lyons and Mâcon. The *Gladiateurs* stopped just opposite our house; when one of them was about to start, there was great activity on the quay, whistling of the boat, shouting from the mariners, and four little heads never failed to watch the proceedings from our windows. On the other side of the water rose the steep hills of Saint-Just and Fourvières, so steep that the principal public access to the top was by endless steps (there is now a funicular railway); but there were several " passages," that is gardens, which by paying two cents one could use: if you were religiously inclined, one there was adorned with representations of the stations of the Cross; if fond of antiquities you had the " Passage Gay," full of Roman remains found on the spot, some magnified by glowing inscriptions, as the one at the entrance where a small rusty sword was seen dangling, and still dangles I believe, from a hook, and was described as " a con-queror's sword, found in a grave," a description which filled our father with merriment.

At Lyons, to the teachings of " Mademoiselle " were added those of various professors of literature, history, music, dancing, etc., for, even when the revenues of the family began to dwindle, there ever was money for what pertained to education. Dancing was in accordance with the old-established rules, beginning with the basic principles of " the four positions " ; the fourth, in which, turned outward, the tip of each foot must touch the heel of the other, the two closely joined, was of especial difficulty. The classical *révérence* was taught, even to the boys, just for the sake of suppleness; and when one of them saw later, at a foreign court, certain great ladies curtsy to their sovereign, he could not help remembering Monsieur Alexandre and his tiny fiddle and think that some lessons by him would not have been amiss to teach those handsome persons the difference between a genuflexion and a *révérence*.

On Christmas Day there were no gifts, no Christmas tree, no mundane festivity. The religious character of the fête was strictly observed; we were taken sometimes to the grand old cathedral, very impressive with its dark walls, its gloom, partly dispelled on such occasions by hundreds of candles, and with the grandiose character of ceremonies performed by the Archbishop in accordance with the ancient liturgy special to Lyons, "*prima sedes Galliarum.*" Gifts, wishes, and compliments were reserved for New Year's Day.

We were, however, usually treated to a puppet play during this season, with serious and comical scenes, the chief of which was a real mystery play, in the purest mediæval style, representing *la Crèche* (the manger), the coming of the shepherds, of the wise Kings of the East, the sky full of paper angels: it seemed to us a vision of Paradise. What made it even more mediæval was, after the arrival of the shepherds and the kings, that of Monsieur and Madame Coquard, plain old bourgeois of Lyons, bewildered at their own audacity, watching their steps with care in those unknown lands: " Pose là ton petit pied," said the good husband to the good wife. Such a mixture of past and present days and manners was usual in old mysteries and pictures; as the kings of England in the Middle Ages were French and spoke French, Herod and Tiberius in English mystery plays spoke French too. Did we ever feel greater emotion at any play? I doubt it.

Spring came, and with it the time to return to Saint-

Haon. Each change, though foreseen and customary, was for us four children a cause of joy. We would see again the garden and the yew trees, the mountains and plain, the old towers, and the faithful servant Pierre. And what would Pierre have in store for us? He always had something. Pierre was our clever factotum, gardener, coachman, serving at table on Sundays. He knew all sorts of beautiful secrets; he could capture birds and squirrels and build for them comfortable habitations in which they led, as we thought, happy lives. Such a cage, in the shape of a two-floor house for a squirrel, had a whirligig that set in motion three sawyers sawing a tree into boards, while a dark-faced chimney-sweep was cleaning the squirrel's chimney.

When he retired for old age to his native village not far from ours, Pierre opened a small restaurant and would now and then indulge in a little poaching. He once gave us a dog of his own training. The dog did not look much, but he was so clever! We had even to un-teach him some of his tricks. We were now allowed to go shooting, and often our sisters accompanied us. Game was exceedingly scarce. The best place to find any was the neighbourhood of Châtel-Montagne, a place in the mountains thirty kilometres from Saint-Haon, sixty there and back, which we covered on foot, rising therefor at four o'clock in the morning. When a shot was heard in the distance, dog Perdreau would rush with all speed to the spot, and while the elegant retrievers of elegant sportsmen were elegantly beating the bush, he would discover the wounded piece of game, and concealing his movements in the underbrush, silently deposit it at our feet; we had to make him understand that this trick was bad manners.

Years came for him too, as they come all too early for good men and good dogs; the trip to Châtel-Montagne ceased to be a pleasure for him. When we started at the usual hour and took the road to the mounts, he understood perfectly what was meant and pretended to be delighted; he wagged his tail, barked and jumped about. But when part only of the road had been covered, he turned round unobserved and sneaked home, leaving us with a greatly diminished chance of finding any game. Years had made of him a slacker.

Long afterwards, when living in Paris, I was sometimes invited to shooting parties on a grander scale; once to a *chevreuil* hunt at Compiègne. All the other guests were men of importance, the Prefect of the Seine, the Prefect of Police, Mr. Jules Ferry, etc. Alined along the roads in the forest we kept watch. It so happened that the fates were unfavourable to the great people, none of them had anything to fire at; I was the only member of the party who saw any *chevreuils* : a pair of young ones, who came within rifle range, so pretty, with their graceful heads and their timorous appealing dark eyes. "Run away," I said to them, "young fools that you are; you will get shot at." They ran away and did not tell, and I reveal the fact now for the first time. When we returned at dusk Jules Ferry fired at the moon in order to have had a shot at something.

The impression more and more grew upon me that while, for a very long time to come, killing would be a necessity, less and less pleasure would be found in killing for killing's sake. Returning home once very late I saw a large bird high in the sky, so far away that I did not think I could hit it. I fired, however, and the bird fell wounded. It was a big owl not of the brown kind, but with a mixture of white and pale-yellow feathers. There was such an expression of sadness and reproach in its large dark eyes that I was touched to the quick and I was beset, so to say, with a desire never to incur such a look again. This shot was the last I ever fired at any harmless creature.

As I was talking of such things, in later years, at Washington, with a diplomatic colleague of mine from

Central America, he told me that he had had a similar experience. In a forest of his country he fired at a little monkey seen in the distance and wounded it. The monkey put its hand to its breast and showed it covered with blood, with an air of silent reproach obviously meaning: What had I done? For my colleague, too, that shot was his last.

CHAPTER II

Two hills face each other on the banks of the Saône, as this river flows through Lyons to join the Rhône a little farther below—the hill of Fourvière famous for its pilgrimage and the hill of La Croix Rousse famous for its silk-weaving. You cannot follow any street in the latter part of the city without hearing the ticking of the looms. If you enter one of the houses you will find yourself in a more than modest, stuffy room, sometimes only one for a whole family, an iron stove in the middle for heating and cooking; the *canut* carefully raising the wrappers that protect his work, will show you, illuminating, so to say, the shabby place, the most dazzling silks that will shine later at the court of kings.

At the summit of the hill, facing the river, is a well-known educational establishment called Les Chartreux, from the name of a *Chartreuse* formerly existing there. The establishment is in the hands of liberal-minded secular priests whose methods in my day were far ahead of those prevailing then in State Lycées. Besides the classical studies, drawing, the learning of one foreign language, physical exercises, gymnastics, swimming, walking, were compulsory. To a park in the country, which belonged to the Institution, the boys were taken during the summer months, on Sundays and Thursdays, to do what they pleased; they had the use of a gymnasium, were allowed to ride, play billiards, etc. A small plot of ground was allotted to the elder ones to design, plant and cultivate as they chose. All pupils at the Chartreux were *internes*, that is boarders; they had two brief holidays, on New Year's Day and Easter Day, and a long one during August and September. The discipline was strict but not unbearable, the hardest thing for those not inured, was to rise every morning to the sound of a merciless bell at 5.30 and to remain silent most of the time, even during meals, when some books of travel were read aloud to us. In the recreation hours our lungs got their free play.

To this place we were sent, my brother and I, when we were nine and ten years of age and the teachings of " Mademoiselle " had become, for us boys, inadequate. It was long before we could cheerfully accept our new fate. To be away most of the year from father, mother, sisters, the servant Pierre, the Grand Roc, the warmth of the family hearth, caused us fits of despondency. We longed for the holidays and counted the days until they came round. Once, on the brief New Year's one, which, contrary to custom, was spent at Saint-Haon (the merchants had probably been slack in buying our crops), my father caused me a pleasure so keen that I still gratefully feel it: he placed in my hands the first real novel I had ever read. And what a novel! Everything so new, so unexpected, so entrancing, people the like of whom you had never seen and whom you now saw and heard, whom you loved or hated or laughed at! Nothing less than Walter Scott's *Ivanhoe*: young people, it appears, now feel differently, but we are not ashamed and we still bless the name of old Sir Walter. The pity was that the holiday being so brief (only two or three days, and there being so much to do, climbing, walking, polite visits to pay, contrary to our liking), I could not finish the wonderful book, and had to wait till the Easter holiday to learn what became of Rebecca, the Templar and the others.

The flood-gate for new emotions was now open, and, without speaking of Jules Verne's wonderful journeys to

the United States or to the moon, Chateaubriand's
romantic stories, *Les Martyrs, Atala, Les Natchez* were put
into our hands.   We read them in a place which deepened
our emotions.   When everybody had retired at night,
my brother and I, risking the severest reprimand, silently
crept out of the house, made ourselves known to the
watch-dog, petted him and persuaded him to kindly not
bark; we reached a diminutive hot-house in the *clos*.
To the light of candles brought in our pockets, surrounded
by tiny plants in tiny pots, breathing a tepid atmosphere
loaded with moisture and the aroma of leaves and flowers,
while all outside was cold and dark, we followed in their
adventures the magic writer's Roman or Indian heroes.
I have since seen the primeval forests of the West, the
real prairies, the lakes like inland seas, the Rockies, the
real " Mechacébé," but they never gave me as vivid an
impression of haunted wilderness, of multicoloured vines
and flowers, of poetical solitude and natural beauty, as
that which we received in the midst of those tiny plants
and their tiny pots in the diminutive hot-house.

When I better understood the importance and charm
of classical learning, I became reconciled to my fate at
the Chartreux, especially when, having reached the class
called *Humanités* (the highest but two), I fell under the
influence of an extraordinary man, Abbé Déchelette.
Belonging to a well-to-do family of the Forez, he had
studied extensively, being equally proficient in Greek,
Latin, English and Italian, and he possessed, moreover,
that secret so important for a teacher, he knew how to
excite admiration for what he was teaching.   While
pupils elsewhere might grumble at learning Greek, of his
he made enthusiasts.   He would now and then set apart
a whole week for Greek, during which nothing else was
taught nor thought of but Greek.   We had reached a
sufficient degree of proficiency to read the *Odyssey* aloud,
for our pleasure, each of the pupils in turn reading and
interpreting a sequence of verses.

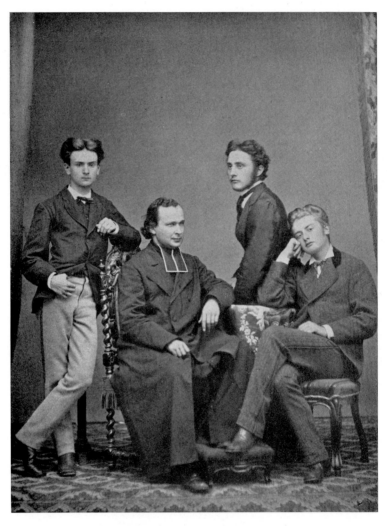

THE ABBÉ AND HIS TRAVELLERS

face p. 21

A good sport withal, the Abbé persuaded my parents to consent to my first trips beyond the familiar way from Saint-Haon to Lyons and from Lyons to Saint-Haon. He took with him two or three of his pupils. In order to accustom us not to be embarrassed by trifles, we were expected to keep, each in succession, the common purse, settle all bills, pay what was due and not allow ourselves to be imposed upon. Our mentor kept an eye on the process but interfered only in extreme cases. Of a cheery disposition, he was ever ready to enter into good-humoured talk with peasants met on the road and plain people sitting at some Italian *osteria*, allowing us to learn something of the ways of thinking and of the manners of men different from those we were accustomed to see. We knew enough Italian to follow the discussions, though a book of dialogues, on which we had counted, failed us in a large measure, applying as it did to times past: dialogues on means of transportation only dealt with stage coaches, and we were treated to the mishaps of Signor Elefante who tries to sit in the coach, where the other travellers loudly protest: "When one is so big, one reserves two seats!"—"But so I did. The trouble is they reserved one inside and the other on top." To travellers on foot or by rail, this was of little help. We thus walked, carrying our knapsacks, to Mattmark, at the foot of the Swiss Alps, crossed the Monte Moro to Macugnaga, reaching those places of wonderful beauty, the lakes of Northern Italy, then the city of the marble cathedral, of Vinci's Last Supper, of museums full of rare works, Milan. The Abbé had so imbued us with the feeling of respect due to the best products of the human mind, whether intellectual, moral or artistic, that we had a heart-beat and felt a sort of sacred emotion when we entered a place rich with so much treasure.

The generality of museums were much better arranged then than now; they had less the appearance of cata-combs for the dead; their rooms resembled rather those in which people dwell, and their collections looked much more as if they still belonged to the world of the living. The iron rod of the pedant has caused great havoc; the fashion for classification has set in; all the works of the same artist and of the same school must be alined together. An easy task, to be sure; not more difficult to fulfil than the classifying of a collection of postage stamps, country by country, figure by figure. Some may suggest that the student, owing to such a system, will better perceive the trend and merits of each school; but one can doubt whether he would not better understand them by observing the differences and oppositions between juxtaposited pictures of different styles.

In one of those journeys we walked from Lake Leman to Zermatt, crossed the Theodule of over ten thousand feet, were rowed across the lakes, and then, mainly on foot, passed on to Chiavenna, Saint-Moritz (an insignificant little village in those days), Pontresina, Landeck, lastly Innsbruck where Emperor Maximilian kneels in his bronze robes, surrounded by his guard of twenty-eight bronze giants, warriors famous in romance or history: the grandest military tomb in existence, after the one at the Invalides where victories, whose names are graven in the mosaic pavement, mount guard over the nameless sarcophagus containing the ashes of Napoleon.

Another journey, after my graduation, included the whole of that Italy which in the course of centuries has been the garden, the museum, the battle-field of peoples and nations. We travelled to Venice, with which we, of course, fell in love, to Florence, whose *Tribune,* one of the brightest spots of artistic beauty in the world, had not yet been submitted to the rules of postage-stamp classification, to the hill cities of Umbria, to Rome, which kept us in ecstasies with its statues, pictures, Saint-Peter's, colosseum, catacombs, via Appia, so much of the history of the world having been written there, defaced, written again; then to Naples, Vesuvius, Pompeii, Sorrento, Amalfi.

The crater of Vesuvius was reached, in those pre-funicular days, partly on horseback, partly on foot. Starting at night from Resina, we followed at full gallop the steep, zigzagging path, vaguely visible in the moon-light, among weird blocks of lava scattered by the previous year's great eruption; each horse was urged on by a Neapolitan boy on foot who never allowed the mount to slacken its speed and who, shouting all the time, was never out-distanced by it. The so-called hermitage was reached at eleven; the "hermit," whose solitude was enlivened by an incredibly numerous army of creeping or jumping little creatures, had but a single bed to offer, a fourth of which was appropriated by each of us, one enjoying a pillow, another a bolster, and so on, all receiving a due proportion of the formidable army. It was a pleasure to rise at three, leave the army at a safe distance, mount our horses again and gallop to the place where rocks stopped and a cone of ashes began, to be ascended on foot. We sent back the horses and the boys, and kept a guide, very necessary in the darkness caused by vapour, mist and smoke, veiling the moon. Those ashes, or rather scoriæ, made of the climb no easy matter; they formed a thick and loose layer, we sank knee-deep into it and, sliding backwards, lost at each step half as much as had been gained. Our guide strongly insisted on our using the good offices of some men, lying there in wait for travellers, and provided with leather belts to be placed around willing waists, the tourists to be each hauled up by one man and pushed forward by another. We saw a troop of sight-seers of rather heavy build accept this help, but we were not of heavy build, and too proud not to climb alone. At dawn, wet with perspiration caused by the heat of the emanations from the volcano, we reached the rim of the crater, a very steep funnel, surrounded by a wall of rock

and ashes, with a dark round hole discernible at the
bottom; a lava rock, pushed down the declivity by our
guide, ran into the hole, and we counted seventeen
seconds before we ceased to hear the rumble, like distant
thunder, which it made after having disappeared. The
sun arose, but a thick black smoke soon emerged from
the crater and we scarcely, for a moment, had a dim
view of Naples and its bay. The air, moreover, was
loaded with the fumes from blocks of sulphur, slowly
burning here and there; the ground was so hot that
eggs for our breakfast were cooked in it.

The descent was helped rather than hampered by the
knee-deep ashes which prevented our bounds forward
from ending in falls. We bought grapes to wash down
the fumes, walked to Torre del Greco and to Pompeii,
the sun shining now in quite undesired splendour.
Pompeii was minutely inspected in the afternoon and
when bed-time came we slept indeed.

Farther south, after pilgrimages to many spots made
familiar to us by Virgil, the Phlegrean fields, the Averna
lake, the Sibyl's cave, Sorrento with its orange groves
and blue sea was visited; a boat took us to Capri of
Tiberian fame and to the picturesque little harbour of
Amalfi, reached at sunset. The light of the vanishing
day lent its warm hue to the surrounding rocks and hills,
while fishermen drew up their boats on the sand and
brought in their catch. More colour was lent by a layer
of corn drying on the flag-stones of the harbour. It
seemed as though we were sailing into a landscape by
Claude Lorrain.

Another voyage was to the Loire valley and the
château region, to Brittany and Normandy, ending with
a brief glance at that dazzling city seen then for the
first time, " Paris la grand' ville."

One result of those journeys was the increase, in us
four children, even those who had remained at home but
heard the story, of an inborn passion for art. We studied

its principles in the *Grammaire des Arts du Dessin* of Charles Blanc and read, pen in hand, all the histories of art and artists we could secure. We decided to form for our instruction and enjoyment a museum or album of the arts of every land and every period, and the collecting of the material, with no special resources for it, was of intense interest. All the engravings we could cut from cast-off illustrated papers, photographs we could get, views of monuments and historical places, were sought with as much passion as that of the great collector with his millions, ready to purchase a Rembrandt. The advertisements for illustrated books at New Year's time were one of our best occasions for valuable catches. We awaited the time with longing anxiety; would the crop of advertisements be good this year?

I was still at the Chartreux when, as I attained my sixteenth year, a grave, saddening note was sounded in my ears: in February 1871 a letter came from my father saying: " I try to hold to life. I would it were possible for me to survive some years more so as to give all of you a good impulsion and to direct you properly. But, alas, I must acknowledge that my sufferings greatly increase and that life, which is ebbing by degrees, may come any day to an end. As I have told you more than once, you are the one to replace me and become the head of the family. You will help your mother, to the best of your ability, and you will watch together over your brother and sisters. In view of this it greatly behoves that you think very seriously of this new position, that you fulfil all your duties so as to end your studies brilliantly and distinguish yourself in the career that you will follow. Then I shall be able to descend to the grave with the consoling thought that I will not be too much missed."

He lingered in great suffering until the following year. I humbly pray and hope that I did not prove to have swerved too much from the line of conduct drawn for me by a venerated hand.

CHAPTER III

WE had not yet finished our studies at the Chartreux when there occurred one of those terrible events that shake the world. From the fall of Napoleon I to the accession of his nephew, France had had no real war. During the reign of Napoleon III there had been several, all of them victorious. And now was happening one of the worst reverses in the millennial history of the country. It seemed to us unbelievable; at the news of each defeat we thought it was a mere accident which would soon be retrieved; we were moved to the bottom of our young hearts. The unpreparedness of the military, the unwisdom of the statesmen, the falsifying of the Ems despatch, the unkept promise of Austria to join France in case of trouble with Prussia, were bringing about the downfall of the Second Empire, the siege and surrender of Paris, the extension of the battlefield as far as the Loire valley, the loss of Alsace and part of Lorraine, the exacting of an enormous indemnity to cover the war expenses of the victors (we exacted nothing on this score in 1919), the excesses of the Commune. One single favourable symptom: the continued resistance to the invader after all hope of victory had vanished, so as to give proof to the world, and make sure ourselves, that France was still France, the country of which Froissart had said at the worst moment of the Hundred Years' War, that " it was never so discomfited that there were not left there people with whom to fight."

Too young to be elsewhere than at our college, part of

26

which was occupied by troops on their way to the front, we saw the elder pupils enlist, most of them being sent to Belfort that never surrendered and thus at the Peace Treaty was saved to France, and it was thrilling to hear those who returned tell of their experiences, and laughingly show us how they had managed to the last to have a service uniform and a dress uniform, this being accomplished by buttoning their doubled-breasted coats to the left on ordinary days and to the right on solemn occasions.

Military drill was taught us, with wooden rifles, in view of the possibility of a long war. Slackers were loathed. Allusion having been made to one before our mother, she said in our presence: " I would much rather my two sons were dead."

But the war was brief. While it lasted, and after, our professors were ceaselessly telling us: " It is our lack of knowledge, our lack of seriousness, of method, of careful application to our tasks, whatever the task, our ignorance of foreign countries, that have caused our country's disaster. If we do not rise, each of us, to a higher moral level, she will never rise again."

The result was an incredible ardour for studying, inuring the body to hardships, becoming complete men. With such a goal in view nothing seemed difficult. Owing to this impulse I, for one, took, when I left college, three degrees instead of the usual one, viz. in letters, sciences and law; became master of arts, prepared a doctorate in letters, studied four modern languages, until my family decided that I could not continue to study in view of a variety of careers; I must choose. I was left one day alone at Saint-Haon, while all the others went as usual to the Bachelard; on their return at night I must have decided.

Communing with myself, having no one to give me experienced advice, I spent some very puzzling hours. Would I continue the study of sciences, prepare for the " Ecole Polytechnique " and become probably an artil-

lery officer, or continue law and select any of the profes-
sions to which it opened the way? The result of my
reflections was that, after such a terrible war, as we
considered it then, there would probably be no other for
a great many years; the career of an artillery officer in
command of silent guns was like to be of little use and
there must be more practical means for being of service.

When the family returned I had made up my mind:
I would finish my law studies and prepare for a civilian
career; which I did, spending one year in Paris and
one in London, learning as much as I could in every
accessible branch, and teaching the body to perform its
duty and not to pay attention to trifles. At Paris I
became master of laws, studied at the same time history,
foreign literature and languages, improved my Latin,
followed courses of palæography, and even some pre-
paratory ones for the Ecole des Beaux Arts, regretting that
no time was left for at least a smattering of medicine.
As for the body, it was put to a rather hard schooling
which included not only swimming in very cold water,
riding, fencing, the avoidance of any means of con-
veyance except my two legs, but the discarding of any
overcoat, whatever be the weather, and sleeping on boards
placed on my bed between the mattress and the sheets.
I found, however, that " Nature is a strict accountant," and
that it will not do to overdraw one's account with her.
When, after some years of this " strengthening " of the
body, a persistent cough set in and a little spitting of
blood began, the method had to be altered, and as this
was done in time, no serious harm resulted.

The year 1875–76 was spent in England. Since I
was not to serve in the military I decided that I would
serve abroad; our ignorance of foreign countries, we
were told, had been one of the main causes of our disasters; this guided my decision. Admittance to the
Affaires Etrangères was to be had in those days by competitive examination for the consular service and through

political pull for the diplomatic one, the latter being my ambition. But I lacked such pull, so I tried the other road, with the hope of bifurcating afterwards, which I eventually did. In order to compete, one had to be at least twenty and an inquiry was made as to one's milieu and family and the possibility of its being able to supply the candidate's needs during the first years, when he was expected to serve without any salary. I was twenty and I sent in my application the day I sailed for London, which seemed an excellent place to prepare the examination and also, while seeing a new land and improving my English, to continue my other studies.

First of all, acquaintance must be made with the country; no sooner landed, in October 1875, at Saint Katherine's docks (for I had read in Taine that the thing to do was to reach London by the Thames; I did it once, but again never), I began a journey north through a green land of endless meadows, with clipped hedges and impressive old trees, heavy with thick foliage, babbling streams, full to the brink, and here and there, in contrast with this quiet of dreamland, the noisy tumult of industrial cities; roman remains dotting the country as far as the great wall built by Emperor Hadrian as a protection against the wild clans of Scotland, norman and gothic cathedrals with square apses scarcely known in France, high, thick, stern-looking norman keeps, early built by the conquerors as far as the Scottish border to show the population that they had come to stay, ruined abbeys, ivy-covered, Elizabethan castles, like Hatfield, with thin brick walls, innumerable turrets and windows, abundant ornamentation, nothing for defence, the owners having evidently preferred to run some risk rather than deprive themselves of plenty of air and light, and of fine views over their trees and meadows; and within, many works of art, sculptures, pictures, wainscoting, ornamented ceilings, things of beauty. In the wars and revolutions castles suffered less than churches. Léon Say asked me once to inquire from Lord Salisbury whether he still possessed the portrait of an Ambassador of France given by the French envoy to the famous Cecil. The answer was: " The portrait is at Hatfield, hanging from the same nail on which my ancestor hung it."

Around the churches and around the ruins, grass of a super-green hue, rare elsewhere; on Sundays the chimes, always the same, giving, in their monotonous melody, an impression of quiet and happiness, a rest for the soul. They are such indeed as to smooth away the troubles and worries of the other six days. Let us hope they will ever continue thus, ceaselessly repeating their few crystal notes. To try and improve them would be to kill them.

In Scotland, Edinburgh was visited, and out of gratitude Dryburgh Abbey and the tomb of dear, admired Walter Scott, to whom were due such moments of delight; the Lowlands; the Highlands with their snow-capped mountains, their glens, lochs, bogs, pools and ponds, their vast expanses of hilly ground, almost uninhabited, heather undulating on it as far as the eye could see. From Inverness reached by the Caledonian Canal, or rather from Dingwall, and in spite of the rain, fog and wind being very much in the way, I started on foot, carrying my knapsack, for the north-west coast. I had, however, to give up the thought of crossing to the Orkneys and visiting that extraordinary cathedral of Saint Magnus, in norman and early gothic style, unique in that latitude. The regular boat service had ceased at this season, and I was told that I might perhaps hire a sail-boat, but with a chance of remaining for weeks a prisoner on the island, awaiting propitious weather for the return.

The places stopped at were then very primitive; I had to learn some Gaelic, many people knowing no other language, and when I spoke to them, answering: " No English." A man who wanted to give me his name in writing, prudently asked me first whether I knew how to read. But everywhere, as soon as I was understood, the

JUSSERAND AT TWENTY

face p. 31

most pleasant and friendly hospitality. I looked even younger than my age and the presence of a man of my race was so rare in those parts that people were interested.

My first stop after Dingwall was Achilty Inn, where I arrived at night drenched; and in fact drenched I was during almost this entire journey, with no second pair of shoes to replace the wet ones: they are such a load to carry! I nevertheless avoided trouble by rubbing my feet with whisky before starting out and smearing them with tallow. I always had in my bag a tallow candle for that purpose. The system proved most effective. At Achilty I was shown into a cold, empty dining-room. But I had noticed, passing the door, that the family, father, mother, sons and daughters, were warming themselves in the kitchen and making merry by the fireside. I asked whether I could not take my meal in that room. " Yes, of course "; and we fell into friendly conversation as if we had been old acquaintances, remaining late by the fire. The next morning I started at six, for daylight is of short duration at that season and latitude; the whole family accompanied me a good long distance on the road. For many years we exchanged greetings at Christmas, and now and then photographs so as to show each other what we now looked like. " We do not forget," they wrote, " the stranger that came to our house that wet Sunday. . . . We have an artist from Edinburgh and he is quite enchanted with the place. . . . I enclose photos of my mother, sister and myself. Mother's is not very good, it makes her much too old; Bessie's is very like her. Everyone says that mine is the best I ever got taken. . . . Weather here was glorious, snow and frost; the snow was six inches deep. . . . I don't think you saw our garden; it is a very bonnie place in summer." I have before me, as I write, a twig of heather which came with one of the letters, and which had grown, bloomed and been vivified by the pure air of the Highlands half a century ago. One year a letter came saying: " This is the last you will ever receive from us; father and mother have died; the sons have emigrated to Australia and the daughters have married abroad," by which was meant Yorkshire.

At various inns I had various experiences; at one farther inland, as I was standing in the early morning in front of the house, about to leave, the landlord asked what country I was from. I said France. He could scarcely believe his ears; he had, he said, never seen a Frenchman, and as he would not have his family lose this unique occasion, he shouted to them to come down and see what there was in the courtyard. I was soon stared at as I had never been before, nor ever was again. On another occasion the innkeeper handing me his bill made this candid statement: " You may notice, sir, that we have charged you a little more than we usually do, but to travel so far you must be very rich." I was not, but as the price had nothing outrageous and I had no means of comparing, I paid with a smile.

Poolewe, which maybe has now a Palace Hotel, winter sports and other "improvements," consisted then of a tiny village of low heather-thatched houses, built of loose stones without mortar, only a ground floor, many of them with three apertures, one serving as a window, another as a door (and one had to stoop to enter it), another, cut in the roof, allowed the smoke of a peat fire to go out if it chose; the chimney consisted of two large flag-stones placed on the ground under that hole.

As I reached the place at dusk, I had noticed in one of those houses the music of a harmonium. I called after my meal and was well received. The inmate proved to be the school teacher. I asked him what he was teaching; he answered: " Mainly English," but he used for that purpose books which, besides the knowledge of the language, imparted useful information. He gave me one as a sample; it was in both languages and dealt with a question of the utmost importance to the population, being called: *An seol air an Glacar agus an greidhear an Sgadan,* in other words, " *Directions for taking and curing herrings.*"

Encased in a setting of steep rocks, Loch Maree is one of the most beautiful of Scottish lakes. It has a number of wooded islands, on one of which are tombs said to be Scandinavian. I crossed by boat to sketch them, then started on foot again for Loch Torridon and Shieldag by the seaside, through a landscape of desert mountains, bogs and heather, of rivulets hastening among stones, of ceaselessly murmuring cascades, whitening the declivities of the mounts.

Roads crossed the country east to west, none north to south. I decided to take my chance and try to reach Applecross harbour from Shieldag, walking through the trackless hills and bogs. I had no compass, but the sun appeared for a moment, and so I could take a good aim; the people at the inn were, moreover, interested and told me what to do: " Go right across the mountains; you see those three pine trees, they give you the proper direction; you then find a number of hills which you will cross, then you reach a deep pass beyond which you see . . .—Applecross?—No, but you will understand that you are on the right way to it." And they made a sketch on the sea sand.

Thus armed and forewarned I climbed the heather-clad steep acclivity, reached the three pine trees, and walked among the hills, in the midst of an absolutely desert country, meeting some deer, who doubtless recognizing a friend did not trouble to move away, the only trace of man's presence, and not of recent date, being a quite unexpected dolmen of which I made a sketch. Progress was difficult; it was not a question of walking, but of jumping most of the time from one tuft of heather to another; tufts being slippery and surrounded by water, care was indispensable. The sight was, however, of striking grandeur, sometimes with gigantic rocks, right

D

and left, smaller ones showing their grey heads here and there through the yellowish glen; a number of little lakes, sleeping in the hollows, clear rivulets singing along the declivities.

Climbing a hill to take my bearings after three hours of this exercise, I found that I had reached my goal; the sea was near by; the usual dark rocks half circling a beach, around which rose the neat-looking small houses of Applecross. I had thought the journey would be a longer one. Happy at the discovery, for the mode of advance had not been of the pleasantest, and some miscalculated jumps had resulted in a knee-deep cold-water bath, I moved toward the little city. Coming nearer, what did I see? It was not Applecross at all, but Shieldag again; I had unwittingly verified the truth of what I had read in accounts of travels, that when you are lost in mountains, instead of following the straight line as you intend, you circle around and find yourself at last at your starting-point.

But I would not be defeated, and some light having by good luck appeared in the sky, I took aim anew for Applecross and set forth again. More bogs, more heather, more jumping, rocks and rivulets, absolute solitude. Day began to wane, I was hungry and tired and all the hills I crossed were so much like the hills I had crossed before that I could not be sure I was making any progress at all. Darkness was setting in, the air was becoming colder and damper; the prospect of spending the night in my soaked boots and gaiters, foodless and roofless on the heather, had nothing cheery. I had now been walking without any stop for seven hours. Before resigning myself to waiting on the spot till morning, I put my faith in one more hill at some distance and climbed it. A happy move: at the foot of a mountainous ridge in front of me I could discover something like a white ribbon contrasting with the darkness around: a road! the end of all trouble, for a road necessarily

leads to somewhere.   With renewed vigour I ran towards
it and chose the direction which would, I supposed, lead
me to the sea.   It did, and I reached a little village fast
asleep under the moonlight.   Applecross?   No; it was
Kisshorn (if I caught the name aright).   An old woman,
the only being I saw on the way, answering my best
Gaelic, pointed out a low-roofed, loose-stone house
which, possessing one extra room, did duty for an inn.
The father, mother, and a number of young children
were asleep in the chief room.   Answering my knock
they rose, dressed, and instead of showing any annoyance
at being disturbed, welcomed the drenched traveller, lit
a bright fire, unhooked from the wall over the fireplace
some drying fish and bacon, the most delightful food I
ever tasted, and after some hearty and cheery talk took
me to the spare room, where, as in the rest of the house,
heather served various purposes; the roof was heather,
the mattress was heather and a calf's long-haired hide
did duty as a carpet.   On the wall, a kind of poster with
the inscription: " What must I do to be saved?   Believe
in the Lord Jesus Christ and thou shalt be saved "; not
so unlike, in spite of the difference of country, language
and religion, to one I had noticed on the façade of a
modest house in the Tyrol, giving the passers-by this
advice: " Pensa, anima fidelis, quid respondere velis,
Christo venturo de cœlis." I slept soundly till eight
o'clock and found to my amazement that, owing to the
clever care of my host, my shoes and gaiters were
dry.

I gave up Applecross, which will have proved to be my
Carcassonne, with less cause for regret than had the
peasant of Limoux, walked to Jeantown and breakfasted
in an hotel where numerous engravings represented
French defeats in the war of '70.   I noticed the same
thing in other places and made inquiries.   The answer
was: our only visitors are Germans, are you not one?
We are deluged with such engravings; they are not

made in our country, but in Germany, and distributed here for nothing.

Passage was taken to Skye, a land of weird deep violet or bluish-black rocks forming at sunset extraordinary indentations on the red welkin. I returned by way of Kyle Rhea ferry at the extreme south of the island, and when, answering questions, I said that I had left Portree, the capital, that morning, my statement was received with a mixture of admiration and doubt, both undeserved. The inn was very primitive, with a common sleeping-room for all comers; the securing of a whole bed for one's self required quite a negotiation. Then to the mainland again, greatly hampered on the road to Glencoe by a tempest of wind which I saw uproot a little wooden hut and scatter its boards in the air as if they had been paper. Reaching at night, very tired, a solitary inn, not so primitive, however, as those I had stopped at of late, I felt an intense longing for a kind of food that I had not tasted for a long time, but not remembering the English word I had to go without it, and only when I reached Glasgow later did I learn that what I wanted so much was called in French an " omelette " and in English an " omelet." I have never forgotten it since.

The journey south then began by way of Glasgow, the Clyde, the Lake country, Chester and Wales. Using the Royal Mail, which, for all the grandeur of its name, consisted of a kind of dog-cart with two seats, one for the driver, the other for the rest of the travellers, luckily represented only by myself, I reached, out of the beaten track, across a desolate country, the picturesque city of Saint David, in a hollow, near the seaside, the centre, long ago, of religious life in Wales, the resting-place of Edmund Tudor, father of Henry VII, of many prelates, and where may be seen the vast ruins of the bishops' palace, the earliest habitation of importance where all was for convenience and beauty, nothing for defence: fourteenth century.

Westward, many cities, Welsh, Roman like Bath, or English; many castles, some in ruins, some inhabited by the great; the most extraordinary and most discussed of all megalithic monuments, Stonehenge, and once more vast impressive cathedrals, Salisbury with its famous steeple that so often tempted Constable's brush, Winchester's noble pile; then London again for serious work.

Serious work indeed, first in order to complete the preparation for the competitive examination giving access to the Foreign Office. But I was informed after a while that there would be none that year, and so, putting away in a drawer of my memory all that I had learnt, I turned the key for safe keeping, and worked at my two theses for the doctor's degree, one in French and the other in Latin. With the Foreign Office examination in view, however, I tried in various ways to improve my knowledge of languages, one way being to go, on Sundays, to a Protestant sermon in English and to a Catholic one in Italian.

Ordinary days were spent at the British Museum; no work after dinner, but sometimes a visit to a theatre, or to that fairyland with so much to learn and so much to be charmed by, the South Kensington Museum, one of the places in the world to which I owe most gratitude; more usually long night walks, in any weather, through the streets and lanes of London, observing the many scenes and sights they offered, very different from the elegant quarters where nothing happens and there is nothing to look at; Punch and Judy with their cock-crowing, battles royal between two people who had disagreed about something, everybody looking on and no one interfering, except sometimes the police, street singers with blackened faces, Saturday markets, in the poorer parts of the city, where the mobile flare of the mineral oil, burning on each push-cart, gave, with its crude light and crude shadows, an unreal appearance to pale-faced customers and to red-faced merchants shouting the praise of their goods, meat, fish, hot potatoes, second-hand books and songs; preaching, at times by a real preacher, oftener by a volunteer, some workman wanting to improve the condition of his brethren. I mingled with the crowd, one afternoon, as I was walking to Greenwich; a work-man, in tattered clothes, pitiful to see, stood on a stool, his back to a fountain and was holding forth with feverish ardour. And what, I wondered, could he be pleading for in the name of his class, with such fire, such intent to convince, such a fervent desire, as it seemed, to inject his own soul into the soul of his hearers? This is what he was saying: "Let public-houses be empty and work-houses will be empty; swear not to drink brandy any more and prisons will be empty. You complain of the price of meat, say good-bye to gin, and meat will be cheap for you, and you will have quiet at home, and you will be men. Shame on those whose money tinkles on the counter!" A credit to his class to produce such men.

Brief journeys to Oxford and Cambridge, to Canter-bury, to Cologne and the Rhine country, broke the monotony of the long working days spent at the British Museum, which began the moment the museum opened and finished when it closed. The journey to the vanished shrine of Thomas à Becket was performed not in pleasant April weather, when "smale fowles maken melodye," but in bleak, snowy and windy March. While, however, it took Chaucer and the pilgrims who went with him

"The holy blisful martir for to seke,"

four days to reach the place, I nearly covered the whole distance in one day, Canterbury to Stone: it makes a difference having no Chaucerian story to listen to. As in the eyes of the pilgrims of long ago, very impressive stood the grand cathedral with its lofty towers, turrets and pinnacles, its splendid choir raised on eighteen steps and its unique historical associations: the spot where Becket fell, the tomb (probably) of Stephen Langton of Magna

Charta fame, that (certainly) of the Black Prince, in a remarkable state of preservation, agreeing to the minutest details with the directions left by the Prince in his will. His reclining figure is " tout armez de fier de guerre," [1] the arms of France and England are quartered on his breast, and the slab is surrounded by a melancholy inscription drawn by him from a long-winded mystical poem of Guillaume de Deguileville, *Le Pélerinage de la vie humaine*: " Ma grand beauté est tout alée " [2]; the will was in French, the only language that he spoke.

Here and there throughout the city, ancient houses and churches, full, they too, of historical associations, and the remains of those defensive walls, the clever devising of which was explained by the Knight to his son according to the continuator of Chaucer.

The news came in June that the competitive examination for the Affaires Etrangères would take place the following month. I hastily reopened the drawer in the recess of my memory where the products of my economic, historical and geographic studies had been stored; they were found pretty well preserved, received some refurbishing, and I left for Paris to try my chance at the examination.

[1] All armed in war iron.
[2] My great beauty is all gone.

CHAPTER IV

PARIS AGAIN AND LONDON AGAIN
1876–1880

On reaching Paris I went to the little hotel in the Latin Quarter where I had lived as a student, and the next morning asked the landlord where the Ministry of Foreign Affairs was. He did not know, so I inquired in the street from a police officer who did know and told me where to find a building with which I have since become pretty well acquainted.

As good luck would have it, and owing to the fact that I had studied beyond the strict limits of the official programme, I was received with number one, and was notified of the fact by the Duc Decazes, then Foreign Minister, a white-whiskered diplomat of the old school, of great experience and charming manners, whose fine features changed expression according to circumstances and the people spoken to, as easily as an April sky.

Years afterwards, giving a dinner at our Embassy in Washington to a new French Ambassador on his way to his post at Tokio, I had on my right the young wife of the Japanese Ambassador. My visitor asked me how my career had begun and what had influenced it. I answered: " The war of '70 and the desire we had to serve; hence so many examinations successfully passed. I was even near becoming a *mouton à cinq pattes*." I did not know whether my pretty neighbour had followed the conversation, which was in French. But when it was finished she said, in her soft voice: " What is it to be a *mouton à cinq pattes*? " (a five-legged sheep). I explained that it was the kind of prodigy, not to say monstrosity, exhibited in shows.

40

My new functions were simple enough and consisted principally in copying the drafts of our chief's letters for the Minister to sign. It was considered that, by dint of copying, beginners would become acquainted with the proper diplomatic style. By degrees they were entrusted with the devising of drafts of the simplest kind, and were taught a few principles certainly wise and worth remembering to-day as in former days: in every letter, state first the occasion that causes you to write, and in a different paragraph say what you have to say concerning that occasion. Never use extraordinary words or extraordinary modes of expression except in extraordinary circumstances; they must not be blunted by being put to common use.

Materially, one did not begin at the bottom, but at the top: in small rooms under the roof of the ministry. On the big beam across one of them a previous occupant had painted, in his leisure moments, the triumph of the " Elève-Consul " (probationary-consul, the first grade one aspired to after Attaché). From the gates of an Oriental city with plenty of towers, minarets and palm trees, the beturbaned dignitaries of the place, escorted by soldiers, musicians and, of course, dancing girls, marched to welcome the Elève-Consul; while he meantime, leisurely reclining in a palanquin, looked very grand, and smoked a long pipe with unconcerned dignity.

The partitions between the rooms and the corridors were of the thinnest; the doors often remained open, so that it was sometimes impossible not to hear what people were saying on the other side. It happened on one occasion that I was the subject of the talk. Some-one said: he looks so young; what he needs is not a consular post but a wet-nurse. Another remarked: he has outranked the others, but he coughs a good deal, he won't last long. I however survived this gloomy foreboding.

Owing to my rank at the examination, this period of

apprenticeship lasted only two years, in the course of
which I went to Lyons, where I had formerly studied
letters, in order to obtain a doctor's degree. The rule
is that you must present your theses to the Faculty,
and in a kind of literary tournament defend them against
the strictures and objections which the professors may
choose to oppose to you. This is called "*Soutenir ses
thèses*," and is, in an attenuated form, the survival of a
mediæval custom according to which a candidate for a
mastership had to remain forty days at the disposal of
all comers and refute their criticisms. My refutations
on November 22, 1877, lasted only six hours. A local
newspaper gave an account of the ceremony and stated
that "the discussion had been always very courteous,
but at times rather sharp."

The subject of my Latin thesis was that strange Joseph
of Exeter who was born in the twelfth and died in the
thirteenth century, having taken part in the third crusade.
His chief work was an epic poem on the Fall of Troy,
and his hexameters were so remarkable for the time,
that his early editors (Basle 1558, Antwerp 1608), unable
to believe them the work of a mediæval writer, boldly
attributed them to a Roman prose writer of the first
century before Christ, Cornelius Nepos. They might
have been troubled by the lines in praise of "flos regum
Arthurus," and those where Henry II Plantagenet is
compared to Hector, which could scarcely be expected
from Cornelius Nepos, but, in their editions, they simply
left out such lines as well as the poetical dedication of
the work to Thomas Baldwin, Archbishop of Canterbury.

What gave some interest to that study was my having
discovered, and printed in part, an unknown manuscript
containing, in a minute, careful hand of the thirteenth
century, a running commentary, explanatory of the text,
just as if it had been a classic, something like the notes
of Muret for Ronsard and E. K. for Spenser. This
compliment to the poem must have been bestowed on it

by the author himself or prompted by him, so impossible
is it to conceive that anyone else could have unravelled
the true meaning of certain passages. Joseph describes,
for instance, the invention of ships as being the cause of
insults to the gods, which rafts are not. How can that
be? Because, the expounder says, the gilded images of
the gods are placed at the prows of ships, which is not
the case with rafts, and when a storm arises, those sacred
images get disrespectfully broken on the rocks, "illas
illidendo scopulis."

My French thesis was devoted to the predecessors of
the immediate predecessors of Shakespeare; it has long
been out of date, but the subject was not so trite then
as it has since become and it was well received. I owe
to it some happenings of lasting consequence in my
life: great Taine desired to know the author, took him
into his friendship, and that friendship lasted without a
shadow until his death. Guillaume Guizot who taught
at the Collège de France, the son of Louis Philippe's
famous Minister, had the same desire, with the same
effect, and I was, moreover, invited by the *Revue Critique*,
"the only paper worth reading" as Andrew Lang
humorously remarked, to become a contributor. It was
an austere publication, founded, some years before, in
order to improve French criticism and erudition and
cause authors to be more severe for themselves, if they
wanted to avoid the strictures of impartial judges. The
only aim was the search for truth, without consideration
for private friendships, relationships or interests. Gaston
Paris and Paul Meyer were then the chief animators;
their group was so small that, so as to better keep careless authors in awe, they concealed that fact, spared no
pains in order to become competent to pass sentence on
all sorts of books, and in the earlier days each signed his
articles by a variety of names. It became more and
more evident, as years passed, that they were succeeding
in their self-assigned task.

After two years I was sent as *Elève-Consul* to our Consulate-General in London. The Consul was M. Lenglet, a man of experience and wisdom. He had been in his younger days secretary to Mignet, the famous historian, and one of the *post-mortem* worshippers of Mary Queen of Scots. Whenever M. Lenglet, in his researches, had brought to light some document detrimental to the lovely lady, Mignet could scarcely conceal his sadness and used it as little as his principles as an historian allowed him.

The Consulate-General was in Finsbury Circus, where all houses were bleak and black, but ours was the bleakest and blackest, which made it easy to recognize.

His constant poring over statistics and his study of the industrial and commercial development of England had not dulled M. Lenglet's kindly and convivial dispositions. He liked to entertain, gave dinners and balls; he had three daughters as pleasantly disposed as himself. The youngest being rather short and plump had been nicknamed *la Boule*. Long after, when I was again at the Foreign Office, I received one day the visit of a Sister of Charity wearing the beautiful large wing-like cornette devised by Saint Vincent-de-Paul for his helpers of the poor. She had some petition to present and after a few words, said: " Don't you recognize me? "—" No, ma Sœur, I do not."—" Why, I am *La Boule*." The poor Boule wore herself out tending the sick and the destitute and died young.

Reserving for himself the more important questions and the drawing up of reports on the greater economic problems of the day, M. Lenglet gave me a free hand in the management of the abundantly visited and very busy Consulate-General. A great boon it was, for one cannot too early in life attain to responsibilities; they temper one's character, and one reaches them much sooner in the consular than in the diplomatic service. I had to deal with the somewhat unruly amnestied com-

munists, recalled from New Caledonia, and sent home
by way of London; with the mutinous sailors of a merchant ship, and to intervene on other occasions obliging
one to act with due reflection, but decisively and
promptly.

Abundant as they were, consular obligations left some
spare hours; they were devoted to history and literature,
my taste for which was becoming real love, and that
passion has accompanied me through life. Work on
these lines acted as a rest from my official duties, and
made them easier to fulfil; so my conscience was quieted
by the thought that these same duties profited by it.

I formed a vast plan; when you are young you
always form vast plans; mine was to write, in as many
volumes as might be necessary, a study of England in
the fourteenth century, the so important period when it
became certain that the country would be neither Anglo-
Saxon nor French, but English; when the chief characteristics of the people, social, political, as well as intellectual,
were acquired; when the first great writers began
English literature in earnest, when a Parliament was
established with all the main attributes it still possesses
and a poet of the day could say of the King: " Might
of the Communes made him to reign." Notes were
accumulated, books read in vast numbers, places of
historical importance visited, sketches made of monuments, ruins, statues, costumes. Fate, however, decided
otherwise, and finding that my official duties would
absorb more and more of my time, I felt I must give
up that vast plan. In order that some trace of the
effort be nevertheless preserved, I wrote an essay on a
portion of the subject which had so far remained the
least studied; it appeared first in a now long dead
English review, then in a French one, then in book form,
first in French, then in English, the latter illustrated,
partly from pen-and-ink sketches by the author. This
casual publication proved the most popular of anything

I ever wrote; it was entitled: "English Wayfaring Life in the Middle Ages, Fourteenth Century," and after so many years and many editions, it still has a public. I have often been asked if I knew my namesake the author.

I had conceived, in the course of those studies, a profound admiration for a poem of the same period, some passages of which I could not read without a heartbeat, much less popular then than it has since become, " Piers Plowman." An excellent edition of it with ample notes had just been published by W. W. Skeat of Cambridge, a leader in such studies. I wrote for the *Revue Critique* a long account of his edition, and dared to propose an interpretation of allusions to contemporary events contained in the poem, different from the interpretation adopted by Skeat. The publication of this article had for me two important results: first, it showed me how far could go the generosity of a man of learning, whereas such are supposed to be usually more prone to wrangle than to agree: *grammatici certant*. Skeat was famous and I practically unknown: he wrote, however, to say that he accepted my interpretations and asked permission to translate my article and print it in his next edition. Secondly, Gaston Paris wanted to know the author of this same article, and to it I owe one of the dearest and most enjoyable friendships I was blessed with in all my life. I wrote a little later (1894) a whole book, the first then in existence, on Piers Plowman. It was merely paying a debt.

Gaston Paris, so well known to all Romance scholars and students of the old French language and literature, was a most lovable man. Of the widest knowledge, extending far beyond his particular branch of studies, he hated sham in all its varieties and people who used sham to succeed in life; for all others he was kindness itself; with nothing small in him, no trace of vanity or self-interest, he always found time to help and advise beginners, to read their proofs, to aid toward the development of what was best in them and which, but for him, ran the risk of never coming to bloom. Interested not only in the past, but in the poetry, the art, the political events of the day, endowed with a wonderful memory which allowed him to make the most telling *rapprochements*, his conversation was a source of constant enjoyment. But though it obviously gave pleasure to all, he never played the part of the autocrat of the library, and on the contrary tried to draw out from each of his visitors what was most worth while.

In everything, irrespective of people, time and circumstance, his criticism, which could be severe, was devoid of acrimony and his sincerity was absolute. A sentence of his is famous: in the opening lecture of a course at the Collège de France which he delivered under tragic circumstances, he said: " He who, in the facts that he studies, allows himself, from a patriotic, religious, or even moral motive, the slightest dissimulation, the slightest alteration, is unworthy of a place in the great laboratory wherein probity is a more indispensable title to admission than cleverness." At that date (December 8, 1870) the speaker and his audience were shut up in Paris besieged by the Germans.

He was at home to his friends on Sundays, and to be admitted to these gatherings was quite a privilege. There one met thinkers, poets, historians, grammarians, who came all of them in the best dispositions, sure to have an enjoyable time, to please and be pleased. Such men as Taine, Renan, Gaston Boissier, Eugène Melchior de Vogüë, Albert Sorel, poets like the gentle-looking, appealing, dreamy Sully Prudhomme, who had been drawn out of obscurity in his youth by a group of young students, Gaston Paris among them, asking the king of literary critics, Sainte-Beuve, for a public recognition of the beginner's talents; imperious, impressive Heredia and many others. Returning from abroad, one had only to go once or twice to these gatherings to be aware of what was uppermost at the time in men's minds.

It was a rule that everybody must be seated, so that little groups could not be formed and there should be no private conversation; the talk must be general. "Assis! assis!" the master of the house would call when any unruly visitors broke the rule. Heredia would, on rare occasions, stand in front of the mantelpiece (the rule being waived for him) and recite one of those wonderful sonnets at which he had worked as long and as carefully as a goldsmith chiselling a gold casket; as he stammered a little, he spoke with some hesitancy, as though he were looking for the proper words and improvising lines which in fact had been for months on the anvil.

During that stay in London I made some literary acquaintances, among others that of the historian James Cotter Morison, one of the last, with his friend Frederick Harrison, of the sincere Positivists. His chief work was a history of Saint Bernard, in honour of whom he named his fine house in Fitzwilliam Avenue at Hampstead, "Clairvaux." The dream of his life had been to write a history of Louis XIV and his time, but he died having completed only the introduction, the proofs of which he gave me to read, and which have since disappeared. Through him I became acquainted with John Morley, who, in his Reminiscences, drew an excellent portrait of him and who was himself one of the best friends I made along the path of life. An excellent linguist, speaking French perfectly, Morison during an illness, diabetes, which he knew was to be fatal, chose as a last enjoyment the re-reading of his favourite Greek authors in their most recent editions. I still feel the pang I experienced when, paying him a visit which proved to be the last, he said in a very weak voice: "Oh! Jusserand, I want you so much to . . ." and after a while repeated: "Oh! Jusserand, I want you so much to . . ." And he could never finish.

In the Hertz family many people of interest were to be met, no grandees, but men notable for what they thought or what they did. Interested in questions of social development, liberal-minded, they had no ambition except that of pleasing their friends and making them know and understand one another. Their fortunes went dwindling; their smiling temper remained unaltered and they continued as keenly interested in the welfare of others. The London " season " was made especially bright in 1879 by the presence of the " Comédie Française," then at the height of its fame with Sarah Bernhardt, Croisette, Reichenberg, Samary, all of them young, pretty, remarkably gifted, and, among the men, Coquelin, the ever young Delaunay, Got, Mounet-Sully, Faivre and a host of others. The success was prodigious, it was very difficult to get seats. Miss Hertz was given one, but it was for a night which she was accustomed to spend with poor women in the East End, trying to enliven and instruct them. She sorrowfully but unhesitatingly gave up the ticket, not the poor women; such was the spirit of the family.

With his big bushy beard, thin lips, flame-darting eyes, in the semi-obscurity of his study at 3 St. George's Square, Primrose Hill, a room darkened by piles of books and papers made grey by the London air, F. J. Furnivall looked a mediæval wizard. Most helpful to those he liked, he was terrible, aggressive, mordacious to all others. A trifle made you sometimes pass from one category to the other, a difference of opinion on a date or the orthography of a name. He had fierce jousts with Swinburne, whom, by an inimical translation of his name, he called Pigsbrook. He never granted me a greater proof of immutable friendship than when he forbore giving me up though I persisted in calling Shakespeare, Shakespeare, and not Shakspere.

He rendered withal great service in many ways to many people and to his country. He caused ancient

E

English literature to become accessible to the mass of students. His magic wand called into existence such societies as the Early English Text Society, the Chaucer Society, the New Shakspere (of course Shakspere) Society and several more of infinite help to many a " Clerk of Oxenford " and others.

He later founded a Browning Society for the explanation of the obscure passages in the great poet's works. He wanted me to become a member of the committee, but I declined, saying: " Browning is still among us; he is to be met constantly at parties and dinners; why not ask him what he meant? "—" We have tried," replied Furnivall, " but without success. When approached on questions of this sort, he says, ' I wrote that long ago; I don't remember.' "

Gaston Paris, to whom I repeated this, said: " He might have spoken like Goethe, who, on being asked the meaning of a passage in the Second Faust, replied: ' When I wrote that, we were two who understood, God and I. Now there is only God.' "

At home meanwhile, family life continued, as before, divided into the usual three parts, spent at Saint-Haon, le Bachelard and Lyons. Such success as fell to the lot of the elder brother excited the enthusiasm of the young sisters, who wrote: " We are amused at the thought that you are considered as a future ambassador; we think likewise, but we did not dare to tell you. We dream beautiful dreams; we change the house into a castle, our rabbits into roe-deer, and in fine gilded drawing-rooms moves a gentleman, well known to us, before whom all bow; it is Monsieur l'Ambassadeur. Such is our train of thought when we are sorting beans or when the daylight falls and we sit around the fire before the lamp is brought in. The background of the story is ever the same, but each adds variants of her own. The first snow has just fallen."

In Lyons, studies were energetically pursued by the

sisters under the best masters of music, literature, etc.
An abundant, most affectionate correspondence from them
and from my mother kept me informed of the slightest
incident in their lives. Sometimes a journey of several
days was undertaken to the villages of the region having
picturesque ruins, which most of them had. Sometimes
when in town an old-fashioned dinner was offered relatives and intimate friends. The menu of one was sent
to me, and as it seems to belong to an abolished age, I
transcribe it as a curiosity. Twenty-seven people sat
down to dinner: how they could sit in our modest
Lyons dining-room I do not know; they were expected
to absorb:

Poules bouillies
Cervelas truffé
Civet de lièvre
Filet de bœuf aux champignons
Saumon à la mayonnaise

Petits Pois au jambon
Champignons à la crème
Dinde truffée
Bombe glacée
Desserts variés.

Following dinner there was music and dancing. " It
was a success," my mother wrote, " though I should have
liked more *entrain*." But how could *entrain* be possible
after such a meal?

In 1880, after two years at the Consulate and having
had the privilege, though only twenty-five, of acting for
two months as Consul-General in London, I was called
back to Paris where our Ministry was being reorganized.

CHAPTER V

TUNIS

1880–1887

In the autumn of 1880, our Foreign Minister was the learned hellenist, Senator Barthélemy Saint-Hilaire, born in 1805, the trusty second and admirer of Thiers, of whom he liked to say: "You may disagree with Voltaire and you may disagree with M. Thiers, but you cannot pretend not to understand what they mean."

He selected me to be sub-chief of his secretariat; the chief being a personal friend of his, René Millet, later Resident-General in Tunis, who went afterwards to the United States to lecture. Of ready pen and tongue, well versed in the classics, Millet sometimes chose, for his amusement, to write to me, even on business matters, in Latin.

Close-shaven, with handsome regular features, austere yet courteous, more indulgent to others than to himself, Barthélemy Saint-Hilaire was a man of principles, a worshipper of Aristotle, to a translation of whose complete works into French he had devoted all the time left by his political duties. He said to me once: "Young man, choose, for intellectual work, a subject so ample that it will not be possible for you to see the end of it; thus will you have, throughout life, a faithful companion. I hear that you think of writing a history of English Literature; you will begin it and finish it, and your life will continue, deprived of that intellectual companion. Happier than you, I have selected a task which I have no chance of completing and which will keep me company to my last day." But the oracle for once went

52

wrong: I was destined never to finish the Literary History of the English People, of which I was then but vaguely thinking, and as for him, his life was so long and his industry so persistent, that he saw the end of his translation of Aristotle. Nothing dismayed, however, he began one of Plato.

He considered that he was wrong not to have married, and said to his youthful secretaries: "Young men: think of all that society has done for you, what protection you have received, what accumulated treasures of art and science are at your disposal, what progress mankind has made, to the benefit of us, who are living now. You will never be able to repay society for its benefactions. One thing, however, you can do, continue it, get married."

An optimist, he also said: "The proof that in society there is more good than evil, is that society still exists."

Of steady mind, he was never upset by anything that occurred and had that disdain for "fortuitous happenings" on which learned Budæus had written a treatise at the Renaissance. Old-fashioned in material matters he would never use any but quill pens and considered steel ones as a mischievous invention: they give one the writers' cramp. Like his mind, his handwriting was steady; neither slow nor hurried and as regular withal as print. His voice too was steady; when addressing the Chamber the sober distinction of his manners, his obvious sincerity and honesty made him impressive; raillery thrown at him would not stagger him, but fall at his feet, *telum imbelle sine ictu.* An early riser, he was at his desk at six, sometimes at five o'clock. We were expected, Millet or I, to enter his room at eight and give him an account of the morning papers and of the telegrams arrived during the night. I wrote to my mother: "I see him often, but only on business. I had to call on him very early yesterday; he was dressing. We talked of a rather important affair while he was changing his shirt. But he was not rising then; he

had been at work since five, without having dressed."
Again, to the same: "He never pays me the slightest
compliment, but he speaks favourably of me to others
who tell me."

The leaders of most nations, in the last third of the
nineteenth century, longed for an increase of their
country's place on the map, the United States being no
exception. Tunis was then for us the chief problem;
the prospect that another nation, perhaps a not very
friendly one, might secure predominance over a state
adjoining and rounding off to the east our Algerian
possessions, gave our statesmen food for thought. This
question was the principal one that Barthélemy
Saint-Hilaire had to deal with in his thirteen months'
tenure of office. I was entrusted with all the work concerning it, under the leadership of Baron de Courcel,
Political Director, later Ambassador to Germany and
to England, a clear-minded, resourceful, well-informed
diplomat who knew when to wait and when to take
risks and decide promptly.

Maladministration, disordered finances, local troubles
and aggressions were incitements to foreign intervention,
ours or that of others. We had fortunately as our representative in Tunis a model servant of his country, Théodore
Roustan, afterwards French Minister to the United
States; all his family, his father, his brothers were of
the same stamp; one brother became an admiral,
another a colonel. Of pleasing manners, more prone
to smile than to frown, he had nevertheless a firm will,
a watchful eye and no other purpose in life than to make
France respected and liked. His services during the
seven years he spent in Tunis were of the highest order.
They are as completely forgotten now as if they had been
rendered in the moon.

On the occasion of the Congress of Berlin, held in
the summer of 1878, after the war which had brought the
Russians to the gates of Constantinople, a number of

nations—Russia, Austria, to whom was given the upper
hand in Bosnia and Herzegovina, England who got hold
of Cyprus, the Balkan states—secured material advantages; Bulgaria that of being born. Our representative,
M. Waddington, then Minister of Foreign Affairs and
later Ambassador to England, seconded by Count de
Saint-Vallier, Ambassador to Germany, wisely limited
himself to our understanding with Bismarck and Lord
Salisbury to the effect that, should circumstances lead us
to interfere in Tunis, there would be no objection from
their countries. Not only did Bismarck and Salisbury
agree, but they went even further than we desired and
recommended an annexation pure and simple which
was not in our thoughts. " Do what you like there,"
said Lord Salisbury to M. Waddington, adding: " You
will be obliged to take it; you cannot leave Carthage in
the hands of the Barbarians." [1] Bismarck said to Count
de Saint-Vallier: " Gather this African fruit; if you
don't it might be stolen by somebody else." [2]

On this point the German Chancellor never ceased to
insist. In a conversation of November 28, 1880, he
revealed to Count de Saint-Vallier the inner thoughts
of our southern neighbours and told him of a visit
received by him four years before from " a certain Mr.
Crispi " (the famous Crispi of later years), " who," said
Bismarck, " offered me with the cynicism of a malefactor
the most shameful bargain. . . . In his cheap generosity
he gave us the territories of Champagne, Burgundy and
Franche-Comté, reserving, it is true, for himself Savoy,
Nice, the Dauphiné, and Provence, with Marseille and
Toulon. I simply asked him whether he counted on
my grenadiers to go and take them. Same offers concerning Austria: to us Bohemia, Silesia, Northern

---

[1] M. Waddington to the Marquis d'Harcourt, July 21, 1878.
Documents Diplomatiques Français, 1st series, II, p. 362.
[2] Count de Saint-Vallier to M. Waddington, January 5, 1879,
ibid., p. 412.

Tyrol; to them the Trentino, Istria, Trieste, Dalmatia. . . . I continued for three days to be pestered by his entreaties and I ended the way I should have begun, by showing him the door. He revenged himself by a flood of mendacious publications which I disdained to refute." [1]

As we did not want trouble with anybody, we had thought of advantages which might be reserved for the Italians, in some other part of Northern Africa or in Albania. Bismarck excluded this latter hypothesis, because he said " it would cause too much sorrow to my friend Andrassy."

As regarded us he never varied, declaring that, moreover, he would with pleasure see us develop our interests in Morocco, Syria, Egypt, etc. [2] His favourable dispositions toward us were caused by mixed motives: he was then in favour of such a *rapprochement* with France as the memory of 1870 would allow. He had been struck by the vitality we had shown after our disasters and deemed that, if not friendship, at least other relations than enmity were worth trying for; the more so that other nations inclined to show that our friendship was in their eyes worth having. He did not conceal his way of thinking and plainly told our Ambassador that he wanted us, by these means, to think less of Metz and Strasbourg. As for colonies, personally, he did not care for them: let others take as many as they pleased, the more busy they would be there, the less active in Europe.

Measures were at once contemplated to turn to account the good-will that had been shown us and the draft of an agreement for the Bey to sign was tentatively sketched, by the first article of which he would have obligated himself never to cede any part of his possessions to any foreign country. But, whatever was the case with some of her leaders, France was then as little colonially inclined

---

[1] *Documents Diplomatiques Français*, 1st series, III, p. 476.
[2] Count de Saint-Vallier to Baron de Courcel, November, 12, 1880.

as Bismarck himself; feelers showed the Government
that they could count neither on the assent of Parliament
nor of public opinion; nothing, therefore, was done and
it remained for Barthélemy Saint-Hilaire to, so to speak,
cash the cheque placed in our hands at Berlin three
years before.

Early in 1881, he and his Political Director, Baron de
Courcel, came to the conclusion, from the information
received, that the time had come for a decisive step if
we did not want to be forestalled. But public opinion,
Parliament, the Press were still restive. The first notes
I was requested to draw up in view of an action in Tunis
were of January 1881. In March Barthélemy Saint-
Hilaire proposed certain measures at a Cabinct meeting,
but only three Ministers sided with him, and without
altering his purpose he had to postpone it.[1] Prime
Minister Jules Ferry is usually considered as having been
the initiator of the enterprise, but he assented to it only
later when the incursions of the unruly Tunisian frontier
tribes on our Algerian territory made it difficult to resist
his Foreign Minister's entreaties. As he was President
of the Council, on him especially the Opposition papers
poured their insults and obloquy, with the result that,
as a compensation, the part played by him became
proportionately conspicuous, and he is usually held to
be the prime mover of a policy which was to yield such
advantages to the Republic, mistress afterwards of a
more valuable colonial empire than that founded, and
lost, by the Ancien Régime. His services were, it is
certain, of a high order and he bore the brunt of many
battles; but the real originator of the movement was,
after Waddington, that translator of Aristotle, he of the
quill pens, Barthélemy Saint-Hilaire.

Following the Kroumir troubles on the frontier, a
military expedition was sent to Tunis in April 1881, a

[1] Courcel to Noailles, March 13, 1881. *Documents Diplomatiques*,
1st series, III, 381.

move highly approved of by Bismarck. "Prince Bismarck," Count de Saint-Vallier telegraphed on the 24th, "has again asked Count Limburg to express to me his wishes for the prompt success of our Tunisian enterprise, which has all his sympathies because it is a civilizing process that will profit all Europe. The Press and public opinion fully agree." [1] England, on the other hand, forgetting the assurances given us at Berlin, remained openly hostile and supported our opponents.

Our military expedition had an easy success; the country was occupied almost without bloodshed. Then were seen the results of Roustan's wise policy; owing to him France had many friends and an important part of the population, much less warlike than that of Algeria or Morocco, had no objection to our coming in. Indifferent to any personal danger, Roustan not only did not leave Tunis, but continued to appear in the streets, making purchases in the *souks*, visiting the Bey, who remained in his palace and prevented his troops from opposing ours. Thus was avoided an open break and a war which public opinion would not have brooked: how could there be war, since our representative remained at his post, and the Bey in his home, where he signed on May 12, 1881, a treaty which was the corner-stone of a protectorate as profitable, the event has shown, to his people as to us.[2]

Now that the undertaking has succeeded beyond

[1] *Documents Diplomatiques*, 1st series, III, 454.

[2] The statement in the *Encyclopædia Britannica* that, "on the 11th of May, the French Foreign Minister, Barthélemy Saint-Hilaire, had officially assured the Italian Ambassador in Paris that France ' had no thought of occupying Tunisia or any part of Tunisian territory beyond some points of the Kroumir country,' " is untenable. Such a pledge on the eve of the treaty, Art. II of which gave us the right to occupy such points in Tunisia as we deemed necessary, would have been at once an act of folly as well as dishonesty. B. Saint-Hilaire, who was neither dishonest nor a fool, handed on the 13th a copy of the treaty to General Cialdini, who made no allusion to any pretended pledge previously given to him. *Documents Diplomatiques Français*, 1st series, III, 511.

expectation, it is difficult to understand the storm of protests raised by the opponents, not so much of the expedition as of the Ministry. Pamphleteers were ready with contumely, insinuations, calumnies, an inexhaustible fund of venom, chief of them Henri Rochefort, feared by everyone. Ferry was the principal mark for his barbed shafts. He did not know Roustan, had nothing against him, but wanted his destruction because that would be one more way to injure Ferry. After an article exceeding the others in violence, and in which, as a recompense for a life of honour, probity and disinterestedness, Roustan was described as having engineered the military expedition in order " to steal millions on corpses," Gambetta, who, in November, had become Prime Minister and Minister of Foreign Affairs, unwisely decided that Rochefort should be summoned for libel before the criminal court. The jury, by one of those whims to which this institution is sometimes addicted, acquitted Rochefort. The Government fortunately stood by its servant and promoted him Minister to the United States.

Eloquent, fearless, warm-hearted, deep-voiced, red-faced, full-bearded, with semi-long hair that he shook like a mane, big-bellied Gambetta read, when he assumed office, a note of mine on Tunis, desired to know the author and showed me thenceforth an affectionate friendship. As my cough still hung on, he would say with his strong southern accent: " Take care of your health, little one (*mong pétit*), we shall have need of it." Later, after he had left office, he desired our relations to continue and I visited him now and then in his home, Rue des Belles-Feuilles, where I was touched to see in place of honour two terrible daubs, representing his father and mother, the retail grocers of Cahors.

In December he sent me on a mission to Tunis, in order to report on the situation there.

I had no trouble in collecting evidence of the absolute inanity of the accusations levelled at Roustan and I sent a memoir accompanied by incontrovertible documents. In accordance with Gambetta's request I also tried to form an opinion on the best way to reorganize the country. The situation was so clear that it did not leave room for much hesitation. All the local organization, from the Bey downwards, must be maintained, but controlled, so that the Arabs should not feel the hand of the foreigner, and yet should no longer suffer from the exactions of petty administrative tyrants. Much might be expected from those same tyrants if they could once be persuaded to renounce, as dangerous to themselves, their bad habits, for they were very intelligent, knew well the temper of the various sections of the population and were quite able to understand that the time for pilfering had passed. They were to be watched, and in serious cases advised or admonished, but not suppressed.

Our establishment should be as unmilitary as the necessity of keeping order would allow. Thanks to Roustan there had been no break and military action had been chiefly against unruly tribes over whom the Bey himself had so little power that he had every year to send his brother at the head of his regular troops to make them pay their annual dues. At his request, and as a sign that we were not at war, we had decided that our army would not enter Tunis. I suggested in my letters to Gambetta and his successor Mr. de Freycinet (for Gambetta's " grand ministry " lasted only two months and a half), that, contrary to what had long prevailed in Algeria, the head of such power as we might exercise should be a civilian, to be called Resident and to be assisted by a very small well-chosen personnel; that the head of the military be a major-general recently promoted, with the understanding that he would rank under the Resident; that the finances should be reformed, as was easy in such a rich country. The public debt should be bought up in its entirety by France, which would rid us of a cumbersome and meddling International Commission, and which we could do without any expense; for we issued a loan at 4 per cent., and the maladministered revenues allotted to the Commission yielded a little more than that. A reform of justice was also suggested with the creation of a French tribunal at Tunis and justices of the peace in the principal other towns, which would allow the suppression of the capitulations; also an extension of public instruction, in a country where such a large proportion of the people were quick-minded, of artistic and literary dispositions and desirous to learn. My plan included even the instruction of Moslem women, of whom scarcely any, even in the capital, even in the richest families, knew how to read. Moslem women of education willing to teach might be brought from Algiers.

The days thus passed in Tunis were busy ones. Much of the time was spent in seeing people, of every walk in life, visiting public establishments, such as schools, hospitals, our consular tribunal, Moslem courts of justice, the mint, following the narrow lanes and examining the *souks* (shops in the bazar), driving to the places of importance in the environs, sketching and painting watercolours at every corner of interest—and all corners in the picturesque capital were of interest.

No visit was worthier of remembrance than one to Cardinal Lavigerie, " once Cardinal Priest of the Holy Roman Church, Archbishop of Carthage and Algiers, Primate of Africa, now ashes," as one reads to-day on his tomb. Tall, long-bearded, of strong build, liberal-minded, a trusty friend and adviser of Pope Leo XIII, he was one of the most impressive men one could see. Living at La Marsa near Tunis he had excellent relations with the Moslem priest of the neighbouring mosque. He was the holder of some *habous* property, *i.e.* religious property, which, as in European countries during the Middle Ages, was usually granted by the original donor on condition that some public obligation be fulfilled, the upkeep, for instance, of roads and bridges. But in most cases those obligations were left unobserved. For his piece of property the Cardinal was expected, under the terms of the foundation, to keep a lamp burning in the mosque. " I keep it lit he said, I consider it a duty; and it is, in fact, the only one that burns there."

He prescribed to his missionaries, *les Pères Blancs*, never to try to make converts by any kind of pressure; to convert fetichists was possible, to convert Moslems almost impossible; the missionaries were to live among them, be helpful in any circumstances, gain their affection, and that was all. Years later, at a ceremony to honour the memory of the Cardinal himself, at the Sorbonne, my wife happened to sit next to one of his *Sœurs Blanches* and spoke of that problem. The Sister said that they continued to follow the same rules and told of a poor Arab woman whom she had attended and who was dying of a dreadful disease; her face was nearly destroyed, she was horrible to look at. One day the physician said that he would not return; nothing could save her, and he could do nothing more for her; he left her in the hands of the Sister, who continued to tend her to the last. As the end was drawing near, the woman said: " I want to be baptized." The Sister objected: " Are you sure that you really want it? Is it not out of kindness, to please me? "—" No," said the woman, " I want it; the religion that moves you to do what you do for me must be the true one."

In those rambles, the hill of Saint Louis was not forgotten, the ancient Byrsa of the Carthaginians, from the summit of which the eye ranges over the Tunis lake, the open sea, the remnants of the harbour of the Punic city, the place where the King of France, Saint Louis, died in 1270; and in the little museum where the Cardinal's *Pères Blancs*, chief among whom Father Delattre, keep their principal finds, is to be seen a small object found on the spot, which we of France cannot see without emotion, a gold piece of Thibault de Champagne, companion of Saint Louis in his last crusade. The great friend, and former companion, Joinville, who did not care to be heroic when he could help it, was not there; " of the journey that the King made to Tunis," he wrote, " I shall say nothing, for God be thanked I was not of it."

Tunisian justice was still as picturesque and mediæval as the *souks* and lanes of the capital. High above all tribunals was the Bey himself, who rendered justice publicly in person every Saturday. The Prophet had rendered justice; the Bey must therefore do the same. I was present once. On such occasions the Prince left his favourite villa at La Marsa and came to his close-by official residence, the Bardo, a mile and a half from Tunis, an extraordinary conglomerate of halls, arcades, staircases, galleries, courtyards with ever-singing fountains, rooms recalling in some measure the Alhambra, so splendidly decorated they are, and of sheer crumbling ruins. The upkeep of any place was contrary to the improvident spirit then prevalent. If any part of those buildings ceased for a time to be in use it was allowed to fall to pieces; if wanted again, it was not repaired, but another was built a little further, so that, ceaselessly increasing, ruins and buildings spread more and more.

In a large hall, the ceiling of which is covered with mirrors partly concealed by arabesques of gilt wood, the Bey Mohamed el Sadock, sat on such days upon a red throne in Louis XVth style. He was good-looking, of noble mien, with an air of majesty, and wore a high and heavy red *chechia* (an Oriental cap special to Tunis, with a dark blue tassel), a black coat of European cut, trimmed with ermine, and military red trousers. He remains almost motionless on his throne, his gloved hands, which are very small, are crossed before him. His ready-lit pipe is brought, a pipe the cherry wood stem of which is seven feet long; the amber mouth-

piece rests on the arm of the throne and a thin spiral of
blue smoke rises from the bowl resting on the carpet
below the steps of the throne. The Bey does not
smoke; the pipe is only an emblem of his power: he
needs no concentration of his thoughts on the cases submitted to him, for he is inspired from above.

Around him, his nephews and other princes, the grand
dignitaries in semi-European costume, the sub-dignitaries
in much more becoming arabian garb, are alined along
the walls, two ranks deep. The heralds, dressed in red
with gold stripes, march past one by one.

Opposite the throne, at the other end of the hall, the
great door under which the complainants appear; two
officers hold them by the shoulders; in the small space
back of them, the Arab crowd, the common people, are
allowed to stand and witness what is going on. Complainants are of all sorts; the poor appear in their
tattered garments, with shoeless feet clotted with mud.
There are Bedouin women, blue-tattooed (country-
women do not wear the veil), Jews with black turbans,
green-turbaned Arabs in some way connected with the
family of the Prophet, soldiers of his Highness' regular
army in black tunics mended with yellowed thread. Each
complainant explains his trouble from the further end of
the hall in as piteous a manner as he can, but in not
more than two minutes. The General *Bachamba* (head
of the *hambas* or gendarmes) sums up their little speech
in a few words, very loudly pronounced so that the Bey
can hear them distinctly. The Bey listens and delivers
his sentence instantly, in some four words which the
notaries register, and it is executed at once.

The Arabs like this promptness; the poorest of the
beggars is happy to think that he can be judged by his
Prince, which happens quite frequently, and that he
has an impartial judge. The Bey, at least, is inaccessible
to gifts, and as he preserves in the eyes of his subjects a
sacred character, people scarcely venture to lie to him,

which makes it easier for him not to go wrong in his awards; his decisions are accepted by everybody without contestation or protest. And there is no need, in order to be admitted before him, that it be a case of assassination or the appropriating of somebody else's fortune. Here is a Bedouin woman in tears who complains that, for having stolen two asses, her son is kept in prison, and has been there for such a long time!— Ordered that she pay for the two asses and the rest of the prison term will be remitted.—A soldier of the Bey's regular army belonged to the troops sent, as a sign of friendship, to help us subdue the rebellious tribes; he was to receive some pay but has got nothing.—Ordered that, as everybody in the country is in the same case, he shall continue to get nothing.

Death sentences do not need any more preparation or time. There had been one the Saturday before. An old Arab, more than sixty, had killed two members of his family. The Bey had listened to him for two minutes, in three words had sentenced him, and ten minutes later the man had been publicly hanged under the windows of the palace. In another case a strange discussion had taken place between the Bey and the murderer. The family of the victim claimed the head of the murderer or 20,000 piastres, which was held a considerable sum in spite of the value of the Tunisian piastre being then only sixty centimes. The guilty man addressing the Bey said: " I am a villain, I am not worth such a sum, let me be hanged." But the Bey was touched by his courage and said: " Do not give up; I will help thee to pay; I will give thee half the sum."— " No, I am a villain, I do not deserve to be helped; it is better that I die." Then said the Bey: " Be it as thou wilt," and the man was hanged.[1]

[1] These same scenes are described in an article of the *Revue des Deux Mondes* (October 1, 1882) signed "J. de Saint-Haon." But J. de Saint-Haon is myself, and so is the " Jacques Tissot " of the Tunisian instalment in the *France Coloniale*, 1888.

F

Not very different from the Bey's justice must have been that of Saint Louis under the oak tree of the Vincennes forest.

Toward the end of February 1882 I was back in Paris. When, at the end of my mission, I had been received by the Bey and he had given me his order, upon which the dignitaries had all exclaimed *mabrouk! mabrouk!* (may it bring luck to you), he had expressed the wish that I should live long and continue to occupy myself with Tunis. I saw the Minister, M. de Freycinet, and found that part at least of the Bey's wish was being fulfilled: a Bureau of Tunisian affairs was to be created and offered to me. My only request, on accepting, was that my authority and responsibility be complete, that the whole question, so far as our Ministry was concerned, be centred in my hands, with no interference from other bureaus, and that all the correspondence and documents pertaining to Tunis be always within my reach and kept in my own office, which was granted.

This arrangement lasted five years and I never worked at any task with a more passionate desire to contribute to its success. It was for France a new experiment, the beginning of a new policy, and it was of the utmost importance to avoid failure. It luckily so happened that the few who had to deal with the problem felt, all of them, the same passion, and were on every point in constant agreement. Roustan, appointed French Minister to the United States, had been replaced by Paul Cambon, who later, as a diplomat, reached well-deserved celebrity, and who, as a Prefect, had become familiar with all that pertains to administration. Of affable manners and with a sense of humour, he had a broad and open mind, neither averse nor favourable to precedents as such, nor to men of various races or origin as such; able to judge for himself, he decided on the merits of each man or each case. Wherever he was employed he rendered immense services.

He chose for his seconds Baron d'Estournelles, later a senator, a diplomat of experience and resource in spite of his youth, and M. Maurice Bompard, later Ambassador to Russia and Turkey, of great administrative experience, both indefatigable workers with a high sense of duty. Finances were in the hands of M. Depienne inherited from Roustan, and no public Treasury was ever better safeguarded than the Tunisian one under his care. The slightest avoidable expense caused him acute pangs; collectors of taxes were more and more strictly watched; we prided ourselves on providing for all the Tunisian outlay, and developing the Regency without having to appeal to the Chambers for funds. The result was that, four years later, the public revenues had almost doubled and we had interfered with taxation only to diminish it: a good example for some greater nations.

What helped above all was the good understanding between us all that never, for one minute, failed. " What most surprises new-comers," Cambon wrote me, " is the harmony prevailing among us. What, no conflicts! No acrimony! Robin on good terms with Bompard; Depienne spending his nights studying a diminution of taxes that breaks his heart; people help each other and at need do each other's work. How different from what happens elsewhere! " The fact is that there was more than harmony between us, there was trust and affection. In the same letter Cambon wrote: " I have asked d'Estournelles to tell you how cold, when I think of it again, our parting seems to me, in that corridor of the Elysée on a rainy day, after five months of life in common. I ought to have held you to my heart and told you how much I love you, but you know it." (June 21, 1884.)

Peace reigned in the country; no insurrections, no riots, even the unruly tribes of the west and the south quieted down, security was complete. Mines, fisheries, agriculture developed. Wherever a roman ruin was

found, were it in the driest sand of the desert, one was
sure that a spring must have existed thereabout, and
search was made until it was found. When found, it
was protected by a low wall against the sand, a little
moss and verdure soon grew, then some bushes, later
some trees, and that part of the land was reclaimed.

Every precaution was taken not to hurt the feelings
of the inhabitants. Not only was their religion respected,
but in many cases we invoked it instead of our own regu-
lations, to make them act properly. At the time when
cholera caused havoc in many Mediterranean cities, we
greatly feared that Tunis would not escape. There were
large cemeteries in or near the city dotted with innumerable small white tombs, often visited at sundown by
relatives of the dead; but the dead were buried very
near the surface, with results, in a warm climate, which
can be readily imagined. There is nothing natives hate
so much as foreign interference with their mode of burial.
We did not interfere, but asked the Cadi Maleki (one of
the two heads of their religion) how a true faithful should
be interred. He answered : " So deep in the soil that a
man, standing in the grave, would have earth up to his
shoulders." We answered: " Would you put this in
writing and seal it with your seal? "—" Certainly." This
was placarded all over the city, a regulation almost
similar to ours was thus enforced; there was no trouble,
and, whether owing to this or by some happy chance,
no cholera in Tunis.

The political opponents of a colonial policy had not
disarmed and, in spite of the favourable results, went
on merrily with their insults and obloquy. The Government thought that by giving them some satisfaction they
might quiet them; but, taught wisdom by the Roustan
affair, they limited themselves to an investigating committee presided over by Count de Saint-Vallier; and
the findings were that there was not the slightest ground
for the Press and pamphleteer attacks.

One day the Minister (Flourens) asked me to call on him and handed me a number of the *Lanterne,* not the famous one of Rochefort, but nevertheless one of the most feared Opposition papers. In it was a virulent article on the policies attributed to me, and which rendered impossible, it was said, the proper colonization of Tunis.

" How do you feel about it? " asked the Minister.

" I feel callous."

" But there is such an article every other day."

" They waste their time, I never read that paper."

The Minister had the kindness to say that this was the proper course. The attacks, I suppose, continued; we, at all events, continued our nefarious policy.

CHAPTER VI

LATE in the summer of 1885, I received at the Ministry
the visit of the afore-mentioned Guillaume Guizot, son
of the famous historian and Prime Minister of King Louis-
Philippe. Lean, deep-wrinkled from his youth, a pack
of nerves, of wide knowledge and wonderful memory,
he had once won a bet that he would remember two
hundred consecutive lines of a tragedy heard by him for
the first time: he remembered three hundred. A hard
worker and excellent talker, prone to enthusiasm, ever
ready to spring to the help of others, he never turned his
rare qualities to permanent account and wrote almost
nothing. He lives in the memory of those who knew him,
and they are becoming scarce.

His only public function was a professorship at the
Collège de France, that extraordinary institution founded
in the early days of the Renaissance by Francis I, for
sciences outside the pale of the normal teaching in
universities. The lectures delivered there do not lead to
a brevet, a diploma, a degree; they lead to nothing
except knowledge. It is one of the few of our institutions
that has never been altered; a number of our master-
minds have taught at the Collège; there are no fees for
the students, no matriculation; any comer is admitted;
he has only to push the door open, be it even a man who
feels cold in the street and comes in to get warm; he will
get warm and perhaps listen too. Some professors fill
the largest hall to capacity, and to get seated the crowd

70

comes long before the lecture begins; others deal with
such abstruse subjects that they have sometimes the
humiliation of confronting empty benches. The professor must in that case wait a quarter of an hour; if no
one has appeared then, he signs the presence sheet and
goes home.

The story is famous at the Collège of such a professor,
who was once favoured with the presence of one single
listener. Delighted, he spoke his best, and when his
allotted time (an hour) was about finished he said: " You
will pardon me, my dear *auditeur*, if I keep you a little
longer; there is one more point of view, of great
importance, that I would like to develop before you."

The *auditeur* answered: " Do as you please, *patron*,
I am your cabby, and you have hired me by the
hour."

Guillaume Guizot was not one of those, and he always
had large audiences. The object of his visit was to
inform me that he was threatened with a serious illness,
and would like me to replace him the following winter.
A great honour to be sure, but I had never spoken in
public and never delivered lectures. A professor who is
new to it, if he falters and feels shy, has a right to indulgence; but a secretary of Embassy who is bold enough to
lecture from one of the most famous chairs in the country
can expect none. I thought the matter over and came to
the conclusion that, since there was a kind of danger in
the attempt, to refuse would be cowardice, and the
proposal should therefore be accepted. The result was that
when I thought of it, in bed at night, I could not sleep.

To my Tunisian occupations, much literary work was
thus superadded; subjects had to be thought of, notes
to be garnered; very little time was left for such a
preparation, as winter was not far away. You were
expected at the Collège de France to deliver two different
series of lectures each week: one for the general public,
the other, more technical, for a more erudite audience.

I chose for my chief series the history of the English novel up to the time of Walter Scott, and for the other, the contemporaries of Chaucer, which included of course my dear Piers Plowman.

My autumn vacation was spent first in London or rather in the British Museum, where I arrived when it opened and left when it closed, and, late in October, at Saint-Haon where my mother was then alone. Except for a brief walk each day in the mountains, all my time was devoted to the preparation for the Collège. In order to accustom me to speak in public, my mother devised an excellent system; she made me deliver a lecture to her each evening after dinner, with no written text, and only notes. I stood at one end of the drawing-room, and my public, that is herself, was seated at the other end; a single lamp but partly dispelled the obscurity. In the silence of the night, that empty space, that single judge, not of the easiest to please, were very impressive. To that drill, and to the one who instituted it, I owe more than I can say.

Back in Paris where Tunisian affairs claimed most of my time, I, however, continued my preparation, using for it every shred of any spare moment. The day before the courses were to begin at the Collège de France (another building which I then entered for the first time), I called on the janitor and asked in what room I would have to speak.

" In the largest."

" Is there anyone who speaks there before my day comes ? "

" Yes, Mr. Boissier."

I went the next day to hear Gaston Boissier and I returned dismayed. He spoke with such eloquence, such wit, such good grace, that I was terrified and thought, if this is what audiences are accustomed to at the Collège, I am disgraced. I wrote to my mother, on December 7th : " I begin to-morrow ; I am still full of apprehension."

An opening lecture is there a sort of solemnity. The speaker does not actually speak, but reads a paper carefully prepared in advance; he is in evening dress and white tie. Guillaume Guizot was present on the platform to see how his substitute would behave, and I could not help remembering what I had been told had happened when he himself delivered his opening lecture. His nerves gave way and he fainted. His august father, who was present, helped to restore him to consciousness, and made him continue his lecture as if nothing had happened.

My luck was better. When, greatly moved, I entered the large hall, packed with people curious to see how a secretary of Embassy would succeed, a sort of pre-rooseveltian thought occurred to me, namely, that there were not two sorts of cowardice, the fear of bullets and the fear of a public, but only one, which must be conquered. The moment I had said " Messieurs " (for in those days, ladies, though present, were not mentioned), all trace of fear vanished; 'twas like a cloud that dissolves. I spoke much longer than the regulation time, and the public paid me the compliment that no one budged.[1]

With his kind-heartedness and his courtesy, Guillaume Guizot wrote the same evening to my mother, whom he did not know, telling her that the opening lecture " had succeeded well and had pleased an audience numerous in spite of the snow which had been falling since the morning. I was not surprised, for I knew the text and found it excellent, full and well ordered, accurate and subtle, leaving the impression that it came from a heart in the right place and a mind that knows its goal. The voice is unaffected and sonorous."

He came also to my second lesson and wrote again: " I can once more send you good news. I was present

---

[1] The text was printed under the title of *Le Roman Anglais ; Origine et Formation des Grandes Ecoles de Romanciers du XVIIIème Siècle.*

this morning at Julius' second lesson or rather his other first, for he treated a different subject and had, not to read, but to speak from notes. The second experience has succeeded as well as the first; it is even more important in my eyes than the first. He spoke quite freely and simply, with equal modesty and assurance, as a young man whose mind is both quick and mature, who masters his subject and his ideas and knows how to impart and explain them with no make-believe imposed on his public or himself."

The total number of lectures for a complete course was then forty. I was replacing Guizot for only a semester, but as he was ill, I tried to leave him as few as possible, and delivered thirty.[1] He was able then to resume his chair, but year by year he grew worse; a cancer finally necessitated the ablation of his tongue. His good grace and equanimity never left him. Admiring his stoicism, suggestive of Cato of Utica, his doctor said to him one day: " One would think you had been born in Utica." The dying man asked for a pencil, and wrote: " You are mistaken, my dear Doctor, Cato was not born in Utica, but he died there."

Life was pretty hard while I was delivering those lectures, two a week, for my functions at the Ministry had become at the same time more and more exacting; to my " realms and empires," and as a supplement to Tunis, had been added Annam, Madagascar, Obok, Congo, the Western Coast of Africa and other places. In March 1886, as my course was about finished, the Minister (Freycinet) handed me a decree carrying an important promotion.

" Are you pleased? " he asked.

" Very much."

" But it is upon one condition, namely, that you cease delivering lectures at the Collège de France."

[1] Those relating to the earlier period were printed under the title of *Le Roman au Temps de Shakespeare*, 1887, and appeared later in English as *The English Novel in the Time of Shakespeare*.

" Have you heard that there was anything wrong in them? "

" Not at all, I have heard them praised, but we want you to belong entirely to us."

ABOUT " TURC "

As I was walking in the Bois early one morning, in February 1887, I made an unexpected acquaintance. Feeling that I was followed, I turned round and saw a tall, big dog, covered with dust, looking as if it had long been lost, but, dust apart, very handsome, with black glossy, curly hair. He had no collar nor any mark allowing the identification of his master. I tried to drive him away, even giving him a few (not very hard) raps; all to no avail. He waited until my fit of bad humour had passed and trotted behind me again, or sometimes in front, for he would go ahead and return as if we were bound by long-established ties. I entered a shop, he politely waited at the door, and continued to dog my steps wherever I went until lunch-time, when I could not forbear inviting him, so he lunched with me. I paid some calls, and he waited outside. At the Ministry he entered my office and settled quietly under a table as if he had been accustomed to do so from his birth.

I was dining far away that evening with the Mimauts, place Malesherbes; Mr. Mimaut, afterwards Minister to Norway, son and grandson of Consuls-General, had been my predecessor in London. I thought, if that dog crosses so many places and streets in the same disposition of mind I shall do something for him. I went on foot, never called the dog, whistled nor made any sign to him. He acted like a dog on a jaunt with his master, ran about, spoke to other dogs, and faithfully returned. The Mimauts, great friends of dogs, asked him to dinner, and we sought to discover his name. We tried on him all sorts of dogs' names. At the word *Turc* he wagged his tail, so we concluded that he must be called Turc.

But what to do with him? Such a vast dog would not be very happy in my bachelor's rooms. Nisard, Political Director, afterwards Ambassador to the Pope, famous among us for his wit, but as kind-hearted as witty, proposed that we jointly adopt him, that he become " *l'enfant du Ministère* "; some of the ushers would attend to his needs. But neither did this plan seem very practical; so I wired to my mother asking whether she would give hospitality at Saint-Haon to a splendid, large dog that had become attached to me. Mother answered: " Send splendid dog if not mad," which was pure wisdom.

I had Turc taken, therefore, to a veterinary who kept him under observation, and after a while reported that he was all right. I had a crate made, for the animal was too big to enter the ordinary dog compartments in railroads, and sent him on his travels, advising that a large bowl of soup be ready for him on arrival, for he was very greedy.

He was received with due honour, adorned with a beautiful collar bearing our name and address, fed, fêted, petted, as well treated as dog ever was.

But then, and then only, was his true nature revealed. That passion for following me which I had deemed so flattering, he displayed in favour of anyone, and preferably of the first man to call in the morning. This was usually the postman, and as we enjoy rural delivery, the man had far to go in the mountains. The dog kept him company, did to death such chickens as he could catch, and, as his collar bore our name, my mother received endless complaints and demands for indemnities on account of slaughtered chickens.

Another trick of my favourite was to go and bathe in a small pool in the garden, covered with water-weeds. He impregnated his glossy curly hair with them, and slipping into the drawing-room, when he found the door ajar, shook himself vigorously and the weeds alighted on mirrors, pictures, clocks and other unlikely places.

This lasted a pretty long time, mother in her kindness being unwilling to be severe on her eldest son's protégé. But the dog made himself more and more unbearable, and had to be presented to the *pati*. The *pati* was, in many villages, a sort of Autolycus, to whom was offered anything one did not know what to do with, but he knew: furniture broken beyond repair, tattered clothes, rags of all sorts. Turc, collar removed, was offered to him, and received with joy. He took the dog to the nearest city of importance, fourteen kilometres away, with a large railway station; he passed to and fro before travellers sipping drinks till their train appeared. He found at last a traveller who just happened to want a good watch-dog. " The very thing I can offer you," said the *pati*; " there never was such a good watch-dog; just look at him; his face denotes his disposition." The traveller agreed that the dog's face was one to inspire confidence. He gladly paid fifty francs, even more gladly received, and he started with the dog for some distant destination and an unknown fate. That was the last we heard of Turc. Moral: Do not too easily trust even good-looking chance acquaintances.

I had promised not to lecture any more at the Collège de France and I never did; I was asked later to deliver a course at the Ecole Libre des Sciences Politiques; I declined; but just like old Barthélemy Saint-Hilaire, I found it impossible to give up all literary pursuits. To indulge in them was not, as I was glad to think, betraying the ministerial trust, but facilitating the fulfilment of my official duties; some rest is indispensable, but a change of work is often more invigorating for the mind than rest pure and simple. So that, in spite of Tunis, Madagascar, Annam, Equatorial Africa, etc., vast plans again haunted my thoughts: that same dream of a Literary History of the English People very different from Taine's English Literature; also the launching of a collection of small books, well printed, with good portraits, devoted by the best French writers of the present to the best French writers of the past. I had been struck by the fact that, in our busy lives, handsome complete editions of the nation's classics had little practical attraction; they were of use for serious study, but not for the vacant hours of more frequent recurrence. And thus the book which opens, so to say, of its own accord at such moments, is the novel last published, while great men's works, complete and intact, as motionless as family portraits, venerated on trust, remain in their dignified array on the upper shelves of our libraries. They are admired but neglected; they seem too distant, too different, too learned, too inaccessible; and the empty hour, filled anyhow, passes and we get accustomed to leaving in loneliness our old authors, mute majesties with whom no familiar talk is being sought.

My idea was of a *rapprochement*, a greater intimacy, a knowledge easily acquired through pleasantly written short books about those famous men living in solemn temples too rarely visited. John Morley had given an example with his *English Men of Letters*; I desired, however, that the French public be offered biographies not only of our great writers of all times, but of their works. For such works have a life of their own, an endless life, in the course of which they may behave well or not, help or hinder, elevate or debase. Not every contributor to the collection, it is true, fulfilled that important but especially difficult part of the programme.

I felt confident that there was room in contemporary France for something else than the frivolous literature that encumbered our book-stalls and for which we were often severely reprehended by foreign critics. The idea remained hatching for several years; I spoke of it to many in the hope that somebody with more leisure, and less subject to transfers from one country to another, would take the project in hand and realize it. Nobody would, but all approved of the idea, especially Gaston Paris.

One night, in April 1885, he and I started for Saint-Haon, where we were to be witnesses at my second sister's marriage. No sleepers in those days on that line, no electric or even gas lighting, but just a smoky oil lamp. Instead of attempting an improbable sleep, we discussed the idea of the collection, which was to be of forty volumes in honour of " the Forty " of the French Academy. But who then would be included or rejected? The hours of the night passed like minutes, so passionate was the discussion as to the comparative merits of the dead of long ago, whose shades we conjured up and whose merits we tried to weigh. At dawn we had agreed; a list of forty names had been drawn up which was not, however, to be faithfully adhered to. As no one was willing to be the editor, I had to assume the task; Hachette agreed to be the publisher, and in 1887 appeared the first volume of *Les Grands Ecrivains Français : Madame de Sévigné* by Gaston Boissier, quickly followed by *Victor Cousin* from the witty pen of Jules Simon; then many others. The success was immediate and has continued up to now; the number of the volumes has reached fifty-eight; Gaston Paris wrote the *Villon*, and the editor of the collection who continued for thirty-five years to read manuscripts, give hints to authors and revise proofs under a variety of climes and circumstances, wrote the *Ronsard*, and dedicated it to the memory of the loved friend with whom long ago he had established a tentative list of the intended series.

Several of the volumes have had as many readers as novels: 27,000 copies of Gaston Boissier's *Sévigné* have been sold; a number of others have reached ten to twenty thousand.

Some were translated into English, not, it is true, entirely to my satisfaction, for one translator, deeming that such patriotism as might be detected in my general introduction

was too tame, added various embellishments of his own
and assured his readers (under my signature) that French
literature had spread as far as wherever La Pérouse had
planted the Tricolour.

La Pérouse! . . . the Tricolour! . . . Déja! . . .

Another relaxation from official labours, and a useful
one too, was the frequenting of some of the leaders of
French thought.   Besides the Sundays of Gaston Paris,
a unique treat, I had much intercourse with Taine,
Renan, Boutroux, Sorel, Gaston Boissier, Anatole France,
Jules Lemaître, and many more.   Taine was superb in
his simplicity, modesty, the evenness of his tone, as
courteous to a beginner as to a celebrity, ready to discuss
any question with either, never reserving for a better
occasion his best thoughts.   When we wanted, Gaston
Paris and I, to have a foreigner gain a favourable impression of France we took him to Taine; the result was
infallible.   But he had a hatred of self-advertisement, of
fakers, of personal publicity; "my books," he said,
"belong to the public, not my person."   He never
granted an interview; his private life (a model) was an
open book to his friends, a closed one to all others.

He liked to entertain, and his dinners in the rue du Bac,
and later rue Cassette, were always of great interest.   When
he was living in the rue du Bac (corner of the Boulevard
Saint-Germain), he had once as his principal guest tall,
white-haired, white-bearded Tourgueneff; Gaston Paris,
young Paul Bourget, and I with others, were present.
Toward the end of the meal, homage, not however in the
form of speeches, was rendered to the famous Russian,
who was told how proud his country must be of him.
"They are very kind to me over there," he answered,
"but I have not in Russia the position you imagine, for
here you know only me, but there are others who enjoy,
among my people, a greater and well-deserved fame."

He described thereupon the merits of a writer absolutely unknown to us, able, he said, " to draw as well as myself those pictures on a reduced scale that you appreciate, but also to paint vast frescoes, great events, masses of personages full of life; a thing that I am unable to do. His name is Tolstoi; you should read his *Guerre et Paix*; a French translation has appeared in Saint-Petersburg; order some copies and then tell me what you think of it."

We did as he suggested and became rapturous over the merits of the unknown author. I lent my copy to a number of people; noticing that their enjoyment was diminished by the difficulty of remembering, in such a vast drama, who was who, I drew up a list of the personages, giving their connections and the various appellations under which they went. The success of the book was such that Hachette, learning of it, decided to give an edition, and hearing of my copy with the list of the *Dramatis Personæ*, asked for it. As it had been lent from one person to another I had some trouble in tracing it. The book turned out to be in the hands of Admiral Gervais, who was to play later such an important part in Franco-Russian relations, but in the course of its pilgrimages my list had been lost, and the new edition had to appear without it.

For several years our little Tunisian group tried with unabated ardour to improve the Regency, develop the best qualities in the natives, and they have many, teach them economy and practise it ourselves, check corruption, endow the country with roads and public works, spread instruction, raise to some extent the standard of living of the many. The results were surprising; in the course of these years, only one European was killed, and that in a brawl; the increase of prosperity struck even the casual observer; when going on their pilgrimage to Mecca, the Tunisians praised our rule to such an extent that sometimes far-away populations would ask us to extend our protectorate over them too. Once the

G

Uganda people sent such a request from their remote place of abode, and we had to answer: "We would with pleasure, but really you live too far." They are now under British rule.

The time came when the work was passed on to different hands, but the more important points of the system which had succeeded have been maintained. Our group was scattered. Mr. Cambon was sent as Ambassador to Madrid, and I, in November 1887, as Counsellor of Embassy to London.

CHAPTER VII

VICTORIAN ENGLAND

THREE years were now spent in London, when the Victorian period still shone in all its lustre, with Browning and Tennyson the poets of the day, Gladstone and Lord Salisbury the statesmen, the one having for his second John Morley, the other his nephew Balfour; Burne-Jones, Alma-Tadema, Sir Frederick Leighton the painters; Meredith, Mrs. Humphry Ward the novelists; Freeman and Lecky the historians, critics and scholars innumerable, Gilbert and Sullivan and their operettas, the Esthetes, the Souls, society leaders bright, handsome, smiling, using, without apprehension of the morrow, their inherited privileges.

The French Embassy was, and still is, at Albert Gate, overlooking Hyde Park. Being Crown land, it cannot be bought and we must rest satisfied with a lease. As it is, however, for 999 years there is no need to worry just yet about what will take place after that.

My new chief, the Ambassador, was the above-mentioned Mr. William H. Waddington, former Minister of Public Instruction and of Foreign Affairs and our First Delegate at the Berlin Congress in 1878. His family had come from England in the eighteenth century and had established in Normandy a prosperous weaving business, thus paying a debt that England had owed us since the time when, at the Revocation of the Edict of Nantes, we had sent her our Huguenot weavers. The Waddingtons had been ennobled by Louis XVI, but had not

83

broken their connection with England; the Ambassador had been a student at Cambridge and had even been a Cambridge *eight* in one of the famous Oxford and Cambridge boat-races. As a remembrance of the event, when the annual race recurred, the carriage horses of the Embassy wore the pale blue ribbons of *their* university; but, as bad luck would have it, the dark blue of Oxford won then every year.

No man was more sincere nor of greater diplomatic probity than Mr. Waddington. His telegrams as accurately reproduced his talks at the Foreign Office as wax reproduces the imprint of a seal.

Madame Waddington, gay and kindly, a good conversationalist, fond of music and of the theatre, was American by birth. On the grand piano of the Embassy was a water-colour representing, as it seemed, a French marquis of the eighteenth century, with a white wig and a green silk coat, but it was the ancestor of Madame l'Ambassadrice, Rufus King, one of the signers of the Declaration of Independence. A charming hostess, she was fond of entertaining and so was her husband.

He however, acting on the same principles as Barthélemy Saint-Hilaire, had, as a companion through life, an intellectual occupation the end of which he would probably and in fact did not see: the drawing up of a complete catalogue of all the Greek coins, his own collection being among the most famous. He did not fail to appear at important functions, but at the innumerable others he allowed his wife and his young secretaries to represent France. He liked to have us go in and see him sometimes late at night and tell him where we had been and what we had seen. We usually found him by his chimney corner, smoking a very long pipe in jessamine wood, and sorting his coins. He got some exhilaration from our talk, " and so to bed," like Mr. Pepys.

Men great in society or in the world of letters appeared at his table. I once met there Mommsen, a good talker, speaking French and English fluently, an image of the typical savant, close-shaven, deep-wrinkled, with very long white hair, largely, though somewhat thinly, displayed on each side of the head. He had come to ascertain how the great catalogue was progressing and went home satisfied.

A soirée was once given in honour of the Norwegian composer Grieg and his wife, both of them to be heard in his music. For days, people were at Madame Waddington's knees; beseeching letters asking for invitations came by shoals, not at all, it is true, on account of Grieg; Saint-Cecilia herself might have come to play without causing such a stir, but it was known that the Prince of Wales would be present and he came indeed, with the Princess, their two daughters and their eldest son, Prince Albert Victor, later Duke of Clarence.

In the midst of this brilliant set, Grieg and his wife, small, unkempt, unfashionably dressed, with a sincere, thoughtful, almost religious air, seemed little figures escaped from a sixteenth-century Dutch picture. Their music of an intimate character, full of subtle nuances, would have been a delight listened to by people having no other thought save to enjoy its charm. But in the midst of this large, festive, gorgeous gathering it seemed a somewhat rustic *musiquette*. No one minded, however; the party was a great success; everybody wanted to see the Prince, everybody saw him, and he had a smile for everybody.

Relations with those of the world worldly were of the pleasantest; everywhere a welcome, a smile, invitations without number, friendships easily begun and yet long continued. The business part of one's functions was less smooth; colonial rivalries and competitions were intense; we thought the British very exacting and they considered us very exacting. More than once a severe clash was but narrowly avoided.

Except for a few months in the late summer and early

autumn, when it was not good manners to be in town at all (but I was, being always then in charge of the Embassy), social life was constantly active in London, but more especially during the celebrated " season," the most brilliant moment thereof being from mid-May to mid-July. All society moved in a whirl, a merry-go-round, in which even political people took part, everybody going to everybody else's house for lunches, teas, dinners, balls, concerts; the streets were impassable for the number of carriages, proceeding at a footpace, bringing very late guests, but no one cared; late comers were received with a smile; during the season, all was smiles. The flat smoky brick façades of the houses were themselves (and certainly continue to be) wreathed in smiles, with flowers at every window of every floor. The prettiest ladies managed to look even prettier during the season; and when it was finished, pale, exhausted, worn out, disappeared in order to recuperate, in which they generally succeeded; some of them had a fad for walking in a fog, of which, as is well known, there is no dearth in England, and which was supposed to be good for the complexion.

Court festivities, levees held by the Prince of Wales for men, drawing-rooms held by the Queen for both sexes, State concerts and balls were numerous. The man in the street saw something of the sight: so many beautiful Cinderella coaches, with fair ladies in them, going to the drawing-room, rarely, however, looking their best because they were tired with waiting, a little afraid, a little famished (some nibbled at provisions they had with them), somewhat anxious about their three feathers, their veil and their vast regulation train. Our Embassy's coach, suspended from on high by leather straps, which gave it a swing like that of a bark on the sea, was blue and silver; so were the liveries; two tall powdered footmen with long canes stood on the little platform back of the coach.

Age and a certain plumpness caused the Queen, who was of short stature, to look even shorter; she was always very simply dressed in black, a small royal crown on her head, not however of gold and diamonds but of jet. On her arm, a large gold bracelet with an oval miniature portrait of the Prince Consort. When, after a while, she felt tired (for her drawing-rooms lasted over three hours), the Princess of Wales would replace her. The Princess also held whole drawing-rooms on behalf of Her Majesty; but what people wanted was the Queen, and on those occasions the attendance was much smaller, though the smile of the Princess, I find in my notes, " was worth going round the world to see."

Everybody managed to have a right to some uniform, and did not fail to use it; very few wore the civilian court dress (black velvet with knee breeches and a sword). I saw Mr. Gladstone for the first time at a levee, he looked an admiral, with glittering epaulettes and a heavy sabre; and why? because he was a " Trinity Brother " and thus belonged to an institution concerned with the lighthouses.

A gathering place of very different sort was the Mansion House, the official residence of that reigning Prince of merchants, the Lord Mayor. As the host was in a way a Prince, one was expected to go there in uniform, but not however in knee breeches as at Court. Many olden-day traditions still prevailed there; not only concerning the garb of the Lord Mayor and his seconds, but in sundry other ways, such as the custom of married men offering their arm to their wives and sitting by them, and the passing around of the " loving cup," a sort of deep gold chalice, from which you drink standing, and while you do so your neighbour stands behind you—— And why so? In order, you are told, to prevent some evil-intentioned person from stabbing you in the back while you drink: an act no longer of every-day occurrence, but the custom has been preserved. A large gold snuff-box with partitions for various sorts of snuff is also passed around when only men are present; I saw this ceremony performed once during the delivery of the speech of the evening. As people are no longer accustomed to snuff, there was from one end of the hall to the other a storm of sneezing which abated for a minute, then began again to the dismay of the orator.

Such speeches are uniformly patriotic, and have for their subject the prosperity of the Royal Family, of the army and navy, the city, the colonies. More than once, in my day, the Duke of Cambridge, for a great many years commander-in-chief of the army, was the principal speaker. Genial and kindly, tall, broad-shouldered with ruddy cheeks, white whiskers and a shaven chin, he was unpopular with the experts and popular with the ordinary people. The experts alleged that he was backward, ignorant of new methods, indifferent to altered circumstances and to the effect of new inventions. There was, already, talk of suppressing the bright red colour of the English uniform, as too conspicuous and easily seen by the enemy. I heard at that time the Duke address Mansion House banqueters and assure them that " it would be a sad day for the army if the time ever came when the British soldier should hesitate to offer his chest as a target to the enemy." This was received with prolonged applause.

Occasions of lesser importance but not without interest were the banquets offered by the " Livery Companies " of the City. Political leaders were allowed greater liberty there than elsewhere and spoke their minds more freely. On May 22nd, 1889, I was present at a banquet of the Goldsmiths (who are Tories, while the Fishmongers are Liberals), on the occasion of W. H. Smith, First Lord of the Treasury, and Balfour, Chief Secretary for Ireland, being made honorary goldsmiths. Lord Salisbury spoke with great warmth in favour of the House of Lords, the object then of violent attacks, especially by Labouchere,

COUNSELLOR OF EMBASSY IN LONDON

face p. 89

whose motion the previous week for the suppression of
hereditary legislators had been rejected by a majority
of only forty-one votes. Balfour declared that those were
wrong who saw a merit in his indifference to the attacks of
his adversaries. Blame, he said in striking words, is like
a bill of exchange the worth of which depends on the
signature. But when he added that it was impossible to
count for anything such signatures as those of Gladstone
and Morley, it was difficult to follow him.

One day, as I was duly adorned with stars and ribbons,
gold embroidery (" I am glad," Furnivall wrote me once,
" that they did not embroider your head "), a sword, a
cocked hat, etc., going from the Mansion House to the
" Private view " of the yearly exhibition at the Royal
Academy of Arts, the opening night being the occasion
for a great gathering of artists, famous writers, society
people, whom it was very pleasant to see, little enough
attention being paid, it must be confessed, to pictures, I
took a hansom, and as I was seating myself I felt something soft and warm that moved; it turned out to be a
black cat whose slumbers I had interrupted. It did not
dispute me a place on the cushions and showed some
disposition to be petted. Reaching Burlington House, I
told the cabby of the presence of his cat and the risk he
was running. " But," he said, " I have no cat."—
" What then will you do with this one? "—" Why? throw
it away."

This seemed too hard a prospect for poor Puss and so
I alighted with it in my gold-braided arms and called
on the door-keeper. I asked him to house the animal
while I should be inside and said that I would send
friends who would probably adopt Puss: I was too much
afraid of my landlady to risk an adoption myself. I went
in and to every likely person I advertised my cat; it is
black, I said; that brings luck. When the time came to
leave I again visited the door-keeper. " Has anyone
called for my cat? "—" Yes, several, but none would

have it." " How did it behave? "—" Very badly; it is
full of fleas and it wanted so much to run away that we
had to tie it to a cord." And there it was indeed trying
so energetically to go that it was nearly strangled by its
cord. I had no choice; landlady or not, I again took
flea-bitten Pussy in my arms, called a hansom, placed it
on the cushions and jumped in after it. But the very
instant the cat was free, it bounded into the street and
ran away in the turmoil of carriages. This means, superstitious people told me, that some happiness was to fall
to your lot and will not. As I had no cause to expect
any particular piece of happiness at that time, I could
have no regret; I did not, therefore, mourn over my
fate, but only over that of poor Puss.

At that time flourished the Souls and the " Esthetes."
The Souls were a group of men and women, but especially women, of the best society, most of the ladies being
very pretty, who wanted not to spend all their time in
adorning their persons, but in adorning also their minds,
their souls. Without any pedantry, they followed lectures, read serious books, discussed important questions,
which did not prevent their enjoying mundane
gatherings and brilliantly playing their part there.
The most conspicuous among them was the ever-con-
spicuous Margot Tennant, later Countess of Oxford and
Asquith. Among the handsomest and most distinguished,
in mind and manners, was an American, the universally
admired Mrs. Margaret White, wife of the American
First Secretary. I did like the universe, and was a
frequent guest at their house at Ramslade, where I
received my first tennis lessons. Among men, a great
favourite was George Curzon, quite young, and even
younger-looking (a friend wrote me later that he had
greatly aged and looked eighteen), with great knowledge
of men, books and the wide world, on all of which he was
inclined to banter and to severity, full of spirits, proud of
what he had done, of what he was doing and of what he

was sure to do in the future. He, the Whites, joined later by the Reeves (Amelie Reeves), journeyed up the Rhine and to Bayreuth in August 1889, and Curzon wrote in verse an account of it, brimming over with youthful merriment:

> There started from England a party,
> A rare and redoubtable party—
> Old Harry so hale and so hearty,
> And Daisy his wife,
> Most adorable wife,
> Who gives joy to the life
> Of the third of that party, a person
> Known to fame as the dashing George Curzon,
> The never defeated George Curzon. . . .

The Esthetes were supposed to live in a state of constant ecstasy, disregarding the vulgarity of life, hating politics, lost in admiration before a feather or a flower or each other. Their clay-footed idol did not, it is true, look like a feather or a flower; Oscar Wilde was tall, of heavy build with ample, drooping, close-shaven cheeks, but he had a creed of his own which he taught, for which he recruited believers, and which *Punch* never tired making fun of. One of the adepts was supposed to express his admiration in the words: "Oh! isn't it too, too?", and another, being taxed with having taken lodgings in a very expensive part of London, to have replied, "Not at all; peacocks' feathers are very cheap there." The Esthetes did not live much longer than the flowers that gave them ecstasies.

In the country houses and castles, where leaders of the nation have lived from the Middle Ages to the present day, the invited guest was as well received as could be a long-expected friend, or even a member of the family. Great freedom, excellent talk, other guests from every walk in life, artistic surroundings full of historical associations, old trees and immense meadows of soothing influence, cheered the visitor in rose-coloured Compton

Wynyates adorned with the pomegranate of Catherine of Aragon; great Cecil's, now Lord Salisbury's, Hatfield; impressive Castle Howard, built by the dramatist and architect Vanbrugh, where reigned supreme, imperious lady Carlisle, firm in her beliefs or rather disbeliefs, rejecting with equal fervour, alcoholic drinks, religion and monarchy; Middleton Park, with a separate garden reserved for simples, those plants which in mediæval belief cured any disease; Osterley, with pink Gobelins tapestries after Boucher, both belonging to those loved friends the Jerseys; York House at Twickenham, first Queen Anne's, later the Orleans Princes', in my days inhabited by Sir Mountstuart Grant Duff and his numerous family of sons and daughters, young, active, cheery, in spite of the eldest girl having founded among her friends (one of them being the well-known Lady Blennerhasset) a pessimist society, but it was pessimism *pour rire*, and in some corner or other of the house, laughter was constantly heard; Woburn Abbey, the Duke of Bedford's, in the midst of a park so beautiful that it gave an idea of what the garden of Paradise must have been like; a variety of animals, deer, buffaloes, cows, sheep, living together; rhododendrons as high as trees, covered with flowers, lining not alleys, but what seemed to be natural glades, the soil covered over not with gravel, but with grass; peacocks moving about like large live flowers; all sorts of prospects, hills and valleys, clear rivulets, desert moors, scenery as striking as that which at the Opera sometimes draws the applause of the crowd. But with all this beauty, that princely house (rebuilt in the eighteenth century, for the old abbey was ruined beyond repair), those rooms full of pictures, one every panel of which was painted by Canaletto, a pall of gloom overhangs the place. " A sort of fatality," the old Duke told me, " attributed by superstitious minds to our having received from Henry VIII too much Church land, attaches to our family: I did not inherit the place from

my father; my son has no sons. As bad luck would have
it, while a pipe was being laid the other day near the
house, the bones of a monk were uncovered and had to
be displaced. We did it quite reverently and built a
little monument for that monk, as a kind of propitiatory
offering." The duke's end, and shortly after that of his
son, were to show, some years later, that the spell was
not broken.

In those beautiful places, really innumerable, shooting
parties were sometimes arranged, but I did not take
part in them. In one case, at Overstone, a modern
house belonging to the Wantages, one of the guns was
Lord Wolseley. The Countesses Gleichen, cousins of
the Queen, who knew the ways of the famous soldier,
suggested that we keep close to him all the time, not
only because he was an excellent talker, but because " it
was our only chance to escape injury." We escaped and
more than one piece of game did likewise.

Artists

In London, the society of writers, thinkers, artists was
most agreeable. Burne-Jones, the painter of sweet,
pensive, sad-smiling women, was often to be met at the
congenial house of Lady Brooke, Ranee of Sarawak,
herself a musician of great merit, one of those ladies
who spent evenings in the East End, using such talents
as they possessed to cheer the poor and enliven some
hours of their dull existence. The Countesses Gleichen,
both very gifted, one as a singer, the other as a sculptress,
were also to be met there. Burne-Jones, of Welsh origin,
offered that strange combination of pensiveness and
humour frequent with the Celt. He lived at Hammer-
smith in one half of the vast house formerly inhabited by
Richardson of *Clarissa Harlowe* fame. But the place had
been much altered, no trace was left of the summer-
house where the novelist wrote and which was the temple
where his lady admirers came to worship. In the garden

a studio had been built of sufficient dimensions for the artist to paint his huge canvasses. I found him once, at the top of a ladder, busy with a composition to all appearances entirely finished. I asked him what he was doing. " I am adding," he said, " those so important last touches which will be the first to go under the brush of the restorer."

Painting was his joy, his relief, his cure when unwell. He wrote me once from Rottingdean, near Brighton: " I have been illish of late, and sent hither and thither by the doctors—you know that silly old game—but I don't believe in anything doing me a bit of good but painting, so I shall go back on Monday."

Grandfather of a little girl, he was rapturous over her and did his best to smooth, for her early steps, the path of life. She would, of course, be now and then naughty and would be sent to the corner: he painted in that corner tumbling cats and other scenes which might alleviate the severity of the punishment. He also devised for her an album in which he gave free play to his inventive mind, showing little dragons going to school, a school for more advanced dragons; and at the risk, as it seemed to me, of frightening rather than cheering the young grand-daughter, a desolate scene of desert mounts and steep rocks showing " the place where it lives." What was it? No one knew, for only its tail was visible emerging, at mid-height of the cliff, from the narrow round hole giving entrance to its lair.

Mlle. Bartet, in our days the loveliest interpreter of Racine, having desired Burne-Jones' advice as to her costumes when performing the great dramatist's Greek plays, and having requested some photographs, I wrote to my friend and received this answer: " At last I have dragged those photographs out of the mendacious and false Hollyar,[1] and I send them to you, not knowing how to forward them, and believing you have power to

[1] The usual photographer of his pictures, who was always late.

charter a special steamer with them or send them by a
Queen's Messenger. . . .

" Tell the Lady how proud I should be to be of service
to her and with what doubts and hesitations I send her
these photographs—which may encumber her rooms and
desolate them.—Ah! don't I know how photographs sit
on chairs, lie on sofas and can't be burned and won't go
into drawers until one dies of them.—I think it is a
cruel thing to send her these.—But tell her they will tear
to bits if she tries, and so can be got rid of.—I have done
this with many a present—and in the next life the donors
will understand and forgive. But I urge her to do this
at once as soon as she has looked at them: and I send
them only to show that it is possible and desirable to defy
archæologists, and set them at naught—for not a dress
in these pictures was ever worn at any time by anyone
under any circumstances; and some such invented dress,
I think, designed far away from all Greek document or
statue, or pottery, should fit a play of Racine's best."

The refinement, delicacy, purity of Burne-Jones' art
was greatly appreciated in France, and, after the great
Exposition of 1889, where he had exhibited his " King
Cophetua and the Beggar Maid," the Legion of Honour
was bestowed on him. " A pretty letter you have sent
me," he wrote, " indeed I think we are good friends for
always, only I wish we could oftener meet, and I think
I should grow younger as well as wiser and merrier—if it
could be.

" But I have not for many a day had such comfort and
pleasure in matters that affect my work as the sympathy
that has been shown to me in France. I cannot tell you
how it has cheered me."

When he died (having been made a baronet by Gladstone in 1894), his son, Sir Philip, wrote: " If I lived to
be a thousand years old, life would never again be to me
what it was when I walked in that garden with my
beloved wonderful Father, my best friend" (Oct. 19, 1899).

As different as possible from pale, thin, thoughtful Burne-Jones was plump, red-cheeked, cheery Alma-Tadema. They resembled each other, however, by an equal passion for their art: a very different sort of art, Tadema painting with the minute accuracy of his Dutch ancestors, but in even more brilliant colours, scenes of Roman life, by preference the most pleasing ones, with marbles, statues, flowers, young girls, plenty of sunshine. It all seemed to come easily to him, as a gift from above, but he took infinite pains, hesitated, decided, reconsidered. I remember a marble slab in the upper part of a picture, painted with the utmost care, veins and all, which he suppressed and through the opening thus created showed, minutely painted, the domes and towers of ancient Rome; after which he thought the marble slab did better after all, and so Rome vanished and the polished stone, shining under the glare of midday, above a procession of young girls carrying flowers, was reinstated as before.

All the members of his family were remarkably gifted; his wife (English, the sister of Mrs. Edmund Gosse) painted Dutch scenes, while he of Dutch origin cared only for Roman ones; a daughter was a talented water-colourist, another, when a mere girl, wrote and published a poetical play called *One Way of Love*, a pale-hued touching fresco.

His house was like himself, bright and smiling on visitors; gay colours everywhere, the dome-shaped ceiling of his studio was silvered, the staircases were lined with shining brass. After having visited the place a lady once asked him: " In what part of the house do you retire when you want to be ill? "

MEN OF LETTERS

I saw a good deal of the Humphry Wards, of Robert Browning, Henry James, Du Maurier, Lecky, Leslie Stephen who had just launched his grand *Dictionary of*

National Biography, Mrs. Green, Andrew Lang, Maunde Thomson of the British Museum, Edmund Gosse, Lady Blennerhasset, Augustus Jessop and many others, some of whom were just beginners and became famous afterwards. Mrs. Ward had, locked up in a drawer, the manuscript of a novel which she hesitated to bring out. She had published one already, *Miss Bretherton*, with little success. Her formidable uncle, Matthew Arnold, had intimated to her that if her next venture was not a success, the honour of the family would forbid her trying again. She remained therefore anxious and hesitating. She gathered courage enough at last to risk one more attempt, and in a few months *Robert Elsmere* (1888) made her rich and famous. In a note sent me a little later she said: " Mr. Taine has written me the most charming letter, I feel quite *tete montée*." To her next novel, *David Grieve*, I was in a minute way a contributor, altering the itinerary of the hero, who had been originally made to follow, in Paris, streets and avenues not yet in existence. The family, who had been living in Russell Square, moved westwards, had a country place (once the E-shaped mansion of patriot Hampden), and not only enjoyed life but helped others to enjoy it too, for in Mrs. Ward, as in many of her sisters of those days, was an apostle's zeal, and she tried to do good to those who most wanted help, spiritual or other. That generous disposition never failed her and inspired her during the Great War.

Mrs. Green, the author of *Town Life in the Fifteenth Century* and many other works, notable not only for her knowledge but her Irish liveliness, outspokenness and wit, in the company of whom, and of the Mimauts, I visited the Malvern Hill of dear Piers Plowman, Gloucester, Bath and other places of beauty in the West, was of the same disposition. At a time when there was much talk about the sweating system, she invited a number of sweaters (nail and chain makers, from the south side of the Thames) to a dinner in her house. They had come

H

over to testify before the Parliamentary commission. Their salary was five shillings a week and they worked more than twelve hours a day. Not one of them had ever entered the house of well-to-do people; they had never sat a ready served table. Their little band included women and young girls, twelve or fourteen years old, pale, worn out, already working in metals. Great was their surprise when they saw the ready table. They spoke sensibly and with moderation. They were seated around the board and did not begin. The hostess was wondering what they could be waiting for. They waited until one of them rose and delivered a sort of prayer expressing gratitude. In order to occupy the evening pleasantly Mrs. Green took them to see the wax figures and historical souvenirs at Madame Tussaud's, and was surprised to find that, owing probably to such newspapers as they could lay hands on, often discarded papers found in shreds on the pavement, they knew a number of the personages represented. In the midst of this crowd of wax people, kings, generals, celebrities of all sorts, the one without compare that interested them most was Voltaire. They had somehow an impression that he had been kindly disposed toward the like of them. They remained before him in prolonged contemplation.

At ceremonies, inaugurations, dinners, teas, Robert Browning was constantly to be met, a rather corpulent, red-faced, keen-eyed gentleman with a white beard and curly white hair. Of simple manners, showing interest in the questions of the day, whatever they were, he was as far as possible from parading his genius, and nothing revealed, to those who did not know, that generosity which caused him to print his *Hervé Riel* early in 1871 and send the hundred pounds he received to the victims of the siege of Paris. Once or twice only I heard him speak, and not on his own initiative, of poetry and of his work. On one occasion we were dining with Lady Stanley of Alderley (mother of the Countess of Carlisle

and of another daughter and several sons, one of whom
was a Moslem, another an agnostic, another a papal
monsignor; only one daughter had remained Church
of England). I mentioned the performance of one of
the great poet's plays, having recently witnessed the *Blot
on the 'Scutcheon*, put on the stage by the Browning Society,
and I had noticed his presence in a box. He said that
he had never been satisfied with any of those performances.
He always conscientiously tried to make the players
understand the kind of passion or sentiment he had
wished to express, but after the second rehearsal, he found
that actors and author were so far apart that there was
no use in insisting; he left them to their own devices.

On another occasion, dining with the well-known
naturalist and alpinist John Ball, then an old man and
who remembered Byron's Guiccioli,[1] remarried and
grown fat (which would have reduced her lover to despair,
as he hated " even moderate fat," and smoked in the
belief that tobacco was a good preservative against such
a calamity), Browning recalled a dinner forty years
before, in the course of which he had been informed that
his health would be proposed and he would have to
answer. At the last moment, he was told that the plan
had to be given up, the chairman, who was the Bishop of
Lincoln, having declared that he would never propose
the health of a dramatist.

When the Taines came to London in May 1889, I gave
them a representative lunch. Taine, Gaston Paris had
written me, " is in higher spirits than ever and he is
going to see England again with young and powerful
eyes." Robert Browning, whom they had never met,
was the poet, Augustus Jessopp represented the clergy,

---

[1] I have it from Gaston Paris that the Countess being in Paris, a
writer who wanted to print something about her, went to see her,
and in order to ingratiate himself with the lady said: " We know
what calumnies have been spread; we shall be careful not to circu-
late them." She quietly answered: " He was handsome and I loved
him."

Sir Philip Currie, diplomacy, and so on. Browning the poet remained quiescent and let only the society man that was in him appear. Jessopp created a deep impression: "a kind of man," Taine said to his daughter, "that we have not."

Often also was to be met in society that American of fame, Bret Harte. He was very much lionized, running the risk of becoming a tame lion. At a dinner of intellectuals and writers, where he was the chief guest, the novelty of his *genre*, the effectiveness and simplicity of his style, his mixture of pathos and humour were praised by all. He modestly answered that he was proud of such success as had fallen to his lot, but that it was of a limited sort, and that it had not reached other countries, France for instance. I rose and stated that, contrary to what he believed, he had in France many admirers. Some of his stories had been translated, and moreover a knowledge of English was no longer a rarity in France as it had been in the time of the Sun-King. Many among us were able, not only to understand what he wrote, but to appreciate the cadence of his sentences. And I quoted as an example, from memory (and I still quote from memory) the wonderful last sentence of the *Luck of Roaring Camp*: " And the strong man, clinging to the frail babe, as the drowning man is said to cling to a straw, drifted into the shadowy river that flows for ever to the unknown sea." The beauty of that long, accented, last syllable! Bret Harte was touched and replied: " I can in a way return your compliment. I was a beginner in California, and during my spare moments, in the office where I worked, I read *Monte Cristo*. When I came to the place where the hero, sewn in a bag, is thrown from the top of the cliff into the sea, the intensity of the effect, the simplicity of the means, the absence of any style diverting to itself the attention of the reader, were so striking that I said to myself: This is the way one should write; the influence on me of that scene has been permanent."

Much oftener did I meet another celebrated American who became a personal friend, Henry James; we saw a great deal of each other, especially when the season was over and I had to stay in town, being in charge of the Embassy. We frequently dined together and went to the play, or we paid a visit to a common friend of ours, Du Maurier of *Punch* fame. Du Maurier's intimates could go and sup with him on Sundays, at Hampstead, unasked. We would stroll with him on the Heath and then repair to his house and up the staircase lined with some of his most famous pen-and-ink sketches, drawn with a bold hand, on a much larger scale than they appeared in the paper. A classical English joint, which he himself carved in masterly fashion, and some good claret, were the staples of the meal. James and Du Maurier offered a lively contrast. That best delineator of British foibles, whims and fads, a sharp-eyed critic but with no bitterness in his criticism, was of French origin, Paris born and a papal count. Like Molière, this judge of manners who, every week, exhilarated countless people, was of a melancholy disposition, his smile was tinged with sadness.

Not so James, who in those days enjoyed and spread merriment and showed a disposition to sarcasm and raillery which did not spare the British, at least as a nation. The style of his most casual letters, always written at full speed, was never simple; it was natural for him, without any research, to adorn his sentences with con-volutions recalling the floral ornamentation of Renais-sance sculpture. His thoughts and his handwriting were on a par in their interlacing volutes, sometimes gentle tendrils, at other times iron ringlets. As a specimen of the first sort, the following was sent me as I was returning from some holiday abroad: " I stood suppliant on your threshold last evening at 7.20, but had to turn away with a heavy heart. I didn't carry my heart to the Embassy —no place for hearts—it is always too much chilled by the damp air of international law *qu'on y respire*. But I want to greet you on your return and tell you how much I feel it to be the return of an indispensable element. Let us therefore dine together some day next week." Both he and Du Maurier were at that time trying experiments outside their usual line of work. Du Maurier wrote me: "New Grove House, Hampstead, Dec. 31, 1890. I am proceeding with my novel;[1] I have already made more than fifty drawings; there will be more than seventy, if all goes well. It will appear in *Harper's Magazine* during the six months from June to December, then in London, with the drawings, a *de luxe* edition at ten and sixpence, cheap and magnificent; I shall send it to you. If it succeeds and finds other readers besides my friends, I shall try to have it published in France, with the same illustrations; the translation is already done. Wish it success.

"And you, are you writing, or do politics entirely absorb you?

"Henry James dined here Saturday. He requested our prayers for his play (founded on his novel *The American*), which is to appear at Southport, Saturday next. The troupe (the 'Compton Comedy Company') that is going to perform it is not of the best and he is very anxious. It is a new experiment for him, though he has been dreaming all his life of success as a dramatist.

"On the 22nd of next month we go to spend our four annual months in Bayswater. At present we are frozen, shivering, prostrated. This is a terrible winter, and here at Hampstead, with nothing between us and the North Pole, a more than terrible one."

But one can scarcely fail to be south of somebody. The Du Mauriers let their house to a Scottish gentleman for whom Hampstead was the south, while they them-

---

[1] I translate; he wrote to me sometimes in French, sometimes in English; this letter was in French.

selves found the south in not very distant Bayswater, north of Hyde Park.

The experiments of the two friends met with very different fates; James' plays never found an appreciative public, while *Peter Ibbetson,* and later *Trilby,* brought to Du Maurier a small fortune: " the Harpers," he wrote me, " are princely." When the first appeared in volume shape in London, I having then returned to France, he sent me a copy, and to my letter of thanks he answered from Whitby, a place where he loved to spend some weeks with his family in the autumn: " I am happy to learn that my poor Peter and his Duchess have not bored you. . . . I compliment you on your fine historical surroundings and especially on the beautiful eyes you speak of (too discreetly, alas) and which are worth more than the most monumental architecture. Here also beautiful eyes are not lacking (but nothing quite phenomenal this year) and I am never tired of the very old town of fishermen, with its red roofs, overlooked by the ancient abbey of St. Hilda, all in ruins; especially when the sky is turquoise as to-day, and the sea, emerald." [1] At the end of the letter, a rough sketch of himself contemplating the sea.

After the triumphal success of *Trilby* he wrote: " Trilby is to be dramatized everywhere, I am submerged by it—here, in Australia, in France, in Germany, without speaking of all the United States. Thus I am made a dramatic author in my old days and this does not amuse me. It is a fact, however, that it brings in money; and as it is not I who have dramatized the thing (which is sure to be rather bad) I still carry my head high and preserve all my self-respect.

" My dear friend, 'tis a beautiful city you live in and I congratulate you thereon, but you must not continue to work ten hours at a stretch without stopping.

" This evening I dine at the Reform Club with Henry

[1] Whitby, Sept. 28, 1892—original in French.

James, to meet Alphonse Daudet and his son; it will be most interesting for me, as I admire him very much and owe him pleasant hours." [1]

I had left London in 1890; on my departure both friends had written me kind letters. Du Maurier, who wanted to visit Paris again and make sketches for his first novel, suggested that we might go together on sketching expeditions at " la rue de Passy, la mare d'Auteuil, Saint-Cloud," and he wished me " all that I could desire and a little more." Henry James, then in Milan, wrote: " I shall retain the most affectionate and most charmed memory of you, and shall be extremely happy to think that any sense of pleasant hours in your London life is counted with the vague image, however occasional, of yours, my dear Jusserand, most faithfully— Henry James."

Indolence made man, activity made man, was Andrew Lang. He spoke leisurely, moved leisurely; his long arms hung leisurely about his body and his longish hair hung leisurely about his face. He was ever ready to do something else because, as it seemed, he had nothing in particular to do. And withal, a productivity so alive as to defy comparison, a true poet, the master of admirable prose, keenly interested in all sorts of problems and mysteries, going to the root of each one, defending his opinions with an approved fencer's agility, throwing new light on all he chose to write about: the mysteries of totemism, of myths and religions, of anthropology and psychiatry, of folk-lorism, of Homer, Joan of Arc, Mary Stuart, Shakespeare, the *Masque de Fer* (" Fate has drawn me," he wrote, " into the coil of the man *au Masque de Fer* "), and many more. Concerning the " Maid of France," he stated in his preface that, being a Scot, he considered himself in good position to speak, for " the Scots did not buy or sell, or try, or condemn, or persecute, or burn, or—most shameful of all—bear witness against

[1] Hampstead, May 9, 1895—original in French.

and desert the Maid." Indignant at the pseudo-historical
work of Anatole France, he wrote me: "I *have* spoken
my word for the Maid; she was not what a vain Anatole
France supposes! He did not verify his references.
Horresco referens, as the lady said."

I asked him how, with so many occupations, so many
contributions to the daily press and the reviews, he could
have found time to write not only his shorter poems like
his *Ballads and Lyrics of Old France,* for which a moment's
inspiration is enough, but his longer work, *Helen of Troy.*
"I composed some of it," he answered, "each morning
while shaving."

Keenly interested in the practice and origin of sports
(whenever he was interested, it was always keenly), he
did not receive with unmixed pleasure a book I wrote
some years later on French sports under the *Ancien
Régime,* and in which I showed that most of the more
popular games, cricket included, had spread from France
to other countries.[1] He wrote me to say that he could
not have believed such a friend as I would have caused
him such grief. He reviewed at great length my work
in (if I remember aright) the *Morning Post,* was extremely
fair to it, and declared that he hoped to be able later
to controvert my statements concerning cricket, but that,
for the present, he must admit that I had the best of it.

He wrote me at the same time, saying that the question was much too important to be dealt with in a mere
newspaper article and that he would take it up again at
greater length. I replied that he would be most welcome. I had some reserve troops which I intended to
bring forward when the battle was renewed; but it
never was, death removed that rare mind, and my spare
troops have remained dormant in their trenches.

To the Athenæum Club I owe a debt of gratitude; a
grand, rather solemn place where everybody spoke in
subdued tones; where plenty of books were accessible,

[1] *Les Sports et Jeux d'Exercice dans l'Ancienne France,* 1901.

the oldest and the just out, the French ones, it is true, of a sort to make a Frenchman ashamed, the work in many cases of absolutely unknown trash-writers. I mentioned the fact once at a dinner where Balfour was, and pointed out that, as for Zola, if his grossness was undefendable, he did not in any case paint vice under attractive colours. Balfour said, But what are the books we should have and that we have not? I mentioned Sorel's *Europe et la Révolution Française* and others of great value. The next time I visited the Athenæum they were all there. The notion, however, prevailed, that French literature of the imagination was in its ensemble, and in order to answer expectation should be, impure. A fair aristocratic lady having gone to the Comédie Française told me that she had been disappointed. And what had she seen? Augier's *l'Aventurière*, splendidly played then with great success. I spoke of the merits of the work. "Yes," she said, "but when one goes to a French play one expects something different."—"When we go to *l'Aventurière*," I answered, "we expect to see *l'Aventurière*."

At tea-time the place took on a more lively aspect, members of the House came across the Park to have their tea, and it was a pleasant and often useful occasion for meeting them.

Foreign ambassadors are members of the club *honoris causa ;* counsellors of Embassy are not; they can only be admitted, like any visitor from abroad, for a fortnight. A remarkable proof of British courtesy and punctuality was given me: a letter in official form notified me, every two weeks, during three years, that I was admitted for a fortnight. No less punctually did I, for three years, express my thanks every two weeks.

POLITICS

In social relations all was smiles; not so in politics. As aforesaid, the period was one of considerable colonial

expansion; all over the world causes of friction existed
bringing nations at times very near a break. Even
Bismarck had changed his mind: " I am not a colonial
man," he said in 1889, " but I cannot oppose the sentiment of the majority of my compatriots." At that date
the German colonies and protectorates, chiefly in Africa,
covered 3,231,000 square kilometres, with three million
and a quarter inhabitants. The Press of most countries
was quite aggressive, openly rejoicing at other people's
dangers or mishaps. When William II ascended the
throne (June 15, 1888), the London *Standard*, a Government paper, chuckled at the thought of the new régime:
" The young monarch has faith in his 'immovably strong'
Army, and his only concern will be to make Germany
respected and feared. . . . We are quite ready to believe
that Germany will now be less patient than ever of
provocation, less indulgent towards those who compel it
to live with its armour on " (June 18, 1888). This
unfriendly lecturing was resented in France; it did not
take the *Standard* and similarly inclined papers long,
however, to discover that the new German sovereign
was a man of many animosities and they had to cease
their chuckling.

On this grave occasion, my friend Francis Charmes,
then political director at our Foreign Office, wrote me:
" Herbette (French Ambassador at Berlin) yesterday saw
Prince Bismarck, who gave him the assurance that the
policy of the new Emperor would follow that of his
grandfather during the last ten years. Let us hope so,
without counting too much on it, and especially not for
very long. As for the sentiments of the new Emperor
toward his mother, they seem to be abominable. . . .
Count Herbert [1] told Herbette that, on the eve of his
death, Emperor Frederick placed his wife's hand in
Bismarck's, looking at him sorrowfully as though to con-
fide the Empress to him. But yesterday Bismarck spoke

[1] Bismarck's son.

of her with his usual acrimony, *i.e.* without any consideration. There is undoubtedly in this great man
something that is not of a gentleman."

For once Bismarck's forecast was wrong: one of the
early acts of the young sovereign was to dismiss him
" without any consideration," and many of the former
Chancellor's friends and creatures hastened to abandon
him. I was at a party in London when the news came
(March 1890), and the German Ambassador, Count
Hatzfeldt, whose fortunes had been made by Bismarck,
was there. He took my arm and without a word of
regret said: " Let us go to the club and see what news
they are posting. Perhaps I shall be his successor."
We went, but no such news had arrived nor ever did.

Colonial rivalry went on. It was thought in France
that, since the British possessed the immense realms of
India (in a large measure taken from us), they might see
without jealousy some progress of ours in much smaller
and less productive Indo-China. But it was not so, and
on the contrary they had themselves entered the Indo-
Chinese peninsula and, in 1885, annexed Burmah. The
scramble for Africa, in which Germans, Belgians, Italians,
French, British took part, was very active, the two latter
especially playing an important rôle. With the increase
of our African possessions, we were thinking, as early as
1890, of a Trans-Saharan railway. The British established a protectorate over Zanzibar, placed Uganda and
the Matabeles under their rule; the seeds of the Boer
war and the annexation of the South African Republics
were sown; a first annexation of the Transvaal had, in
reality, taken place in 1877. They saw with displeasure
our occupation of Madagascar, rivalry with us sprang
up in West Africa; they detested being reminded of their
unkept promise to withdraw their troops from Egypt
and, in spite of their pledge, opposed our progress in
Tunis. Trouble was hatching besides, between the two
countries, in Newfoundland: it had been hatching since

the Treaty of Utrecht in 1713, but it was now getting worse. Friction went so far in a number of places, that the hideous word war was at times pronounced, especially somewhat later, when Lord Rosebery was in office.

When I was counsellor in London, the Conservatives were in office. The descendant of great Cecil of Elizabethan fame, broad-minded, of great experience in foreign and internal politics, Lord Salisbury, Prime Minister and Foreign Secretary, was a forceful debater, ready-witted, the possessor of a pungent tongue and a sharp pen; careful not to tie up his country with any of the two groups into which Europe was divided, he inclined, as made evident by his biography recently published by his daughter, toward the German one, although perhaps not as much as the biographer would seem to indicate. Tall, bulky, with a tendency to stoop, a full beard, with some white amid the black hair curling about his ears, he was perfectly indifferent to his personal appearance. His clothes hung upon him anyhow; he seemed to be satisfied with any sort, provided they were not the fashion; his top-hat always had the appearance of having been purposely brushed the wrong way. But his receptions, either at the Foreign Office or in his home, were splendid. His wife wrote, his numerous children wrote; a most clever *milieu*. A peculiar trait of his was that, slight as it might be, the comical, humorous or ridiculous element concealed in the folds of the gravest questions never escaped him. When he signed with us in 1890 an agreement concerning, besides Zanzibar and Madagascar, our zones of influence in the Niger Valley, Lake Tchad and the Sahara, he justified, before the House of Lords, his having yielded so much ground by the remark that much of it was "light ground," a joke which was not found in France altogether funny. An article in the *Matin* by John Lemoinne, of the French Academy, on our rights in Newfoundland, was so sensible and witty that he was as rapturous over it as if it had been a defence of his own cause. What a pity, he said to me, such a piece of writing should be lost! What could be done to save it? I suggested that he should write to Lord Lytton asking him to send the article officially to the Foreign Office, and it could thus be included in the next Blue Book. Lord Salisbury seized upon the suggestion with alacarity and the article forms No. 208 of the *Correspondence respecting the Newfoundland Fisheries*, 1884–90.

The fourth son of a Scottish baronet who had made a fortune in Liverpool as a corn merchant, a descendant of the Gledstanes of Gledstanes, Lanarkshire, who had anglicized their name, William Ewart Gladstone, born in 1809, was then at the head of the Liberal party and of " Her Majesty's Opposition." He had presented his Home Rule Bill in 1886 and was chiefly busy with the Irish question, bitterly reproaching the Conservatives with their system of " coercion." But he was also interested in everything that went on in the round world; with an eye especially on the Austrians and the Turks, whom he considered, in different degrees it is true, as tyrant nations. In complete contrast to Lord Salisbury he never noticed the comical side which even grave questions may sometimes offer. Nothing in his eyes was too insignificant to be taken seriously; he was always in earnest, derided on that score by a few, admired and respected by the many.

About all sorts of problems, all sorts of people consulted him: he never failed to answer, always in his own handwriting, address included. He often used postal cards to reply. *Punch* drew up for him a list of questions to be answered by postal card; the last was: " What is your opinion on things in general? "

An excellent classic scholar, speaking French and Italian, he found time for literary work, wrote on Homer, translated into English verse the Odes of Horace, published innumerable articles and essays on moral, literary or political questions, was ever ready with a speech on any subject, eloquent, thoughtful, earnest.

By a happy chance I had a hand in settling one of the numerous causes of trouble between France and England, namely, that same question of Newfoundland on which John Lemoinne had so wittily written. On the part of Newfoundland called the French shore, the treaties had reserved to us the exclusive right of fishing. The English reproached our fishermen with capturing, which was a fact, not only fish but lobsters, which, they claimed, have nothing in common with the genus fish; we reproached British fishermen with capturing lobsters on a shore where they should not have captured anything at all. One can scarcely realize now the amount of bitterness caused by that conflict and the danger it entailed of a serious clash. In order to avoid it I was empowered to negotiate with the level-headed, honest and equitable assistant Secretary of State, Sir Thomas Sanderson, a *modus vivendi*. After some unavoidable haggling over the social status of the lobster we came to a simple enough agreement: the encroachments we reproached each other for would be condoned, but no new ones would be tolerated; an exact *statu quo* would be maintained; not one French or English lobster-pot beyond those already existing would be tolerated.

Minds were so excited and the Press so acrimonious that we had difficulty in reaching even so modest an agreement, and it seemed doubtful whether our respective Governments would ratify it. But we thought we had done well in halting for the first time since the Treaty of Utrecht the perpetual disputes and ever-increasing irritation. We exchanged congratulations; we did well, for we received no others. The Press of each country declared that its delegate should have secured more. The two Governments granted their assent with ill grace, in March 1890, insisting on the fact that our agreement was, luckily, for just one year and no more.

It was; but when next year came, and the next and the next, with increasing alacrity each said to the other: Shall we not renew the *modus vivendi*?—Of course we shall.

Sir Thomas (later Lord) Sanderson and I chuckled at the sight and exchanged little gifts on the birthday anniversaries of "our child," the *modus vivendi*. I have still a silver lobster claw and other souvenirs that came from him, and he received once from me a whole paste-board lobster, full of sweets which I had bought in Paris as a *poisson d'Avril*. Sir Thomas, who had not been spared by his country's papers, nevertheless vented his satisfaction in a poem "Private and confidential and strictly anonymous" that he wrote in French and which began thus:

> Du homard examinons
> L'épineuse question
> D'une façon calme et sage;
> Que de grâce la triste plage
> Où cette bête se promène
> Ne devienne point la scène
> De lutte et de ravage
> Où le pêcheur sauvage
> Tout en faisant usage
> D'effroyable langage
> Ira chercher la solution. . . .
> Par la voie des coups de bâton.

The metre is somewhat halting; not so lame, however, as in Lord Byron's attempts in the same language.

The French plea was, I think, easy to defend; and I intended to explain to the arbitration tribunal which was to settle the dispute definitively, and where it was understood that I would represent France and Sir Thomas England, that the lobster was a fish, that "Crustacea" was a dignity something like knighthood, conferred on him at a later date, but that at the time of the Treaty of Utrecht, whence our rights were derived, it was a mere fish. Quotations were in readiness, drawn from a number of contemporary dictionaries.

But the arbitration never took place and the whole of the Newfoundland difficulties were included in the general agreement, so important in its consequences, which settled in 1904 the ensemble of our still pending differences with England and was perhaps the greatest service rendered to his country by Paul Cambon, then Ambassador of France in London.

The exchange of gifts between Sir Thomas and myself ceased thereupon, but we decided not to mourn the disappearance of our child, for it had gone to heaven.

A Journey to Egypt—Kitchener

In the autumn of 1888 I had been granted a two months' leave, the longest I had ever obtained. What to do with those many weeks? Maspero, met in Paris, said: "Everyone's, or almost everyone's, experience is that when one has left this world, one does not return to it. Wise it is therefore to see, before leaving, what it contains best worth seeing, than which nothing is better than Egypt." My predecessor in London, now Minister at Cairo, Count d'Aubigny, and his wife, pressed me to come and be their guest; so after a visit at Saint-Haon, I started, saw my brother who was continuing his career as an engineer of the Suez Canal, and visited my friends in the Egyptian capital. Maspero was right; nothing can be compared to the remains of that prodigious civilization, so colossal in its architectural conceptions, so minute in its chisellings and paintings, so pregnant with thought, a meaning attached to every object, form, flower, gesture, attitude; in its day the most advanced in the whole world; now no more. An elegant layer of Arabian art at its best, especially in Cairo, as different as possible from the Egyptian, renders even more apparent the unique character of the Pharaonic times.

Not far from the capital, the great pyramids rise in the midst of a sea of fine reddish-yellow sand, strewn with ruins; many deep excavations appear, bored in

I

the rock, and which have been tombs. Following the
base of the Great Pyramid, rose-coloured by the sun,
and the slope of the ground, one reaches the Sphinx, an
awe-inspiring sight; the huge being seems, with those
tranquil eyes, first opened thousands of years ago and
which have seen so much, to observe and judge the men,
the city of to-day, the landscape, the valley of the Nile—
modern Egypt.

To climb the Great Pyramid a crowd of Arabs offer
their services and, according to what they suppose to be
the nationality of the visitor, babble to him a few words
in his tongue. I was favoured with: "Bonaparte,
quarante siècles!" a very abbreviated reminiscence of
Bonaparte's famous order of the day: "Soldiers, from
the heights of these Pyramids forty centuries look down
upon you."

To reach the said height, owing to the magnitude of
the blocks, some of which are shoulder high, several
Arabs are usually hired, some to pull, and some to push
the climber. But, once more inspired by a pre-Rooseveltian spirit, I avoided the humiliation of such help and
reached the summit at the same time as the others:
nothing very remarkable; the Arabs remembered it
however, for, having recognized me later, on my return
from Upper Egypt, they said: "Toi, monté seul."

The climb is worth the trouble, for the sight from the
top illuminates the story of Egypt: as far as the Nile
water can reach, either naturally or by artificial means,
the fecundity of the soil is prodigious, the earth is green
with a variety of crops. At the very spot where the
inundation stops, the desert begins, dry sand which the
wind moves like the waves of the sea, pushes back, pushes
forth, scatters in the air; immensities where nothing whatever grows, no sage as in the American desert, no cactus,
nothing. The line of demarcation is as sharply drawn
as if by a pen; there is no transition. Life and death
touch each other.

In Cairo I saw a good deal of Kitchener, whom I had
known in London and whom I found, with his tall
stature, his steel-blue eyes, the wound which had recently
broken his nether jaw, looking even more soldierly than
before. As Adjutant-General in the Egyptian service,
he wore the fez, and had now and then to leave Cairo
in order to give battle to the Mahdists or Dervishes.
He told me, and this remained long unknown to the
public, that his first battles had been in France and for
France. His parents had taken him as a child to Dinan,
in Brittany, where life was cheap. When he left Wool-
wich, the Franco-German war was going on and he
wanted to serve the country where part of his youth had
been spent. He asked his Government's permission to
enlist; it was refused. He enlisted all the same, risking
his future career. He served under Chanzy in the army
of the Loire. The greatest moment for him was when
the small body of troops he was with having crossed a
river, it was important to destroy the bridge behind
them. His engineering knowledge was called upon:
" You are the only officer of engineers among us, you
must blow up the bridge." He was greatly embarrassed;
theoretically he knew from books how to blow up bridges,
but he had never tried his hand at it; what if he failed?
But he reflected that, if other things were wanting, there
was no lack of powder, and moreover no one was wise
enough to object to anything he might do; he therefore
had sufficient powder laid to blow up " a city "; the
bridge was scattered into the air and he was warmly
complimented.

At home his " breach of discipline," for which he was
duly blamed by the Duke of Cambridge, was condoned,
and then began for him the extraordinary career that was
to take him, for forty-five years, wherever there was any
fighting to be done or even merely some military knowledge to be gained—Palestine, Cyprus, Egypt, Zanzibar,
the Sudan, Southern Africa, India, the Russo-Japanese

battle-fields, Singapore, Australia, New Zealand, Turkey, British East Africa. . . . He was to end it as he had begun it, in the course of a French war, sinking with his ship in the turbid waters off the Orkneys, having rendered the invaluable service of divining from the first that the war would be a long one and that England would need not only a great fleet but a great army. When in the early days of August, 1914, the British troops began to arrive at Havre, great was the surprise of the people there at Kitchener's leasing for three years buildings for the British army.

In my intercourse with him in Egypt I admired how fair he was to the enemy and the warm praise he bestowed on the bravery of the Mahdists, even small boys in their ranks fighting with desperation. I asked him once, after he had been wounded, whether he did not feel more secure, having paid his debt to bad luck. He answered: " Not at all; I had a vague impression that bullets were not for me; I know now that they are "; which had, however, no influence on his conduct. When our party started for Upper Egypt, he left also, to command the troops against the advancing Dervishes, as the Mahdists were now called, the Mahdi having died; we wished him success and no wound. We found, on our return, a telegram from him, dated Suakim: " Victoire sans blessure." We answered: " Bravo Kit! "

He, a fighter, was of course against any evacuation of Egypt at any time by the British troops. The subject often recurred in our conversations then and later; he imagined all sorts of combinations in order to reach an agreement with us, implying that we would not hold the British to their promise. Our discussions on this and other colonial questions were sometimes so ardent that, being once at Osterley and pacing the lawn in front of the house, we were so visibly absorbed by our subject that a friend watching us from the steps of the castle, said to Lady Jersey: " You should send someone to tell

Kitchener and Jusserand that there is a canal ahead of them; they are sure to walk into it."

Our correspondence long continued after I had left Egypt, he using sometimes French, sometimes English, a French written *currente calamo* and pleasantly faulty. Example: "Le Caire, 3 Dec. 1889. . . . J'espère que vous vous êtes bien amuser à Paris, mais après cela il faut venir passer un peu de l'hiver au Caire. J'ai une chambre à votre disposition avec liberté complète. Justement il commence à venir du monde. Joe Chamberlain avec tous sa famille est à Shepherd's, dans laquelle il est tout à fait difficile de savoir quel est sa femme.[1]

"Les d'Aubigny et tous le monde que vous connaisez sont à marveille et aussi gais que possible. Madame d'Aubigny porte des costumes ravissantes et tous les autres dames sont vertes de jalousie. Ecrivez moi bien vite que vous viendrez passer quelque temps.—Kit."

Most of the correspondence was, however, about what took place in Egypt and the difficulties with France; the Dervishes were still threatening; Kitchener wanted the Egyptian army to be increased, but our consent to part of the economies resulting from the conversion of the debt being thus employed was necessary, and as the British showed us no good-will, we reciprocated their dispositions. Kitchener wrote: "People will certainly say that Lord Salisbury was quite right in his statement that if we had more assistance from France the evacuation might be accelerated. The note to the Powers asking for £60,000 for increase of the army goes in at once. Do what you can, like a good fellow, to help your old friend.—Kit." (Dec. 11, 1892.) But we doubted Lord Salisbury's purpose and I could not help remembering conversations I had had in Paris with Kitchener himself in the spring of 1890, in the course

---

[1] His pretty second wife who looked as young as his daughter.

of which he had declared that the promises of Lord
Salisbury or Mr. Gladstone meant nothing; any renewal
of them would mean nothing. England was determined
to remain in Egypt at any cost, even at the cost of war.
" This French antagonism inclines us toward the Triple
Alliance," he said; " the Germans have often made
advances to us which we have declined; our dispositions
are no longer the same; we would help them not with
troops, which they do not need, but with money, which
they lack; now that we are on good terms with Germany
we might do many things, even establish a protectorate,
without your risking a war with us."

I. " Don't be so sure of that; we do not always
calculate the strength of our enemies; we have more
than once accepted the challenge of all Europe, Fortune
not proving wholly unfavourable to us. But suppose the
reverse: What fine plight would be yours? In what
tone would the Germans address you? Be sure that the
day France ceases to have one million soldiers, Egypt
and India will change hands."

Kitchener. " We look to our interests before all; we do
not hate France, we should like to please her, but in
some other way, give her something elsewhere; several
plans are being considered; a cession of Jersey and the
Channel Islands might be thought of."

Just then an agreement with Germany concerning
various colonial questions was being negotiated by
England; it was signed on July 1, 1890; by it Heligo-
land was ceded to Germany; hence probably the idea
of a cession of islands to us.

Even later, when I was in Denmark, his longing for
an agreement with us securing the permanency of the
British occupation continued, and he asked me once
whether I could not leave my post, unobserved, meet
him somewhere in Europe, and discuss the question.
But this was impracticable. The Egyptian problem was
after all to be settled in accordance with his wishes, not,

however, in connection with the Channel Islands, but with our interests in Morocco (April 1904).

We journeyed up the Nile, as far as Assuan and the island of Philæ, one of the beauty spots of the world now spoilt by a barbaric barrage, and where amidst hieroglyphics may be seen an inscription which would have greatly astonished the builders of those temples, to the effect that French troops under Desaix camped there in 1799. Our fleet consisted in a dahabeah; ahead of it a small steamer; and behind a little boat with live food: sheep and poultry. As bread was baked on board, and no letters or papers could reach us, we were separated from the world and had a most restful journey. Friends in London had said to me: we hope for your sake you do not care for the friends with whom you are going to travel in a dahabeah: you are sure to quarrel with them; the exiguity of the accommodation causes bad humour and there is always trouble. But we proved an exception; our company included two ladies, four men and a dog; we returned as good friends as we had started. The dahabeah had two sails and, when the wind was favourable, helped the little, not over-strong, tug; each assisted the other when one went aground, which could scarcely be avoided owing to the shifting shoals, and in spite of the good-will of the natives, whom we found ever ready to warn our *raïs* or captain of the dangerous spots.

Maspero was indeed right: nothing more beautiful, more restful than such a journey on the huge river, dotted with white sails, the water at sunset iridescent with purple, green, red, blue streaks; lined with cliffs, golden yellow when you are near, in the distance pink with blue shadows, an incredible number of huge monuments whose every stone has a meaning, buildings so colossal that they seem to have been the work of giants, so solid that it needed the passage of thousands of years, earthquakes, the hand of enemies to make them totter; their ruins cover miles, and much is still standing, the images of the kings of old are in many places *in situ*, with the three signs recalling the gifts of the gods to them: " Life, Stability, Force "—life, until they went to sleep for ever in their minutely chiselled and inscribed sarcophagi of pure gold, a brief " for ever," as are so many human for evers.

The race of those builders who no longer build is not extinct; their descendants, tall, dark-skinned agriculturists most of them, live as they always have, along the banks of the Nile, and sometimes one is suddenly struck by the resemblance of the features of some tiny girl to those of the enormous Sphinx. But those descendants no longer pray in stone temples nor help to build palaces; their hovels consist of matting, sugar-cane most of the time, standing on end and lined with mud; when any rain has fallen the women gather mud and reline the " walls." Many have no roof; if it rains, which is rare, they get wet, the sun soon returns and dries them; sometimes the hovel is built around a palm tree, whose starry leaves form a sort of roof. Whole villages are thus mud-built and mud-coloured, and only the house of some important man or public functionary is white-washed.

When we returned to Cairo, Sarah Bernhardt was there playing *Adrienne Lecouvreur* to a half-empty house where no one knew who Adrienne Lecouvreur was, nor cared; and a pacha being asked whether he was enjoying himself answered: " I do not know." The great actress took no trouble, scarcely acting at all; but as the drama proceeded, the part gripped her; voluntarily or not, she became more and more herself, and finally played splendidly, not for the sake of the audience but because she could not help it; she played for art's sake.

The Anniversary of the States-General

By the beginning of 1889 I was back at my post. The 5th of May was the hundredth anniversary of the calling together of the States-General by King Louis XVI, which had been the beginning of our Revolution and of our liberties. The Government of the Republic decided that this date should be duly celebrated and sent to its agents abroad a circular prescribing that they take the measures necessary in order that their Embassies or Legations be open to all French people on that anniversary.

When the day arrived the Ambassador was away in France and on me devolved the duty, as Chargé d'Affaires, of organizing the celebration. Some caution was needed because, although taken as a whole the mass of the French established in England were excellent, just a few, however, as in every group of men, were not so very excellent; and, moreover, General Boulanger, who at that period of his career should have been considered as not more than a spent rocket, was in London, receiving invitations right and left (one from old Baroness Burdett-Coutts) and had announced his intention of holding a rival reception.

I took such little precautions as I could. In order to better impress our guests with the solemn character of the occasion, I requested the personnel of the Embassy to be, like myself, in uniform; the doors were open to all, and the rooms were soon filled to suffocation with people standing, for there was no space for chairs. A guest book was placed at the entrance, which obliged all those who honoured us with their presence to inscribe their names and addresses. I had next to me the Chancellor of the Consulate-General, who had long been in London and knew everybody, and I asked him, if he saw any signs of disturbance in any corner, to inform me. After a while he pointed out a place where some Boulangist or other trouble seemed to be brewing. I made straight for this group, and addressing them in kindly tones, pointed out how unworthy of our courtesy it would be if, on this day, differences were not forgotten. They proved quite reasonable and bowed acceptance.

A buffet had been provided; the servants had been instructed to give champagne to everybody; but warned that if anyone left the Embassy unsteady on his legs they would be dismissed.

An address which I delivered was well received, a number of workmen forming part of the assembly being especially warm in their applause. The papers published glowing accounts of the occasion; the *Daily News* (Liberal) said: "The commemoration of yesterday was not confined to the French Embassy in England. In every part of the world where a French tricolour floats, and where there is a Minister, a Consul, or other Government officer in charge of it, something of the same sort was going on. If the Eiffel Tower had been high enough to command a view of the habitable globe from Paris to Tonquin, its watchmen would have detected the signs of festivity in every settlement of the Republic. The Embassy at Albert Gate was bound by its importance and by other considerations to take the lead in these demonstrations *in partibus*, and to enable it to fulfil this obligation, the doors were thrown open for several hours to the whole French colony in London without distinction of class. . . . Some of the visitors belonged to the *élite* of French society in London, others were as manifestly persons engaged in the humblest pursuits. . . . Even infants of tender years were not excluded, and the wail of plethoric infancy for more cake was frequently heard in the refreshment room. . . .

"On this occasion M. Jusserand appeared more especially in the character of the genial host. There was nothing of the diplomatist but the dress, and that with its heavy embroidery of gold lace and the orders was very fine indeed. . . .

"He made a short speech, but it was very much to the point. He spoke without notes and with that ease which is a gift of his race. After a few words of welcome to his visitors, M. Jusserand proceeded to say something of the importance of the anniversary. . . . 'Our liberties date from that epoch,' said M. Jusserand in a significant tone, ' and though they may have sometimes been violated, no one has been able to abolish them. We hope they may never be violated again; we are sure they can never be abolished.' It is needless to say how this passage was received. 'We have endured the hardest trials that can fall to the lot of any people; yet after our misfortunes, and to the confusion of the prophets of evil, France is still erect. The Republic has restored her finances, her army, her fleet, her rank in the world.' M. Jusserand then alluded to the opening of the Exhibition to-day by President Carnot and to the interest manifested in the event by the whole world. The English section would be one of the finest. . . . A warm tribute to the Republic and to its President concluded this short and interesting address and brought the official part of the celebration to a close. The Embassy was illuminated in the evening."

From Furnivall I received this note: " I hope you saw the *Daily News'* account of your reception on Revolution Day; the *Star's* too. You evidently made a brilliant success. That is as it should be. Time 'll see you at the top of the tree."

Gaston Paris wrote: " Have you killed General Boulanger? We don't hear of him any more." He was no longer to be feared, but I had had very little to do with that; he had been his own undoing.

In the course of the following year I was called back to Paris, to be placed at the head of the Northern Department, which included England, Germany, Austria, Russia, the United States, China, Japan, and other countries.

CHAPTER VIII

POLITICS

THE Minister, Mr. Ribot, had assured me that I was
being called back to Paris only for an interim and that I
would be sent abroad again as soon as I should be no
longer needed at the Ministry. This provisional arrangement lasted, however, nine years. Eventful years: in
every respect France was progressing; in her army,
navy, finances, public security and in her colonies: a
larger domain than she had ever possessed. Boulangism
had come (1888), but it had gone; the republican
régime proved more and more solidly established. In
1890, at the suggestion of Cardinal Lavigerie, Pope
Leo XIII had declared that the Church opposed no form
of Government; and therefore not ours. But all that
France reaped was sometimes wonder, sometimes jealousy,
no friendship. She was the only great republic in the
midst of great monarchies. These now and then concluded alliances and ententes among themselves, all, to
say the least, unfriendly to us. To the Austro-German
alliance of 1879 had succeeded, by the adhesion of Italy
in 1882, the famous *Triplice*, and in her enthusiasm for
her new companionship, Italy had renewed, even before
its expiration her treaty originally concluded for five
years. Led by our arch-enemy Crispi, King Humbert
visited the Kaiser at Berlin and was most warmly received.
By one of those sudden inspirations which often astonished
the world in the course of his reign and which he con-

sidered as master strokes, whereas they were sometimes
boomerang strokes, William II thought that he should
improve the opportunity; he would arrange that the son
of that Victor Emmanuel for whom we had fought at
Magenta and Solferino should visit, of all " German "
cities, Strasbourg. The plan miscarried,[1] but the news
of the intended journey leaked out and increased our
feeling of mistrust and isolation.

One nation only in Europe, as years went on, showed
an inclination to good-will towards us: the most im-
perialistic and dictatorial of all, the one with a régime
most opposed to ours, Russia. The possibility that a
friendly hand might be stretched out to us in our derelic-
tion went to our hearts, and as the Russian favourable
dispositions grew, so did our enthusiasm: our new friends
were in many respects very different from us, but we felt
the more grateful; we should be no longer alone.

The chance came by degrees and was, so to say, in the
air long before it took shape and became apparent to
all eyes. Taking a cure at Royat in 1887, Nisard,
Political Director at the *Affaires Etrangères*, had written
me: " The Russian Ambassador (Baron de Mohren-
heim), who is taking the waters . . . has told me of the
views of his Government. They can be summed up
thus: Russia will enter into no agreement with anyone.
If we act likewise and have a stable Government (an
almost *sine qua non* condition, always mentioned first) we
two will render war impossible. . . . To say that these
revelations have opened to me new horizons would be to
exaggerate; but I want you to know, on account of the
insistence with which this order of ideas has been re-
introduced in these conversations *inter pocula*." (The
contents of the *pocula* were Royat water.)

There was, however, something in those ideas, but the
evolution was at first a slow one. It was accelerated by
that same Emperor William who, according to the hopes

[1] See chapter XI, p. 293.

of foreign papers hostile to France, would have reduced her to a definitively subordinate rank. His system of advances, shows of open-hearted friendship, enticing familiarity, with no abatement of his inward dispositions and plans for the rejection, if not destruction, of his best welcomed guests, has been fully brought to light in these latter years, but was suspected from the first and caused ever-increasing mistrust: advances to Russia, to Denmark, to Belgium, to Holland, to England, to the Boers, to the United States, to France. He posed early in his reign as an earnest partisan of Great Britain's joining the Triple, which would have thus become a Quadruple, Alliance: but when he saw the beginning of the South African trouble, he despatched to England a note equivalent to an ultimatum, which by the merest chance did not take effect,[1] sent to Kruger his famous telegram of January 3, 1896, and, counting on our constant differences with the English, asked us to join him so as to "limit, in agreement with Germany, the omnivorous appetite of England."[2]

The Russians were approached by him in similar fashion. All of which did not prevent the same Kaiser from devising a plan for the crushing of the same Boers; he forwarded it to his "dear uncle" the Prince of Wales,[3] and vaunted himself afterwards that it had been followed by Lord Roberts in his victorious campaign. When, broken and defeated, his country on the verge of ruin, Kruger came to Germany, the Emperor had him notified that he must move on and would not be received: the reverse of what we preferred to do, for we had sent no telegram, but when, after his disaster, the old man came

---

[1] Through a casual absence of Lord Salisbury from London. *Die Grosse Politik.* Instructions to Hatzfeldt January 2, 1896, and his answer of the 3rd.

[2] Letter of the French Ambassador Herbette, January 1, 1896. Archives of the French Foreign Office.

[3] December 21, 1899, and February 4, 1900. Text in Sidney Lee, *King Edward VII,* Vol. I, Appendix.

to Paris he was at all risks honourably entertained (November 1900).

"When Queen Emma of Holland and her daughter," says Prince von Bülow in his *Memoirs*, "visited Berlin in October 1898, the Emperor spoke of the Boer war in such an anti-English spirit, with so much fire and exaggeration, the Queen-mother told me after the meal, that, though being herself pro-Boer . . . she wondered whether it was prudent for the Emperor to exhibit with so much violence his anti-English sentiments." If Queen Emma had suspected with what enthusiasm the same Emperor would six weeks later navigate the English waters, she might have spared herself this anxiety.[1]

To what extent she could have done so was even better shown by a toast proposed, at Marlborough House, on the 5th of February, 1901, by the Kaiser, then in England for the funeral of Queen Victoria: "We ought," he said, "to form an Anglo-German alliance, you to keep the seas while we would be responsible for the land; with such an alliance not a mouse could stir in Europe without our permission." On December 30, same year, William II was writing in a similar strain to his dear uncle: "Our two countries . . . belong to the great Teutonic race which Heaven has entrusted with the culture of the world, for apart from the Eastern races, there is no other race left for God to work His will in and upon the world except ours." [2]

In spite of this and of our being apparently unworthy of a rank among the cultured nations, we were the object of new blandishments in view of a *rapprochement* which would certainly not have been pro-English. To our Ambassador, Marquis de Noailles, von Bülow said in January 1900: "The Emperor has more than ever a desire to entertain with France good relations which could lead to a *rapprochement*, an understanding, profitable

---

[1] *Memoirs*, Vol. I, Chap. XIX.
[2] Sidney Lee, *King Edward VII*, II, 11, 135.

to the two countries. . . . He has made of it one of the
leading ideas of his reign. He thought of it even in his
youth. . . . He is tenacious; Prince Bismarck also was,
but when he was attached to an idea, he became brutal,
almost inhuman. The Emperor is misunderstood; he
is supposed to be impulsive, but he is so on the surface
only. In reality he follows his designs with a firmness
of will which knows neither alteration nor lassitude." [1]
So spoke Bülow in those days.

At the same time the Kaiser was paying a personal
visit to the Russian Ambassador, Osten Sacken; and to
the stupefaction of his host, "suggested an attack on
England." [2]

William II showed us, moreover, in numerous circumstances, that familiarity which usually betokens well-
established trusty friendship, as when he asked for the
formula of the paint we used to diminish the visibility
of our battleships (the *Toile mouillée*, or wet canvas colour).
Why should there be secrets between friends?

His sentiment against the United States at the time
of the Hispano–American war was so marked that von
Bülow had trouble in preventing his expressing it too
loudly. He nevertheless, not very long afterwards,
despatched his brother Henry to America in order by
such a compliment to conquer the good-will of the States
and " to renew old traditions dating back to the time of
Frederick the Great and of great Washington," says
Bülow, who chooses to forget that Frederick's relations
with the insurgents consisted in refusing them any help
in men and money and declining as firmly to receive
their envoy, Arthur Lee, as his successor refused to receive
defeated Kruger:[3] Emperor William later thought in
the same way, that by according to Mr. Roosevelt in

---

[1] Telegram of Marquis de Noailles, January 26, 1900. Archives
of the French Foreign Office.

[2] Osten Sacken's dispatches seen by Sidney Lee, *King Edward VII*,
I, 762–3.

[3] *Memoirs*, Vol. I, Chaps. X and XXVI.

Berlin quasi-regal honours, he would make of him a
tool with which to do what he pleased, when he pleased:
a strange tool that had ideas of its own, as he afterwards
discovered.

The strange thing is, that while the Kaiser courted
President Roosevelt and reserved for Americans his
choicest smiles, favours and invitations, he really, in his
erratic policies, considered the possibility of a war against
them, after having dreamt, at the time of the Morocco
trouble, of a war between the United States and Germany
against us. During the *Kiel Week*, June 1907, Mr.
Etienne, former Colonial Minister, and one of our foremost politicians, was there as guest on the Prince of
Monaco's yacht; they saw the Kaiser several times and
were asked by him to a reunion of Germans, on land,
at some little distance from Kiel. There, in a *bierhalle*,
Emperor William and Etienne had a serious conversation.
The Emperor, reviewing the state of the world, said:
" Our enemies of the future are the Japanese and Americans." He complained very much of England. If
France and Germany were united, they would have,
however, nothing to fear from any quarter. " What is
needed is an alliance." " Sire," replied Etienne, " you
would first have to remake France." [1]

The worst suspicions entertained from the beginning
as to the Kaiser's unreliability were more than justified
by the documents subsequently published, and which
have shown how, deeming in 1904 that a war with England
for hegemony was unavoidable (hegemony was from the
first to last his aim, and very naturally since he considered that it agreed with God's will), he explained
without restraint his real views to von Schoen, the same
who was later to declare war on us, and who had been
appointed by the Imperial Ministry of Foreign Affairs
to accompany him and be at his disposal during a journey
to Silesia. In case of such a war, he said, France,

[1] Conversation with Etienne, Paris, July 17, 1907.

K

Belgium, Holland, Denmark will be requested to state
whether they will act as " friends and allies " of Germany;
and " the German army will take action at once against
any of those countries that does not declare itself
for us clearly and immediately." [1] His ambitions were
limitless; the future of his nation was, he declared, on
the water, but it was also *nach Osten,* and also round the
world.

Notwithstanding all blandishments, and suspecting
what they might conceal, we thought that we had a
better chance of emerging honourably from our solitude
by reciprocating that only good-will which, in the early
'nineties, seemed reliable and accessible to us.

A great friend of mine was Admiral Gervais, whom I
had known long before, when he was naval attaché and
I *Elève-Consul* in London; tall, slight, brown-haired,
austere in his ideas and his looks, and yet a charming
companion, made attractive by his unfailing sincerity
and his dominant and indeed unique passion, the service
of his country, which he had begun in the war of '70, no
other dream, no personal ambition ever crossed his mind.
He would serve, that was all. He was now in command
of the Northern Division of battleships at Brest. On the
18th of April, 1891, he had written me:

" MY DEAR FRIEND,—There is much talk in the papers,
perhaps too much, of the Northern Division being sent
to Cronstadt, but I hear at the same time that nothing
as to this is taking shape and that there is still incertitude.
You know already how ardently I should like to be
authorized to visit this summer the North Sea and the
Baltic, not for my personal pleasure, since alone among
all the rest I shall have scarcely anything for my lot
except heavy responsibilities and worries. But because
it is, as I think, of great importance for us not to remain
confined in our territorial waters, and to show that we
consider ourselves, as is proper, the equals of all and do

[1] Schoen's report to Bülow, Dec. 2, 1904, in Bülow's *Memoirs,*
Vol. II, Chap. VII.

not hesitate more than they to show our flag in foreign waters. Add to this the interest of such a trip for our officers.

"I would be, therefore, extremely grateful to you, first for putting, as much as you can, your shoulder to the wheel, so that the northern journey be made, second for letting me know confidentially and quite between ourselves, what I may hope or apprehend in this respect.

"I believe that, in order to arrange matters for the best, and if, as I hear it is desired, we should arrive at Cronstadt about the 24th of July, to leave after Aug. 3rd, I ought to be allowed to weigh anchor about the end of June, sailing toward Norway, then Sweden, Stockholm included, then Russia, with a stop at Copenhagen on the return journey. . . . In arranging visits to Norway, to Sweden with Stockholm, and Denmark with Copenhagen, besides Russia, we organize a geographically reasonable tour which should not cause misgivings. I am sorry not to be able to talk the matter over with you, but I count on you, dear friend, to remove obstacles and facilitate decisions. Keep me informed and believe in the devoted and cordial affection of yours.—GERVAIS."

I wrote back that I would do my best to help, and I did so, adding, however, that a visit to England seemed to me indispensable. We had our troubles with the English, but not insuperable ones, and we should not, by an appearance of discourtesy and neglect, increase among them the number of our enemies. With this addition, his programme seemed excellent.

The admiral answered that a visit to an English port appeared, to him also, quite natural and even indispensable, adding: "You ask me, on the other hand, whether our Northern Division is, as regards the ships included in it, above criticism, whether British or other. To this I must answer that it does not presently—the *Marengo* beginning to age—count any specimen of the great modern battleship giving an adequate idea of what we conceive it should be. If, however, the *Marceau*

were added, as it has been seriously considered, I deem
that my division would not cut a bad figure. . . . But
if you knew what anxiety is already gnawing me at the
thought I might fail in the mission destined to me! To
leave a good impression, profitable to our country, is
what I wish with all my soul. To wish, however, does
not suffice, and I am nervous at the thought I might
prove deficient. Again my thanks."

He did not prove deficient; everywhere he passed,
he, his sailors and his ships, to which the *Marceau* had
been added, left a favourable impression; the success
of the visit to Cronstadt went far beyond our most san-
guine expectation. The two nations proclaimed to the
world their friendship, soon to be confirmed by a military
convention (definitive in 1893), then an alliance.
Alexander III, the princes, the court, the population
vied in the tokens they gave of their good-will and enthusiasm; the most telling one was the playing of the
Marseillaise on board the imperial yacht, in the presence
of the Tsar and autocrat of all the Russias, he standing
(July 25, 1891).

The English visit was scarcely less successful and, as
the event showed years afterwards, scarcely less useful.
Queen Victoria postponed her departure for Balmoral
and reviewed our squadron. Admiral Gervais was
delighted, as well he might be, and sent me from Portsmouth a card on which he had hurriedly written in
English: " With best wishes from the Portsmouth sailor
to his friend the very jolly good fellow, Jusserand."
Anxiety had certainly ceased to gnaw his heart. He had
written in the history of France a page of lasting import.

We were no longer isolated in the world, and the
settlement of our difficulties with other nations became
easier. One of the more important agreements arrived
at in this period concerned Indo-China; a war with
England, to which Lord Rosebery strongly inclined, had
been barely averted at the time of our blockading Bang-

kok for a brief while (1893). The British Government
wanted a buffer state to be established between its possessions and ours, and a small commission was formed to
consider the question (1893). I was the chief French
delegate, but soon found that the geography of the region
was so thoroughly unknown that no reasonable delimitation was possible. Besides, a buffer state did not seem
an ideal solution; for in such states, intrigues by their
neighbours seeking to outdo each other in their hunt for
influence are scarcely avoidable, and much better it is
in those cases to try and be on speaking terms and see
each other at close quarters, face to face.

Missions to gather information about the country were
accordingly sent by the British and by us; ours including
the well-known explorer Pavie and my future counsellor
in Washington, Lefèvre Pontalis, both sensible, fearless,
personally disinterested, belonging, they also, to the
category of those servants of the State who think of
nothing but serving it well. The work took them several
years and the result of their labours, printed on their
return, proved of exceptional geographic and ethno-
graphic importance. It made possible a delimitation
without any buffer state, and an agreement, which has
since given satisfaction to all, was signed by France and
England on January 15, 1896.

Counsellor *ad interim* at Constantinople

Mr. Ribot, who knew of my preference for serving
abroad rather than in the bureaus, had told me that,
without releasing me from my duties at home, he would
send me wherever there should be a temporary vacancy.
This occurred shortly after my return and, by the end of
July 1890, I was ordered to Constantinople as Counsellor
of Embassy *ad interim*. The Ambassador was Count
Lannes de Montebello, both he and his wife, handsome,
brilliant, enjoying life and a position for which they
seemed to have been made, possessed a large fortune

which they did not care to increase by economy. They
were cheerily kind and serviceable to all and thus escaped
envy. The Ambassador was so transparently honest and
straightforward that when there were contradictory statements from foreign Envoys, the Sultan would ask:
" What does M. de Montebello say? "

He had volunteered very young for service in the war
of 1870; the numerous other descendants of Marshal
Lannes had all done the same, there were nine Montebello's under the flag. He told me that being with the
troops which lost Blois to the Germans, when the order
came to cease fire, one gun was still loaded and the men
said: " A pity not to fire it," and they fired. A few
moments later Montebello was sent with some others on
a parley to Blois. A German officer said to him: " You
are wonderfully well informed of our slightest moves: a
solitary last shot came from your lines and fell on our
ammunition depot causing considerable havoc."

As the Montebellos whom I had long known were then
in Paris, we travelled together by rail to Constantinople,
which made us cross all Europe: Bavaria, Austria,
Serbia, Bulgaria, Turkey. I was at the window, all
eyes, so many countries to see, so many landscapes,
peoples, monuments! What struck me most, however, were not the differences, but the similitudes, in
Christian Europe at least. In my travelling notes this:
" What is especially surprising is the resemblance of most
of what we have seen to what can be seen here or there
in France. From Paris as far as here (in Bulgaria),
under this same sun, amid their well-cultivated fields,
in slightly different garb, work the German, Austrian,
Serbian, Bulgarian peasant, the same peasant, of peaceful
aspect, who casts at us a vague and rather kindly glance.
These good, simple folk form, however, the bulk of the
European armies, and under uniforms which, like their
national garb, differ but slightly, will win or lose battles
and mercilessly destroy each other."

When reaching Turkish territory, a real change:
" Nothing remains—rivers, trees, inhabitants, crops, all
have disappeared; nothing is left, nothing. One sees
yellow ground on which nothing grows, where some yellow
weeds remain, but they are dead and of no use; a few
brambles can be detected in the less arid parts. Nobody
passes, nobody lives, the inhabitants are gone. At
intervals a railway station, back of which there is no
village."

Nearing Constantinople trees reappear, inhabitants,
villages, one of them being San Stefano where the
Russian peace was signed in 1878, at the gates of the
capital. The train enters the city by a breach made
for it in the huge wall built by the Byzantine Emperors.

This interim allowed me to have a glimpse of the far-
famed, time-honoured Eastern question, of the intense
rivalries between the European Powers, of the complicated
problems of the Holy Places and the unholy animosities
between Latin and Greek monks; of the difficulty of
preventing those uncontrollable explosions of wrath
causing massacres, by the thousand, of those Armenian
Christians with whom under ordinary circumstances the
Turks lived on good terms.

The reigning Sultan was Abdul Hamid, a Sultan of
olden days. On Fridays, for the ceremony of the *Selamlik*,
he left his usual place of abode, Yildis Kiosk (Palace of
the Star), and was driven in a gilded coach to a near-
by mosque, all white, built for his use. " Opposite him
in the coach sat the Ghazi Osman, of Plevna fame, white-
bearded, who seemed to be of good health and merry
disposition. The troops shouted in mechanical fashion
the hurrahs prescribed by their German teachers. The
music played, the wives of the Sultan were there in closed
carriages but did not enter the building. The Sultan
walked in; chants were heard in the distance. The
prayer once said, the Commander of the Faithful drove
in person a smaller and simpler carriage drawn by two

white horses and stopped at a kiosk where his guests (ambassadors, their *mustechar* or lieutenants, of which I was one, travellers of note, etc.) had come to present their compliments.

Very lean, Abdul Hamid had a long hooked nose, a sharp pointed dark beard, a sallow complexion. On his long black, red-trimmed mantle no gold lace nor decorations. He had the anxious and unhappy look of a man harassed by worries, who wishes that all should go well but knows that it does not. He stooped as if under the weight of his troubles. A strange mixture, he seemed both appealing and autocratic, with possibilities of kindliness and of ferocity."

I did not know when I wrote this how he was to justify the latter impression by ordering, after other massacres of Armenians, the cold-blooded, unspeakable one at Constantinople in 1896. A Christian of another race asked a Turkish friend while the slaughter was going on, whether his coreligionists had anything to fear. " No," was the answer, " there are no orders concerning you."

But the Sultan's kindly disposition was real too, and he had a pronounced ideal of morality as he understood it. When he engaged foreign advisers, he caused inquiries to be made as to the way they behaved, whether married and living properly with their wives.

Going the round of his guests after the *Selamlik*, he had a courteous word for each of them, translated by an interpreter. He knew French and sometimes remonstrated in strong language when he found the interpreter guilty of a mistranslation, but his dignity forbade his using any language save his own.

Business was transacted at the Porte, the " Sublime Porte," by the Grand Vizier and his seconds. The Grand Vizier was Kiansil Pacha, old, lean, dark, a hooked nose, the upper teeth gone, a white beard, very intelligent eyes, shrewd and sickly-looking. There was much wit

in his talk, a sour kind of wit; he had a thousand and
one ways of not giving an answer, muttering incompre-
hensible sounds, taking back what he had said, in order
to say it otherwise, neither way being an answer.

Abundant as it was (besides the greater political
problems), with claims, counter-claims, petitions, requests
for concessions, protests on account of imperfectly fulfilled contracts, religious matters, financial matters,
archæological excavations, etc., business did not prevent
one's enjoyment of the brilliant life that was led in the
city and, in summer-time, along the Bosphorus: balls,
dinners, garden parties, trips in the richly-carved *grand
caïque* with ten oarsmen embroidered all over, to the *Eaux
Douces d'Asie*, sailings along the Bosphorus, which bristled
with fortifications of every period, provided with appropriate ammunition: white marble cannon balls of
Mohammed II, steel shells of Mr. Krupp; visits to the
Symplegades, those rocks which in Greek times closed on
passing ships, at the entrance to the Black Sea, and
smothered them, to Prinkipo island, to the lovely capital
of former days, Brussa, to what was built, across a fertile
and fruitful country, of the railroad to Angora. Tennis
parties were frequent, in which I had more than once as
my playmate a young German diplomat whom I was to
know later in very different circumstances, Count
Bernstorff. All those gatherings were, so to say, illuminated by the good grace and inexhaustible good-humour
of the French Ambassadress. In my travelling notes:
" Aug. 21st. A dinner and reception at the Embassy;
incredible fund of gaiety and good grace of the lady of
the house. At one o'clock in the morning the provision
does not seem to be even touched. It is one of the
curiosities (and of the charms) of the journey."

I too sometimes received compliments for my *entrain*
in the early hours of the morning, but I must say (in
confidence) that I did not deserve them. When the party
was of too long duration I quietly retired to my room,

and after one or two hours' rest returned quite fresh to resume my rôle. For I lived at the Embassy, established during the summer in the large turkish Palace of Therapia built of wood and given to France by the Sultan, so spacious that the chief drawing-room had seventeen windows, and that it housed all the secretaries, young, active, sportive most of them, several having renewed Leander and Byron's deed, swimming the Bosphorus. Embassies were organised then in the grand old style; the personnel of the Ambassador to Turkey was his family and his court, lived with him and ate at his table. He was something great; he had uniformed and armed cawases as his guard; one of ours wore such enormous mustachios that their upturned points reached under his fez; he looked terrific but was as timid as a hare. His Excellency had also an armed *stationnaire* (a small war-ship) at his disposal on the blue Bosphorus.

Several of the foreign diplomats were men of note— Nelidoff the Russian, Radowitz the German, Baron Blanc the Italian, of Savoyard origin, who, when made a Baron, had selected for himself the punning motto: *Savoie est ma voie ;* shrewd and learned Sir William White the Englishman, of much experience and knowledge, book knowledge and philosophical knowledge of men; young, brilliant, handsome Sir Edgar Vincent, British delegate to the Council of the Ottoman Debt, and with whom thirty years later I was to go to Poland under grave circumstances, he as Lord d'Abernon.

Time was found also to visit a capital unique in the world: everything there out of the common; even what was mean and vulgar was so in an unusual way; tiny old wooden houses, scorched by the sun, each floor overhanging the other, huddled together in the intervals between the mosques, the ruins and the palaces, the easiest prey for flames; domes and minarets without number, and as a background the soft blue of the sky and the intense living blue of the Bosphorus; packs of dogs belonging

to no one in particular and leading in perfect liberty
their lives of free citizens of the metropolis and, obeying
their self-imposed rules, each clan living in a particular
quarter of the city, none of them stealing anything from
a stall or a shop-window, but if a morsel fell on the ground,
it was theirs. They were destined to a tragic death.
We followed the great wall breached in 1453 by the
hundred and thirty cannon of Mohammed II, when his
army marched on to Saint-Sophia, filled with people in
prayer, and massacred them. According to the legend,
the priest at the altar, holding the Sacred Host, walked
to the marble wall that opened and then closed upon
him, and the day will come when the temple raised by
Justinian to " Holy Wisdom " shall be Christian once
more, and the priest will walk out of the wall and finish
the mass begun centuries before.

(*Travelling Notes :*) " Took a drive outside the walls,
and followed along them a sunburnt road, made uneven
by an abundance of disjointed flag-stones and pieces of
rock. The sight is impressive. At some higher points a
long stretch of the wall is visible, made of wrought stones
intersected by lines of bricks. The towers are numerous,
thick-set, of every form: round, square, polygonal.
Such of them and the parts of the wall as have preserved
all their height, are crowned with large battlements.
The whole has remained as it was at the end of the siege,
nothing has been destroyed, nothing repaired; some of the
towers are cleft from top to bottom, and yet standing.
The vast breach through which the conqueror's army
entered the city is there untouched and is the chief
opening for the communications between town and
country; portions of the demolished wall lie in the ditch,
fig trees covered with fruit grow vigorously in their
crevices.

" On the other side of the road, cemeteries begun, it
is said, at the time of the siege, so as to bury the dead
fallen there, succeed one another endlessly. Under the

black shade of cypresses, innumerable white marble
stelæ, topped with sculptured turbans, lean to right or
left, stagger unsteady.

"All this region within or without the walls is dotted
with tombs; the dead invade the living. Such is the
case everywhere in Stamboul, but more especially here.
Some verdure appears between two houses: is it a
garden? No, a little cemetery, an intimate one for a
dozen people who seem to have gathered here together
so as not to be too far from the living and not to be
separated from the every-day life, the noise and bustle
of the streets; sometimes the cemetery, being a little
larger, is surrounded by a wall, but, according to a
constant usage, the wall has openings, so that the colour,
the movement, the rumour of the city, may reach the dead
and enliven their rest. The walls even of private gardens
have such openings, to the advantage of the passer-by.

"In the Eyoub quarter, sanctified by the tomb of a
companion of the Prophet, the most truly Turkish part
of the city, the dead are so numerous and occupy so
much space with their flag-stones and turbaned stelæ
that the living recede before them and are more tightly
huddled together. Not an inch of ground is lost, the
slightest space between two houses is filled with tombs."
It is like the Aliscamps at Arles, a sacred place where
everybody in Gallo-Roman times wanted to be buried.

Incredible events have happened since these lines were
written; for the first time from the days of Emperor
Constantine sixteen centuries ago, Constantinople has
now ceased to be a capital; it has no longer any emperor,
sultan or caliph; the number of the living has decreased,
the dead have more and more available space.

My interim at the Embassy having come to an end in
the early autumn, I bade good-bye to Constantinople,
but visited it again the following year, 1891, returning
by way of Athens, Corfu, Trieste and Venice.

English Visits and English Visitors

For a while I went back to London almost every year, sometimes with a mission, sometimes just to keep in touch, to see friends and continue my literary pursuits at the British Museum. Some papers wondered at the motives of these visits and said that it was difficult to ascertain, because, when asked, the traveller answered that he had come to verify the text of the second stanza in a poem by Hoccleve. And this was known to be true, but was it the whole truth? Furnivall wrote: " You really must finish your ' Literary History of the English People.' . . . It is much more important that you should complete the History than circumvent our Foreign Office." Guillaume Guizot wrote: " Tell me how long you mean to stay there. Not for ever I hope. You are not going to play us the bad trick of taking root beyond the Channel before the bridge has been built? You have, it seems to me, a double programme of mundanity and of work for this so-called holiday which will cause you to become even thinner; are you training to run for the *Grand Prix de Paris* on your return? I remember the time when Waddington was trying to get thin so as to play his part in the Cambridge boat against Oxford, but he had a capital of fat which you lack, and he could cut into the quick without reaching the bone. The day when you are reduced to your lowest terms I shall unfortunately not have much to lend to round you out."

I acted, during those stays in London, in perfect agreement, and as if I had become once more his second, with my former chief, Mr. Waddington, who received me at the Embassy and whom I kept aware of all I did. Most of my conversations with Lord Salisbury and his assistants concerned the thorny colonial questions so much to the front in those days. An autograph note of Mr. Ribot in 1892 instructed me to talk with the Prime Minister, of Madagascar, Uganda where some of our

missionaries had been massacred, Newfoundland, etc.
I saw a good deal on those visits of Joseph Chamberlain,
who proved immovable in his view that England should
keep Egypt in spite of all promises, costs and dangers;
Sir Thomas Sanderson, who was finding, he told me,
the seals of the Bering Sea more dangerous animals than
even the Newfoundland lobsters; Sir Charles Dilke, who
was with us in the matter of Egypt, and against us concerning Madagascar and Newfoundland; and many
more, among whom the lovely group of the Souls, but
especially John Morley and Mr. Gladstone.

Both had come to Paris in December 1891, accompanied
by Mrs. Gladstone and by Mr. Armistead, a gigantic
white-bearded Scot, ardent worshipper of the G.O.M.
After some days in Paris they had gone to Biarritz, and
as Mr. Gladstone wanted to visit Cannes, I had mapped
out for him an itinerary through Toulouse, Carcassonne,
Nîmes, sending him some books on those cities. Morley
had returned earlier to Paris and we had spent in January
1892 several days together, seeing museums, visiting
people of interest; I had taken him to a " dinner " of
friends who used to meet now and then and where he
saw Pailleron, author of *Le Monde où l'on s'ennuie*, Vandal,
Vogüé, the Charmes brothers, Mézières, Aynard the
financier, most of them members of the French Academy.
He was very pleased with all, even those with whom he
did not talk. " Such intelligent faces," he said; " it is rare
to meet so interesting a group of men." Pailleron struck
him by his expression: " the melancholy of Molière."

Many years later, when I was in America, I received
from him the following letter:

" *Oct.* 16, 1917.
Flowermead,
Wimbledon Park, S.W.

" My dear Jusserand,
I know not by what unkind motion of the stars our
correspondence has been so long suspended. For some

considerable portion of that time I do know why. I
was knocked off my perch early last December by in-
fluenza and was laid in my bed for some months, with
the Arch Fear occasionally reported to be near at hand.
I am now chasing Youth and Strength with the amount
of success that usually attends an octogenarian (almost)
in that exhilarating exercise.

" Now a more practical word in which you are directly
concerned. I am on the eve of publishing some
souvenirs, and in them I could not resist the temptation
to include a jaunt I had in Paris in company with you
in 1892. It was your kindness which made that jaunt
happy and memorable to me, and I have devoted a few
pages to it and to your benignant share in it. I have
been haunted in the last few days by the thought that
in this I may have been taking an awful liberty. It cuts
me to the heart that to you too this same thought possibly
occurs. If it does I beg for your indulgence. It would
be sorrow indeed for me to leave the world without being
followed by your good-will, that has been so long one
of the prizes of my days. Let me remain, in spite of any
negligence of a rather distracted life, your affectionate
friend—MORLEY."

I have no copy of my answer, but it was to the following effect:—" Have no scruple, I beseech you, about
what you have written; there is not in it a word to which
I can have any possible objection. I have not seen the
book, but I know you too well to feel any doubt as to
that. And since we are speaking of reminiscences let
us see what man's memory is worth. I look up no notes
and this is what I remember of the ' jaunt ' you allude
to."

I mentioned thereupon the places we had seen, the
visits we had paid, even on one occasion what we had
eaten; except for a misdated visit to Versailles all proved
accurate. The eating had taken place at one of the
restaurants on the left bank of the Seine, either *La Pérouse*
or *La Tour d'Argent*. Morley had desired that we should
order something uncommon, and as I passed to him the

bill of fare his eye was struck by the word " Marcassin "—" What is a marcassin? "—" The young of a
boar."—" Let us by all means eat the young of a boar."
The food was served and, in spite of the supposed youth
of the animal, proved so tough that we did not know
whether we were actually cutting the meat or the plate.

Our principal visit was to Renan, then very near his
end; he died on October 12, 1892.   Morley wanted
greatly to see him once more.   I had applied to Madame
Renan, who had answered : " It may be possible, but
it is not sure; according to my husband's desire I continue to receive on Friday evenings; he does not appear,
but he is pleased to think that our usual train of life
continues; come Friday, if he is well enough I shall
take you to his library."

We accordingly went, and after a little time spent
with the other visitors, were taken to the illustrious
man's library.   We found him dressed in a long black
garment, looking very ill, pale, bowed down, the cheeks
flabby, the eyes glazed.   The conversation was dull,
banal, aimless.   I thought we should not stay and was
about to rise, when Morley said : " It is a long time since
I saw you first, Mr. Renan; you were then returning
from Jerusalem."   At that magic word, a wonderful
change; the eyes brighten, the head stands erect, the
long white hair shakes.   Juvenile impressions are re-
awakened and our host now talks with extreme charm
of his youthful years yonder there, of the Jews, the Turks,
the Latins, the Greeks, the Holy Week, a variety of
superstitions, the holy fire of the Greeks and many other
subjects.   He had become inexhaustible and I was afraid
that now excitement might injure him.   So I rose;
Renan rose too, accompanied us to the first door, to the
second, and we parted.

When we were alone Morley inveighed against French
habits and that lack of physical exercise which had
wrecked the health of such a man as Renan.

We took a fiacre and were driven to the Opera, where two fair ladies were expecting us. As we alighted and mounted the steps of the perron, we turned toward the gaily lit boulevard and avenues, full of people, leading to the "Académie de Musique et de Danse." Morley remained a moment thoughtful and said: "I cannot take upon myself to go in. I want to remain on the remembrance of that man, near death, who has spoken to us with so much lucidity and charm, and has shown us so much urbanity, accompanying us to the first door, and the second door,—that man whose voice has shaken the world."

In my before-mentioned letter I added something like this: "There is one thing that cannot possibly appear in your reminiscences, but will be included in mine if I ever write any. In May 1891, as I was paying one of my visits to London, you asked me whom I would like to meet at dinner. I answered, of course, the G.O.M., but that I knew with all that is going on, this was impossible.—Not at all impossible, you answered, and on the contrary very easy to arrange; he will come and I shall ask no one else of particular importance so that he may have all the talk to himself."

So was it done; Gladstone spoke on a number of subjects—our difficulties in Newfoundland, Italian literature, too much neglected in England, recent happenings in America. His memory was wonderful, not only that of events of long ago, as is frequent with old people, but of more recent ones, remembering, for example, statistics of marriages in certain States of the Union, having read them the year before.

He asked me news of Barthélemy Saint-Hilaire, and was greatly pleased by my answer: "He is very well, quite active, enjoying all his faculties and he is three years your senior."

When the evening came to a close, he offered to take me home to the Embassy, and as we were driving together

L

he said: " I made the acquaintance of our host of to-
night late in life, at an age when one does not usually
form new friendships. From the first moments of our
interview I felt that I had formed one, and I thought to
myself: if there was a secret on which depended my
own and my family's honour, I would trust it to this man
without a moment's hesitation. And every single thing
that Morley has done since has justified that first
impression."

In February Mr. Gladstone returned from the South
and remained in Paris from the 26th to the 28th. His
party was composed as before, with the addition, however, of an extremely pretty daughter-in-law. Busy as
usual collecting information, he had lost no opportunity
of talking with prefects, mayors, bishops, etc. He had
found them intelligent, knowing, worthy of their positions. His impression of the country was favourable;
the luckier it was that *La Terre* of Zola had given him,
as well as many readers in London, a very different one.
I find in my notes of an earlier date: " A visit to the
Whites at Ramslate, Aug. 4, 1889. Mrs. White has
recently seen Gladstone, who had just read *La Terre* of
Zola. He spoke of it with sorrow and horror. He has
met people so well informed as to have told him that
the French peasant was exactly what Mr. Zola had
described. Gladstone has concluded that France is lost,
that he had been wrong in expecting up to now that a
regeneration and resurrection of our country was possible;
it is hopelessly rotten."

When an occasion had offered I had tried, but with
little effect, to persuade him and his " well-informed "
advisers that no country could live which resembled the
descriptions in *La Terre*, and that France was still living.
A visit to the man toiling on that *Terre* had been more
efficacious than any reasoning. Mr. Gladstone was very
much struck by what he had observed; he had found

our Government settling for good and getting stronger:
" I am a royalist in England, but a republican in France."
The country, he thought, is firmly attached to the Republic; a change is not to be desired from any point of
view.

One morning we went together to the Louvre to see
what he had not seen before, the Victory of Samothrace
now erected on the prow of her galley, that filled him
with admiration, " the most beautiful statue in existence,"
he said, " after the Venus of Milo "; the excavations of
the Dieulafoys at Susa, bringing to light the ruins of the
palace of Darius, unique in their ornaments, form and
colour, known up to then only through the descriptions
of Herodotus, whose accuracy was once more demon-
strated; some gold masks which the G.O.M. wanted
to compare with those discovered by Schliemann at
Mycenæ. Quite alert, though being in his eighty-third
year, Mr. Gladstone would not leave the place without
doing homage to his preferred Venus of Milo. He
admired the way our museums were kept, the moderate
heating, the atmosphere of respect and veneration:
" an honour to the race," he said. As we were leaving,
two of the guards, tall men in long mantles with cocked
hats, who apparently recognised the visitor from having
seen his photograph in the near-by rue de Rivoli, stood
on each side of the door and bowed to the ground. The
family seemed pleased.

Early in the month I had received a letter from Morley
saying: " He does not like to importune you, but I take
on myself to tell you that he has been reading Taine on
Napoleon, and has conceived an ambition to know him.
Could you bring about an interview? I think Mr.
Gladstone is only in Paris for three days. He would
be enchanted to see you, but he knows that *I* wearied
you almost to death, and fears to finish that operation.
Do not let him be fatigued, je vous en prie."

Taine and Gladstone met at a lunch prearranged by

an English lady, of her own accord and with the best intentions, but the interview was not very satisfactory; the fact that the two great men were unavoidably separated at table by the lady of the house, the semi-deafness of Gladstone, the meritorious but not perfect pronunciation of each other's language, the stentorian voice of Prince Borghese at the other end of the table, hampered a heart-to-heart talk. Hearing of this, Morley was not pleased and wrote: " I am truly disgusted at that feminine intervention. I wanted Mr. Gladstone and Taine and you to be alone together. It is absurd. But 'tis not the first time in my life that I have had to curse the folly of that gender."

After Mr. Gladstone had gone home, I had some correspondence with him and saw him each time I returned to London, lunching once (June 14, 1892) *tête-à-tête*, no one else than we two and Mrs. Gladstone, when that momentous general election was impending which was to bring him to office for the last time. He dismissed the servants so that we could talk more freely; he himself served the meal, trotted with a light tread to the sideboard, fetched the dishes and cut the meat with a perfectly steady hand. He addressed his wife, calling her " darling," with as much tenderness as if he was in the first year of his love; she watched him admiringly. The talk was about every imaginable subject, from Egypt and the colonial questions to the history of Corfu and the influence of Dante on France and on England, but it dealt especially with the great problem of the elections, the result of which was for him certain: " Name me," he said, " one Conservative who expects a majority."

With the exception of the great leader, who found time for Corfu, nobody thought then of anything but the elections; the very aspect of London was altered, scarcely any trace was left of a season; Mr. Waddington had written me some time before: " There are no receptions;

people economize in view of the elections. I have never seen London so empty and so calm. This week we did not have one single invitation to dinner, which is prodigious at this time of the year."

Mrs. Tennant, of Richmond Terrace (not the same family as the celebrated Margot Tennant), whose handsome and talented eldest daughter had married the famous explorer H. M. Stanley, asked me to dine on the 8th of July with Lord Acton and other men of note; she added: " Mr. Stanley has been asked to stand for Lambeth, and I and my daughters have devoted ourselves to visiting from house to house; so much is done by women on these occasions. . . . One of our most distinguished judges once said to me: ' If a man wants to weep, let him read the police reports.' I should say, if a man wants to weep, let him visit these slums."

She wrote a few days later: " It sounds almost ridiculous, but not *one* of my *promised guests* can come to me on the 8th. All London is in a ferment with these elections, and everybody is helping somebody or other, either in the London boroughs or in the other parts of the kingdom. It is a great and passionate fight between the two parties!

" The door of our carriage was wrenched off on Friday night, and there was no possibility of anyone being heard at the hall. Our adversary got a band and drums, and each time Mr. Stanley tried to speak, the drums struck up—an infernal noise! and then threatened to storm the platform."

Stanley, who was a Unionist candidate, was defeated as well as his party; [1] Mr. Gladstone and the Liberals won the day, securing a majority of about forty.

But while the campaign, in which he took a most active part, was upsetting the country, with Home Rule and other great reforms to the fore, the G.O.M. continued

---

[1] A candidate again in 1895, he was elected, but did not prove a success in Parliament and did not seek re-election in 1900.

to find time for very different trains of thought, and so
prepared a lecture on the value of Oxford and Cambridge
during the Middle Ages, as rearers of great minds. He
wanted to compare them with Paris, and Morley asked
me, on his behalf, for some data. I did my best, wondering at that magical power which allowed this political
leader to deal, at such a moment, with the past as with
the present. Mr. Gladstone wrote me of course in his
own hand, as usual:

"*Sept.* 15, '92.

" DEAR MR. JUSSERAND,
        To relieve myself of any suspicion of magic, let
me say that my idea of a lecture at Oxford was worked out
in my head before the General Election, and this was the
chief matter. I admit that it was put on paper since:
partly owing to our friend Morley's sympathetic recommendation. I shall not again be found in any such
galère.
        " My want as to which you have been so kind is
definite but not very broad. I have the work of Denifle,
which gives an account of the University of Paris generally,
and the book of Budzinsky, which shows the amazing
confluence to it of eminent foreigners both to study and
to learn. But while I am tolerably informed as to the
young who were reared at Oxford during 1200–1400 A.D.,
I have no corresponding information as to Paris: of
course I mean young men who began there and who
afterwards attained to great eminence.
        " I know that Paris reared our great Archbishop
Stephen Langton : as all can credit her with Abélard
and William of Champeaux—but I have not yet found
any book which enables me to form a list of great men
reared by her as she reared Langton.
        " Oxford was then relatively richer than she has ever
been, and what I wish to learn is whether she was more
feracious as a mother of minds at that time than *even*
Paris.
        " I venture to send you herewith a paper contributed
by me (at the desire of some among them) to our recent
Congress of Orientalists.

" Our success at the election constitutes for me a very formidable fact : may it serve the end of truth and justice.
" Believe me with many thanks,
" Most faithfully yours,
" W. E. GLADSTONE."

I met again the G.O.M. several times in 1893, once at a dinner at the Henry Whites'. " March 22nd.— Mr. Gladstone; his eyesight is failing; his hearing grows worse, but he is as good-humoured and lively as ever; he still has his earnest air, whatever be the subject; he talks much, he is full of life, his hand all the time to his ear forming a sort of funnel so as to improve his hearing. After dinner he had a succession of *tête-à-tête* conversations in Mrs. White's boudoir, one with me. He courteously apologized for not having vouchsafed a better lot to Paris in his university lecture, then talked of Egypt and expressed the hope that the sending of reinforcements there would not be taken *au tragique* in France. The Government of the Queen arrived at that decision only on the receipt of telling reports, not merely political (by Lord Cromer), but military ones from the officer in command (whose name he did not remember; it was not Kitchener), who insisted and declared he could not guarantee order."

" March 23rd.—Dined at Mr. Gladstone's 10 Downing Street (the famous residence of the Prime Minister); an ordinary brick house blackened by the weather; the ground-floor bare, empty, unlovely; the first floor, indifferent; but the dining-room handsome, with portraits of the predecessors, Walpole and others.

" With the sole exception of myself, all the guests are members of the House. Home Rule is the chief topic; Mr. Gladstone is, as usual, full of spirit; his wife, by the side of whom I sit, follows all his movements with an expression of admiring tenderness. The host complains of the number of questions (in Parliament), which become a horrible nuisance. They arrive in shoals, eighty to a hundred of them. They have replaced the trouble formerly caused by speeches on petitions. In those days one introduced a petition from anybody, on any subject and could, if so inclined, make a speech on that subject: hence an incredible loss of time.

"The customs of olden days were then discussed. After the Reform bill, the manners of the new members were not of the best. An absurd and irritating custom began, of cock-crowing. My neighbour at the table, old Mr. Whitbread, remembered this crowing, and that the last time it was heard, the cock was the late Duke of Bedford (the one I knew), then M.P. and not yet a duke.

"Mr. Gladstone spoke of the way the Paris streets are kept, and asked me for information as to the rules we followed for the sweeping of them, the result being very superior, he thought, to what prevailed in London."

"March 24th.—Dined at the Reform Club with Morley; Lord Acton, Lord Spenser, Lord Houghton, Viceroy of Ireland, quite young and agreeable. Accompanied Morley to the House; met the very youthful Home Secretary, Mr. Asquith; talked with him of Lord Rosebery, who sees with displeasure my friendship with Morley. 'He considers (said Asquith) that France is the unavoidable enemy of England, as well as are Russia and the United States. Only the *Triplice* has, according to him, tendencies favourable to England. He is a sixteenth-century Italian politician.'"

PERSONALIA

As I defended my country's interests, in a fair way as I believed, and ever in the open, but with undoubted zest, some like Lord Rosebery, thought I must be anti-English, but very few did. I was surprised to see, when my friend Henry White's papers were published, that he was one of these, and that at the time of my appointment to Washington he had warned President Roosevelt of my supposed propensity: "He is as I told you, extremely prejudiced against this country and attributes deep designs and base perfidy to its policy, which are usually without the least foundation." [1]

In France, meanwhile, the sentiment for Russia had become a passion and I was the object of persistent attacks from various papers who deemed that one who spoke English and wrote about England, were it mediæval England,[2] must surely be anti-Russian. As some English, nevertheless, thought that I was anti-English, I began to wonder whether, in order to avoid obloquy north and obloquy south, I should have to go and live midway in the Channel Islands?

The attacks became so violent that I had to refer the matter to the Minister (Casimir-Perier), who highly approved of my intention to, just as before, say nothing, answer nothing, and who wrote me to that effect in flattering terms.[3] Admiral Gervais, with whom I lunched now and then, also approved of my silence. His formula for such occurrences was: "Let scoundrels lie and fools believe them." So fierce was the tempest, that the Minister, however, advised me to postpone the publication of Vol. I of my *Literary History of the English People*, though, as it dealt with the Anglo-Saxons, with Chaucer and Piers Plowman, it was improbable anything anti-Russian could have crept into it. The work appeared later in the year and occasioned no commotion.

There were, for these passing troubles, many compensations: serious work at the *Affaires Etrangères* with collaborators who had become personal friends was one, serious work at the *Bibliothèque Nationale* was another; the day being begun by an early game of tennis in the pleasant *Ile de Puteaux* and ended by a swim in the muddy

---

[1] *Henry White*: *Thirty Years of American Diplomacy*, 1930, p. 223.
[2] I had published in 1893: *L'Epopée Mystique de William Langland*, which appeared the next year in English as *Piers Plowman*.
[3] May 6, 1894.

waters of the Seine, kept up as late in the season as a
single swimming establishment remained open, we having
for the microbes about the same sentiment as Farragut
for the torpedoes. Mundane life had many attractions;
visits to friends in their historic country-places offered a
pleasant intermission in the scribbling of official notes:
at Stors, belonging formerly to the Prince de Conti and
now to the Montebellos, to Epoisses the property of the
Comminges-Guitaut family—part of the castle dating
back to the tenth century, the room of Madame de
Sévigné kept intact, a mass of letters in her hand, addressed
to a Guitaut ancestor, many from the Grand Condé;
Grosbois in the midst of an immense, walled park, where
the honours were done by the clever and lovely Princesse
Berthe de Wagram, the place full of souvenirs of Alexandre
Berthier, among which, as at Versailles, a gallery of
battles, including all those he took part in, which means
all the chief ones of the Napoleonic era, plus one, York-
town, where the future Prince of Wagram and Neuchatel
fought, minus one, Waterloo, where his participation
might have changed the issue.

In spite of ominous clouds following each other in
the international sky (colonial disputes, Crispi's wiles,
the alternating smiles and threats of the German Kaiser,
political wranglings, the Sino-Japanese, Greco-Turkish,
Hispano-American, Anglo-Boer wars), there prevailed
somehow in France (except at the time of the Dreyfus
affair) the usual *douceur de vivre*. People thought more
and more that wars were barbaric and that, between the
great European Powers at least, they were becoming
improbable, impossible; that wrongs would be righted
some day by other means. Society gatherings, artistic
expositions, the theatres, offered many attractions;
there was only one *Salon* a year instead of the present,
practically continuous art displays, and its opening was
quite an event: what will So-and-so have sent? What
great man of to-day will have been painted by Bonnat

in front of his usual dark cavern? What nymph by
Henner, what lady by Carolus Duran? The theatres
had a number of incomparable actors—Sarah Bernhardt,
Bartet, Réjane, Coquelin, Got, Mounet Sully; the
announcement of a new play by Sardou, Alexandre
Dumas fils, Rostand, Brieux, Pailleron, Lemaître and
others gave a thrill; Antoine's " Théâtre libre " introduced new ways of acting and of transferring to the
boards actual life, a life, at times, so low that it is doubtful
it was ever actually lived; Sarcey's comments, full of wit
and forceful common sense, were eagerly awaited.
Novels by Daudet, Voguë, Bourget, Maupassant, Zola
(detested for his filth by men of taste), Loti, France,
Barrès, and their peers; poems by Sully Prudhomme,
Hérédia, Coppée, the symbolist Mallarmé (a protagonist
of the school of darkness and impenetrable mist; hearing
that he had been translated into English a Frenchman said :
" what luck, we shall at last understand him "); Victor
Hugo's posthumous *ultima verba*; important works by
Taine, Renan, Sorel, Vandal, Berthelot, interested a
considerable public and were ardently discussed; the
mad pranks of " Le Chat Noir " amused everybody.
The discoveries of Pasteur filled us with pride and joy.
The success of our explorers and colonial leaders showed
that the vitality of the nation was not exhausted : nothing
more characteristic as to the value of our methods than
the decision spontaneously taken on the occasion of the
recent Colonial Exhibition, in Paris, 1931, by the sons of
those barbaric chiefs whom we had vanquished and
captured, to erect a statue to the conquerors, as being
in reality the benefactors who had brought peace and
civilization to their country.

The art of conversation, supposedly dead, flourished
in many quarters, at such a dinner, for example, as the
one to which I had taken Morley, at those Sunday
afternoons of Gaston Paris, meetings of peerless variety
and charm, where literature, politics, philosophical

views were freely discussed; at the hospitable board of patriarchal Taine; at the Chantilly lunches of the Duc d'Aumale (a touch of history had secured to me his friendship, a date in the history of Sweden, which, while talking with diplomats after a dinner, he wanted to mention and I had been able to suggest); at the house of Count d'Haussonville and at his uncle's, the Duc de Broglie, whom we found once alone in a corner, lost in his dreams, as if unaware of the presence of his guests. As Mr. d'Haussonville asked him: " But, my uncle, what is the matter? " his answer showed us how far his mind had been travelling, for it was: " I cannot console myself for the death of Henri IV."

Among the most famous dinners were those of Madame Aubernon. Of imposing proportions, square-headed, with a sonorous, high-pitched voice, an active mind, pushing to the fire of conversation the most unexpected, crackling fagots, in her heart of hearts very kind, Madame Aubernon gave dinners and soirées where she gathered a number of men of intellectual fame, and the chief star of which was, for a long time, Alexandre Dumas fils. Her admiration for him was boundless. After hearing his *Discours de Réception* at the French Academy, she sent him this message on her card: *Gloria tibi Domine.* Dumas returned his with the inscription: *Ne nos inducas in tentationem.*

A quarrel arose between her great man and a mere youngster, as he was in those days, but clever and promising, Paul Deschanel, in after years President of the Chamber and then of the Republic. Dumas was wrong. Madame Aubernon, who was for justice above all, took the side of the young man, and the star of her salon never shone there again. This was, on her part, nothing less than heroic.

At her dinners, as at Gaston Paris' receptions, separate conversations were not allowed; the talk must be general. She had a porcelain bell that she rang in case any one infringed the rule, and few were so bold as to risk the terrifying effect of that faint tinkle.

At her soirées plays were sometimes performed and poetry heard. On one occasion an actor recited some poems of our dear, admired Sully-Prudhomme. He delivered them actor-wise; tenderness, simplicity, depth of thought, were replaced by conventional emphasis and gestures. Gaston Paris and I were in despair. A lady, relative of our host, came to us and said, all smiles: " Was it not lovely, entrancing? How well he rendered those verses ! "

Gaston Paris answered: " Madam, allow me to tell you two stories. First story. One day under the late Empire, Gambetta, a great friend of the celebrated Spaniard, Emilio Castelar, wanted to offer him a treat and took him to the *Corps Législatif*, where Berryer, the great lawyer and orator, was to speak. Berryer, Gambetta said later, was admirable that day, better even than usual. After the sitting the two friends followed the quays arm in arm; the Spaniard remained silent. Gambetta at length could stand it no longer and said: " But how did it seem to you? What do you think of it? Were you not thrilled? " " Well," Castelar answered, " it was not bad; but if you heard me, my dear friend, in Spanish, *that is* a marvel." (*C'est une merveille.*)

" This," Gaston Paris continued, " is my first story. Here is my second: I too recite verses by Sully-Prudhomme."

One of the best houses for serious talk was closed when Taine died of diabetes on the 5th of March, 1893. I saw much of him in the last period of his life. I used to leave the *Affaires Etrangères* as early as I could, swallow a hasty dinner and hurry to him. He was very weak, feeling chilly, even by the fireside; sometimes I found him stretched on the floor before the hearth. He continued to be keenly interested in what was going on in the world, hence his desire to receive my visits. I kept

him informed.   He used to say: " I have been struck by a
passing cart, and have fallen by the roadside, but I am
still interested in the passers-by."

It was not simply the thought, no more works from his
pen, which saddened the minds of Taine's friends, but
the loss of the benign influence of his personality.   There
was something catching in his wholesomeness.

On October 14, Morley wrote: " This, I trust, is to
prove the happiest event of your life."   It was.   On the
following day I married in Paris, Elise Richards, Paris-
born, of a New England family.   I received a considerable
number of letters expressing all manner of good wishes.
Thirty-seven years now after the event, I can say that,
without exception, they were all fulfilled.   One of the
letters came from Mr. Gladstone; it was most affectionate,
and ended in characteristic fashion by a recommendation
that, in my happiness, I should not forget the poor
Armenians.

We settled in the Avenue Marceau, near the Arc de
Triomphe, at the top of a house, in an apartment with a
large balcony along the whole front, and the first thing
we did was to establish on it a flower garden and a kitchen
garden.   We had been told that at that height and with
the prevailing winds nothing would grow; but we
persisted, so excited, that sometimes, returning from a
dinner or from a ball, we went with a lantern to see
whether our seeds were doing their duty.   They did it,
our display of flowers improved the appearance of the
whole house and, as we thought, of the whole avenue.
As for the kitchen garden huddled in a wooden box at
the extremity of the balcony, it produced radishes and
nasturtiums.   We took pride in the visits we were favoured
with by a few caterpillars: our garden was a real garden.

My principal rest from official duties consisted in visits
to Saint-Haon or brief journeys in France or Northern
Italy.   Sometimes, instead of devising an itinerary of our

own, we selected a famous personage in whom I was interested and visited all the places where he had lived. One year, as I greatly needed a vacation, I was granted a few days with the understanding that I would not fail to be back at a fixed date: the autocrat of all the Russias, Emperor Nicholas II, was to pay France an official visit, proclaiming to the world the union of the two countries and that the French Republic was no longer isolated.

On reaching home that evening I suggested that we should start early next morning for Vendôme with Ronsard for our guide. We took his works with us on the train, divided them between us, and marked all the places mentioned by him. When we reached Vendôme, a fine old city built on several little islands in the midst of the river Loir, in olden days a celebrated place of pilgrimage where the faithful came to worship the " Holy Tear " (shed by Christ at the death of Lazarus), we had traced on the map our Ronsardian itinerary. It took us, across Vendômois, Anjou, Orléanais and Touraine, to a succession of lovely spots made famous by the poet's writings, from the castle of La Poissonnière where he was born, to Blois where he met Cassandre, Croixval and Montoire where he was prior *in commendam*, and the ancient romanesque abbey, now in ruins, of Saint-Côme-en-l'Ile near Tours, where he died.[1]

After a dash to Saint-Haon, we returned in time to witness the entry into Paris of the Emperor and Empress of Russia, who proceeded down the Champs-Elysées in the midst of an enormous crowd of people, happy and cheery, but self-possessed, and too deeply moved for exuberant gesticulation and shouting. (October 6, 1896.) A detail which, told, must seem ridiculous, had a charming effect. The horse-chestnut trees having long since shed their blossoms, pink-and-white paper flowers had replaced them. All the festivities, the naval review at

[1] " Ronsard and his Vendômois," in *Schools for Ambassadors and other Essays.*

Cherbourg, the gala performance at the Opera, the military review at Châlons, were a success; the visit of the young, good-looking imperial guests, the Empress especially handsome, terminated without a hitch, leaving in the whole country a feeling of satisfaction, of increased security and gratitude.

Our brief journeys to Northern Italy were numerous. We carefully avoided grand international hotels for tourists of importance and put up at Italian ones, ate at local *osterie*, made stays in mere villages, becoming friends with the simple folk of those places. Not to draw attention, I did not mention on hotel books my official rank, but as I would not make a false statement, I inscribed such innocuous generalities as " French functionary " or " landowner at Saint-Haon." At a certain place, this time not a village, as I was then a Minister Plenipotentiary, I added to my name a capital M accompanied by two or three small letters and a capital P, similarly followed. The landlord a moment later came radiant, with open arms, exclaiming: " Those were the good old days." As I saw no reason to contradict him I echoed: " They were indeed." From that moment there was nothing good enough for us in the hotel; he lent us his carriage and would not allow us to pay for it. I was at a loss to understand the cause of this favour, which we experienced again on subsequent visits. I learnt by chance at last that he had understood my scrawl to mean " Master of Posts "; he had been one himself and thought that, in the good old days of post-horses, we had plied the same trade.

The village where we made the most numerous stays was Battaglia, to the west of Padua, in a fertile, well-watered plain at the foot of the Euganean hills. We alighted at the " Albergo All Italia," formerly the villa of a local personage of some importance, and were given a large room with three windows overlooking the volcanic hills, the fruitful fields, the elms linked by

SAINT-HAON-LE CHÂTEL

face p. 160

festoons of vine as in Virgilian days. We had the good luck to become friends at once with the manager of the place, Signor Bonatti, his wife, the faithful old maid, Anetta, the great black dog, and the *vetturino* of the village, Domenico Giorra, who drove a small open carriage, the only one at the disposal of the public. I explored on foot the neighbouring country, and when I found anything of interest, which was usually the case, we had recourse to Giorra and I took my wife there. We visited thus Este, Monselice, Monte Ortone where remarkable frescoes of the school of Mantegna had just been discovered under the white-wash; Teolo, in the hills, said to be the birthplace of Titus Livius, and the *osteria* is called, of course, Tito Livio; Carrara San Stefano in the plain, the cradle of the Carraresi, lords of Padua, where in a miserable ill-kept country church, the second of them, Marsilio, is buried in a splendid tomb of white marble, on the fronts and sides of which crowd angels, the Virgin, patron saints in the smiling style in favour toward the end of the fourteenth century. Around the cornice, as glowing an inscription as any Paduan lord could wish explains how, " after they had expelled the ferocious tyrants, the criminal Scaligers, the sublime soul of the Carraresi had risen to the Stars."

But our chief pilgrimage was to Arqua in the Euganean hills, where Petrarch had spent the last years of his life and where he rests in a great red marble sarcophagus in front of the church. About his house, just outside the village, he had written to his brother the Carthusian monk: " All told and weighed, I have decided to give up that glitter, envied of the vulgar, and to lead a modest and solitary life. . . . I have built here for myself a small but delightful house; I have olive trees and a vineyard, the product of which is enough for a family, not numerous and with no great needs, as is mine. I suffer from maladies, but my mind is at rest; I am far from troubles, errors and temptations. I read and write ceaselessly."

M

In spite of remodellings the house still answers the description; it is small but delightful, built apart, outside the village, with a lovely view from every window. The principal relic preserved there is the mummy of the poet's cat, under glass, in a sculptured stone frame of more recent date. Latin verses engraved beneath, reveal to the visitor the sentiments of that tabby: " The Florentine poet was consumed with a double love. His most ardent flame was for me, the other for Laura. Do not laugh. If Laura could charm him by her divine beauty, I deserved that incomparable lover by my fidelity; if she excited his genius and inspired his verses, it is thanks to me that cruel rats did not devour his writings. Living, I chased them from these sacred precincts . . . and now, dead though I am, I still by my presence cause them to tremble with fear; and thus, in this inanimate body, survives my pristine fidelity."

We once remained several years without visiting Battaglia; then, one day on our way from Padua to Bologna we passed there without alighting. As our train pulled out of the station, Domenico Giorra, who was present with his carriage as he was at every train, and who in spite of the lapse of time and of our unexpected appearance at the window, recognized us, stretched his arms towards us, reddening with excitement and regret. We had the painful feeling of having done wrong and decided that, whatever happened, we would next year visit Battaglia and our friends there.

We did so in October 1901, as usual without giving notice of our coming: there was no need to do so, Giorra was sure to be at the station, and he was. When we alighted from the train he was busy making an arrangement with an old gentleman. I touched him on the shoulder; he turned round and said: " Ah, Signor! . . ." and addressing his son told him to take care as he could of the gentleman, and begged us to enter his carriage.

Driving us to the village, which is at some distance, he said: "Do you know? We have got a new mill, would you not like to see it?"—"Certainly we would, of all things," and we inspected the mill. The Bonatti family, the old servant maid, received us with open arms. We drove, of course, to Arqua, but Giorra asked permission to take an unusual route, so as to show us something curious. As we were driving along a garden wall, he stopped and asked us to stand on the cushions of the carriage and look over the wall. We would perhaps have wondered what there was so remarkable to see, if he had not exclaimed with glee: "Tennis!" There was, in fact, nothing less wonderful now, in those hills, than a tennis court.

Some time later, being then stationed in Denmark, I learnt that Gaston Paris and his wife were going to Naples. I wrote to them suggesting that they return by way of Padua and Battaglia; that they ask Giorra, who would not fail to be at the station, to take them to Arqua, where they would see Petrarch's tomb, his house and his cat; I had written on the chance, not knowing whether my letter would reach them. In the course of the summer (1902) I received from them a telegram: "Petrarch, we two, Giorra and the cat send you our remembrances." Paris added in a letter: "I cannot thank you enough for having suggested, not to say imposed, on us the journey to Arqua. If I had time I would write to you at length about it, but the pack of correspondents are barking at me. I must at least regale you with a passage I copied for you in a memoir written by one Leoni, in our century, on Petrarch's house. He speaks of the cat: 'But I must add concerning this poor cat that the French, ever jealous of our glories, have not failed to argue and deride, contesting the authenticity of the relic, though it be testified to by the document discovered in the ancient communal archives at Arqua.' Is not this delicious?" I for one can plead not guilty, for I not only never said anything to the detriment of the cat, but I drew a portrait of her so as not to forget her features.

In our last visit to Battaglia we found the village ever more prosperous, but the albergo *All Italia* had dwindled into a mere *osteria*, the *Leone Bianco*; Signor Bonatti, his wife, the old maid and Giorra, welcomed us with as much glee as ever, but a friend was missing, the great black dog. As we inquired about him, the eyes of Bonatti moistened and he said: " He had become old and ill, he slabbered. One day, as I was very busy, he came to me, and in a moment of impatience I said: Go away! Go away! It seems as though he had understood and felt that he should spare masters who had been kind to him all his life the sight of his infirmities and death. He left the house; I did all I possibly could to find him and call him back; but I never discovered any trace of him."

The Hispano-American War

During the last year of our life in Paris, an event happened of world-wide importance, the Hispano-American war, caused by the state of misgoverned Cuba, the first war between the United States and a European Power since the second war of Independence, 1812. It lasted only three months, from the latter part of April to the latter part of July 1898. How far would it go, politically, geographically? Would not consequences develop, involving other countries? The Old World and the New World were astir with anxiety; all sorts of rumours were afloat, some of which still continue to float, like the belief in an unseemly *démarche* made by the European Powers remonstrating against the policy of the United States toward Spain. The *démarche* of the six European Ambassadors really took place at the White House on the 8th of April, but there was nothing unseemly in it; that appeal " to the sentiments of humanity and moderation of the President and the American people " having been concerted in advance with Mr. MacKinley, who was very far from sharing the radical views of Congress; the text of the brief note had been shown beforehand to, and corrected by, Secretary Day, who, after the presidential audience, received the Ambassadors at the Department of State and said to them: " The President, in his answer to you, has spoken in his personal name; I want you to know that your *démarche* is highly appreciated by the Government of the United States."

Somewhat later Jules Cambon cabled from Washington to his Government: "News from London allege that the Ambassadors, with the exception of the English one, have made representations to the Washington Cabinet concerning the operations pursued against the Philippine Islands and Porto Rico, whereas war was to have for its only object Cuba. Neither my German nor Italian colleagues have, any more than myself, made any such representations." [1] The legend has, however, survived and is brought out from time to time.

I received in Paris, on the 12th of June, 1898, a visit from Henry White, still Secretary of Embassy in London. He said [2] that " his Ambassador, Mr. John Hay, was on terms of special intimacy with President MacKinley; they keep up an active private correspondence.

" The American Government would be disposed to sign peace, *if Spain asked for it*, on the following conditions:

" Independence of Cuba and Porto Rico. The Philippine Islands left to Spain, but the United States to have two coaling stations, one in the Philippines, the other in the Mariana (or Ladrones) islands; no war indemnity. If war continued, those conditions would be aggravated.

" I answered, firstly, that they seemed to be known, if not to the public, at least to the diplomatic corps in Washington, Sir Julian Pauncefote having mentioned them to several of his colleagues. Secondly, that one of

---

[1] Telegrams from M. Jules Cambon to his Government, April 8 and May 12, 1898.

[2] Precis of the conversation written as he left.

the clauses appeared to be excessive and even dangerous
for the United States themselves, the one concerning the
coaling stations. The States have no use for them; they
would not be on a road leading to any centre of American
interests. More than all, if the Americans formed establishments in those islands, others would doubtless do the
same; certain rumours as to English and German
intentions were significant. The question of the Philippines would in such a case unavoidably arise under
conditions rather dangerous for the United States at a
great distance from their shores. They would be, more
than ever before, entangled in the whirl of European
rivalries, losing several of those advantages (no big army,
no big navy) which have helped toward their development and the upbuilding of their prosperity. It would
be wiser, from every point of view, to leave the Philippines to their present owners, without touching them.

" White deplores the state of American opinion toward
France. He renders homage to the correct attitude of
our Government and our Minister for Foreign Affairs
(insisting very much on this), but he adds that it is nevertheless a fact that private manifestations in favour of
Spain have had the more effect that they were unexpected. No one could imagine in America that France
would show interest in a ' backward and decaying
monarchy '; some irrational newspaper articles, certain
Paris manifestations, have been magnified by the Press;
the English and the Germans, especially the English,
have done their best in that line. At the present time,
the friend is the British, sentimentalism prevails; English
and American flags are to be seen everywhere together;
the former popular sympathies for France are obliterated.
Later, doubtless, facts will be better known, and there
will be a reaction in favour of France, but that belongs
to the doubtful future, and the present situation deserves
attention."

White recalled the numerous causes of friction of late
years between England and the United States: " The

Sackville incident, the question of the seals, the Venezuela trouble, creating such untoward dispositions that Joseph Chamberlain, speaking to him, White, at a reception at Marlborough House, two years ago, considered an Anglo-American war as a quasi-unavoidable certainty, and used such strong language that, in spite of his being known for his irrepressible flashes of speech, it had been found necessary to verify with the proper authority the real bearing of his words. All this is altered. The English have succeeded by their *démarches*, the warmth of their assurances, the influence of the Press, which ceaselessly opposes their attitude to that of France, in being considered as friends and quasi-saviours. It is commonly believed that their intervention has spared the United States the humiliation of a more or less comminatory remonstrance from Europe.

" I rectified," being well aware that the before-mentioned legend was a legend. " But," said White, " those facts are nevertheless considered in America as certain, and with the lack of measure to which an impressionable people can be addicted, fanatics are found over there to speak of a possible Franco-American conflict."

Spain delayed her appeal for peace. The conditions made known to her by the end of July included her resigning all rights on Cuba, the cession, as a war indemnity, of Porto Rico and of one of the Marianas (Guam), and the occupation of Manila by the Americans, the definitive fate of the Philippines being reserved for subsequent negotiations. " It seemed to me," Cambon cabled on August 1st, " that the President inclines not to keep the Philippines, but to have an establishment there."

I received thereupon another visit from Henry White, who told me that his chief paid me the compliment of desiring to know what I thought would be the effect in case of an annexation of the total Philippine archipelago.

I answered that if I was an American I would hesitate to proceed with such a plan: " You are victorious; you have framed your conditions; to add such a huge postscript now would be considered going very far. Note, moreover, that if you create for yourselves interests at such a distance from your country, you must prepare to build a vast and expensive navy; one cannot go without the other."

Different views prevailed, strengthened by the uncertainty as to what would become of the islands if left in the hands of a Spain weaker than ever. The presence, to Dewey's great irritation, of a German squadron at the entrance of Manila Bay, at the time of the naval battle, had seemed symptomatic, and the documents published since by von Bülow in his memoirs have more than justified the American admiral's misgivings. William II, who was persuaded that Dewey would surely be smashed, but that Spain would be unable on the other hand to quell the Philippine revolt, telegraphed to Bülow: "Tirpitz is absolutely convinced that Manila must fall to our lot and that it would be an enormous advantage for us. As soon as the revolution shall have detached it from Spain we must occupy it." [1]

An imprudent move by some of the English papers had a like effect. Cambon cabled on the 10th of August: "The attitude of the English Press strikes all my colleagues. A campaign has already begun to induce the United States to establish, with England, a condominium over the Philippines." Another impossible dream.

The annexation was decided; an indemnity of twenty million dollars was paid by the States to Spain. For this (and for other reasons) a huge fleet has since been built, and it can be said to-day that the results have justified the decision. The archipelago has become more prosperous than ever before and it is desirable for its interests that the guiding hand which has brought about such a result be not soon withdrawn.

Toward the end of 1898 I was appointed Minister of France to Denmark.

[1] *Memoirs*, Vol. I, Chap. XIV, April 1898.

CHAPTER IX

The Danish Country

A LARGE city, this " Harbour of merchants " (Kjøben-
havn, otherwise Copenhagen) by the sea, and almost in
the sea, where we arrived, for a stay of several years, in
February 1899. Salt-water canals bring fishing and
other boats to the very centre of the town; its well-
appointed harbour has ramifications far into the place,
and ocean-bound ships on the way to America or the
Far East are seen silently gliding between rows of houses
and the flowers of public gardens. The King can see
them pass along the wall of his palace. A fit capital for
a nation of sailors.

Historical associations abound, some glorious, some
sad, all cherished. The taste for art is deep-rooted,
museums are numerous: the Thorwaldsen Museum
devoted to the works of the great national sculptor of
immense fame in his day, a little too sedate for modern
minds; the " Northern Antiquities " containing many
remains coeval with the Vikings and Sagas, strange
specimens of the pilferings brought home by the North-
men after their plundering expeditions, among which a
large silver bowl, with Roman deities in relief, the rough
work of a Gallic craftsman; the Rosenborg Museum,
entirely filled with historical souvenirs belonging to the
Royal Family; another with antiques; another with
well-chosen modern French sculpture, both the gift of
the rich brewer Jacobsen; one of old armour, containing
the complete armament in guns of a ship of the early

fifteenth century; and among several more, one, unique
I believe in the world, a museum of whales.

On the land side, avenues planted with trees lead to
the city. These are due to a society founded of yore
and which well deserves imitation: "The Society for
the Benefit of Posterity." The members did nothing for
the advantage of themselves or their contemporaries,
but all for the people who would come after them; the
little twigs they planted are now huge trees, a pleasure
to the eye and a comfort to the traveller.

Like the capital, the country is by the sea and almost
in the sea; it includes many islands, in the chief of which,
Zealand (Sjælland), is Copenhagen; sinuous inlets reach
from the sea far into the interior; lakes are numerous,
but the kingdom prides itself on the possession of just
one mountain, decorated with the imposing name of
Himmelsbjerg; those who perform the ascent have the
name burnt into their alpenstock, as tourists do in
Switzerland. The "Mount of Heaven" is, however,
less high than the Eiffel tower.

Meadows abound; cattle-breeding and the products
of the dairy are of prime importance. Cows are not
allowed to eat unmethodically where they please;
alined in straight rows they have to browse on what is
in front of them; six times a day a man changes their
places and they dutifully continue their ceaseless meals.
No dog is allowed near them; they must no more be
troubled than a poet at work on an epic; occasionally
they are carried in carts to their pasture. Some cattle-
owners do not allow strangers in their stables for fear the
visit might agitate animals one would not suppose to
be so nervous. Danish butter is famous.

A large portion of Jutland was barren or covered with
unprofitable heather. A patriot soldier, Colonel Dalgas,
who had taken part in the disastrous war of the Duchies,
when Denmark had to bear alone the onslaught of
Prussia and Austria and lost Slesvig and Holstein (1864),

vowed to himself that he would restore to his nation as much profitable land as it had lost, and made it his life's task to transform vast territories of useless heather into useful forests. The valuable tree, giving masts and boards for ships, is the fir; but young fir is smothered where heather spreads, and the problem was to find a means of destroying the latter. In the course of his researches he found in France the solution: a pine tree that does the work; he imported quantities; where that pine grows, heather dies; pines and firs are planted together, the former protecting the latter during their infancy, and, when the infants are strong enough, the protector is removed. The firs are sown in a nursery and the diminutive future trees are constantly watched by women who remove from them the least insect and who tend them until they can be planted; they now form an immense forest intersected by large avenues. Dalgas too has worked for the benefit of posterity.

Many picturesque castles, churches and public monuments dot the country; the chief castles belong to the Royal Family and the old nobility (but, owing to heavy taxation, the latter find it, as in England, more and more difficult to keep them). The King, in my days, spent part of his summers at Bernstorff, a small place close to the capital, "Honesto inter labores otio sacrum"[1] as reads the inscription on the door, and part at Fredensborg, a larger establishment further off. His eldest son, the Prince Royal, had Charlottenlund, and the latter's heir had Sorgenfri (Sans-Souci), both near Copenhagen; the living apartments in all those places were full of portraits, photographs and souvenirs, tokens of an affectionate family life.

In some of the older houses of the nobility, remnants of mediæval customs remain, as at Gissefeld, the property of the Daneskiold Samsøe family, where the night watchman walks, every hour, from one of the bridges over the

---

[1] Devoted to laudable rest in the interval of labours.

moat to another, announcing the hour and invoking, in a
sort of canticle, the blessing of the Powers above on the
inmates of the place. Which done, he sits on the steps
outside, and resumes a less poetical part of his duties,
that consists in cleaning the shoes of the guests.

A number of churches, chiefly brick, are of great
interest, such as the Roskilde cathedral, the Saint-Denis
of the Danes, most of their kings being buried there, as
well as a number of their princes, the latter in coffins
draped in black velvet and laid on the pavement.
Important families have chapels of their own, in one of
which is a list of names with armorial bearings, dated
1666, the two first ones being "Rosenkrans" and
"Gyldenstierne," of Shakespearian fame. At Bjernede
a twelfth-century round church; other churches of the
same period at Sorö, Ringsted, Viborg, Ribe, etc. The
Saint-Mary church at Elsinore had, fixed, mid-height
against the pillars, closed boxes with roofs, doors and
windows, and bearing the coats of arms of the owners
who came to attend the services and were thus protected
to some extent against the winter cold. The Danes had,
however, a kind of Viollet-le-Duc called Meldahl, whose
rule was that monuments should be restored as the
original builders had, if not built them, at least planned
to build them. He was impervious to the fact that old
monuments have lived with the nation, and must needs
bear signs of age; the passing centuries have left their
mark on them, and it is a pity, the reverse indeed of a
reasonable national feeling, that they should be cleared
of each and all of the souvenirs with which successive
generations have piously decorated their naves. Owing
to Meldahl, the Viborg church, for one, was not, in the
twelfth century, so very twelfth-century as it is now. I
did all I could to save the strange boxes at Elsinore, even
appealing to the Prince Royal and the Prime Minister
in their favour, but failed; one or two have alone been
preserved, I am told, as specimens.

Though radically restored too, the castle in the same Elsinore is of great beauty; part of it is exactly contemporary with Shakespeare, the date 1584 being engraved on one of the towers. The vast halls, secret passages, thick-walled keep, immense subterranean vaults where the shade of Holger Danske (Ogier the Dane) is supposed to still roam, the near-by cemetery, perfectly fit the events in the story of the Prince of Denmark; but the landscape in the play is as imaginary as the story itself; instead of rising on the top of those precipitous cliffs described by Horatio to Hamlet and which overhang the roaring waves, the castle is on the level of the narrow and quiet sund: poets are free to create or to increase beauty at will.

The Danes have a proverb according to which winter in their country lasts eight months, and the rest of the time the cold continues. It is one of those satirical remarks that come naturally to them; they are easily ironical about themselves and others; they excell in good-humoured caricatures. Their summers, it is true, are brief, but lovely, resembling a continuous spring abundant in flowers and embellished with leaves which have not time to wither, but remain young till they die. Their winters, less cold than those of Russia or Norway, are, however, more severe; the sky is cloudier, the alternatives of frost and thaw are more frequent; the wind is almost ceaseless, so strong that it sometimes makes walking difficult, and that out of pity for the sentries, stalwart though they be, their boxes are on pivots and can be so turned as to insure protection against the hurricane. The general health is nevertheless good, epidemics are rare, longevity frequent. The Duc de Chartres, father of Princess Marie, often came to Copenhagen, and used to say that those strong winds blew all microbes out to sea, hence the healthy condition of the inhabitants.

No Government except the British had then a house for its Legation; I established ours in an apartment

which had over all the others the advantage of fine
Gobelins tapestries, some of them magnificent, supplied
by the State; its three drawing-rooms (in Copenhagen
any dignified establishment must have three drawing-
rooms) overlooked the gardens and moat of the citadel,
where we could observe, among other interesting sights,
with what austerity parent swans brought up their young,
the latter, with their still grey down, being forbidden to
make chance acquaintances, and having to swim in well-
bred fashion between father and mother; if an intruder
swan came near, as though to enter into conversation,
the father gave him chase and the unwelcome visitor
had to hastily withdraw, which he invariably did without
the slightest resistance, realizing that he was in the wrong.

A Journey to Russia

Shortly after our arrival in Denmark, we received a
letter from Count de Montebello, our Ambassador to
Russia, and his wife, saying that, as we were now
" neighbours," we ought to go and dine with them,
" sans cérémonie," in neighbourly fashion. We answered,
" Certainly," and started in March for that next-door
house, two days distant. At Berlin the sea and land
journey was broken by a dinner at the Embassy: the
cheery welcome of Marquis de Noailles, who came with
flowers for my wife, the warm, well-lit rooms, the finely
appointed table, the instructive, friendly talk with a
diplomat of great experience, were in contrast with the
darkness, the cold, the dreariness outside. He too asked
us to come again and visit him as neighbours; he accompanied us to the station, in his carriage drawn by two such
beautiful horses that they were rarely allowed out at
night for fear of their catching cold. " The Marquis,"
the secretaries told us, " could not give you a rarer proof
of his friendship."

The Russian, to-day Lithuanian frontier, Wirballen,
was reached on the next afternoon; a muddy rivulet

marks the limit, and there, at once, without any transition, Russia began; all inscriptions were in Russian without the bounty of a translation or even a duplication in Latin letters. We found there, however, a group of com- patriots whom our knowledge of French allowed us to help, namely geese and chickens, real beauties of their kind, being sent in crates to a poultry show. On the crates was an inscription apparently unintelligible to all except to us: " Donnez-nous à boire s'il vous plait." We fetched a decanter, but its neck could not pass between the wooden bars; a young man, who looked a student, came to our help, and drawing from his pocket an old newspaper, formed a funnel by which the water could be carried to the empty receptacle of the feathered travellers. They were so pleased and so thirsty that they at once crowded together, pushing all their heads under the jet, which resulted in much splashing and no filling of the basin. We could at last make them understand, the water finally went where it should, and we parted with the grateful poultry, wishing them the glory of all the first prizes.

The country offered the same aspect on both sides of the frontier; flat and muddy; the roads were even muddier on the Russian side, tracks rather than roads, with deep ruts in the soaked ground. The day was gloomy and so was the landscape; scarcely any in- habitants, no villages, not a monument, not a castle; dismal grey immensities, dismal yellow immensities; now and then a small wood of stunted birch or pine trees, which, however, were a restful sight. The next day the immensities were covered with snow as far as the eye could reach.

Our " neighbourly dinner " lasted a fortnight, during which the Montebellos, who held in St. Petersburg, as they previously had in Turkey, a pre-eminent position, tried to make us see as much of Russian life as was possible in that space of time, from the streets and the passers-by

stopping to warm themselves at the braseros, to the
palaces and their imperial inhabitants—the streets full
of life, with innumerable sleighs and carriages, workmen
busy removing the snow which fell again and was again
removed; in the intervals when it ceased, the sky became
blue and the sun shone again; the Neva, so deep frozen
that tramways, quickly taken away when the thaw
threatened, were established on its surface—churches full
of historical souvenirs, such as the Church of the Citadel,
where emperors were buried and on their monuments
were laid gold and silver offerings, among which a golden
olive branch placed by President Félix Faure on the
tomb of Alexander III; with that, some more modest
souvenirs, and maybe more touching ones, including even
paper flowers. Where are they now, " mais où sont les
neiges d'antan? " At Our Lady of Kazan, besides a
profusion of silver objects, were a number of flags captured from the enemy, many dating back to the time when
the French were the enemy and Napoleon their Emperor,
silk flags, very much torn, but the bees and the eagles
still visible. In all those places, worshippers were praying,
lighting candles, kneeling on the ground, touching the
flag-stones with their forehead, making numerous signs
of the cross. Museums for old and modern art were
visited; the famous *Ermitage* especially, one of the most
splendid shrines in the whole world, where " things of
beauty " from all countries were displayed and where
we went, with increasing admiration and enjoyment,
almost every morning.

Imperial audiences were granted us. I was received
first at the Winter Palace by the reigning Empress,
Alexandra Feodorovna, *née* Princess Alice of Hesse, grand-
daughter of Queen Victoria. A long series of staircases,
corridors, drawing-rooms, abundantly painted and gilded,
were traversed; officers, sentries, lackeys, a considerable
personnel stood at every turn. A long-gaitered courier
in dazzling livery, wearing a strange hat with an enormous

black and yellow tuft on one ear, and a small one on the
other, led the way; the soldiers presented arms; after
having followed a long gallery lined with portraits scarcely
visible in a semi-obscurity, the two first representing
Emperor Frederick III of Germany, and opposite him
Marshall von Moltke, I waited in a large white and gold
drawing-room; Count Benckendorff, grand-master of
the Empress' household and brother of the Russian
Minister in Copenhagen, kept me company. At the
appointed hour a tall negro dressed in red and gold, with
a gold turban, opened the door, and after having crossed
one more drawing-room I reached the one full of flowers
where the Empress was standing, tall, very handsome,
with beautiful chestnut hair, a brilliant complexion, large
clear eyes, a finely cut mouth, a gracious air, but very
reserved and timid.   The conversation was of the innocuous kind usual on such occasions, and dealt with the
former and the new President of the French Republic,
the imperial journey to Paris, the recent excavations at
Kertch.

   From thence I was led to the apartments of the Emperor; I did the waiting in a room adorned with pictures,
all of them French, representing the military review at
Châlons, by Detaille, the ceremonies for the coronation
of Alexander III by George Becker, Emperor Napoleon
in his berline, etc.   Nicholas II received me in a library
the walls of which were lined with bound books, in the
fine dignified array of volumes not often disturbed in
their slumber. Wearing a dark green uniform, fair-
bearded, with large eyes, a gentle look, and an expression
of resigned fatalism, he seemed to be on that day, or at
least at that moment, in a happy disposition and talked
with more spirit than, as I noticed later, was usual with
him, the subjects being, besides some of the unavoidable
ones of the talk with the Empress, the question of disarmament, the new military law in Germany and what
it was foreboding, the Hague conference, convened on

N

his suggestion and in which he showed much interest, without (his fatalism again) great illusions as to its immediate results. The total impression was good-will, honesty, lack of force.

My wife also had an audience of the reigning Empress, and we were received together, at the Anitchkoff Palace, by the Dowager Empress, Maria Feodorovna, *née* Princess Dagmar of Denmark. She was in deep mourning, had an air of extreme sadness and it seemed at times as if she were about to weep. Her lady-in-waiting told us that she was leaving that evening for Copenhagen, and this, her first visit since the death of the Queen her mother, her most intimate confidante, to whom she had ever been devoted, revived her sorrow.

At official dinners at the Embassy or at those midnight suppers which were a second dinner, and were followed by a musicale lasting till the small hours of the morning, we met other members of the imperial family, among whom Grand Duke Constantine, a Shakespearian scholar who had views of his own about Hamlet, himself tall, young, handsome, " the glass of fashion and the mould of form." The Emperor had decided that the Grand Duke would produce his own translation of Hamlet and play the part, before the court, in the little theatre at the Winter Palace. Endowed with an extraordinary memory, he was said to know by heart the names of all the saints in the calendar, an accomplishment more remarkable by its rarity than its usefulness.

Among the interesting personages met on such occasions were the Foreign Minister, Count Muravieff, General Kuropatkin, Minister of War, his chief of staff, General Sakaroff, other Ministers, and the Governors of several provinces. The emotion caused by the recent abrogation of the liberties historically belonging to Finland (February manifesto, 1899), in spite of their having been sworn to by the Emperors, was at its height; it had been deeply felt in Denmark and the other Scandinavian countries, and was wholly unjustified. Finland was the most loyal part of the empire, the one where the Emperor's life was safest; the effect had been deplorable. "This must be the work of Pobedonostseff" (the intractable Procurator of the Holy Synod), I said to Count de Montebello. "Not at all," he answered, "it is the work of Kuropatkin and he is proud of it; at our next dinner we shall seat you next to him; he is full of his subject; he will tell you himself."

The dinner was arranged. Kuropatkin revelled in what he had advised the Emperor to do, refused to see any of the glaringly bad effects of the measure, and tried to justify it by puerile reasons of levelling, regulating and bringing the huge empire with its various populations, races, languages and creeds into subjection, willy nilly, to a strictly uniform Tsarism.

Deep as was the impression one carried away of the importance of an alliance with a country of such magnitude and vast resources, it was impossible to avoid misgivings as to its future, on account of the way it was governed: all the defects of an autocracy, and no autocrat.

THE KING AND HIS FAMILY

Shortly after my arrival in Denmark I had, on February 10, 1899, presented my credentials to King Christian, in his palace of Amalienborg (four palaces surround the place of the same name; one in which he lived, one bearing the name of Christian VII, used for the receptions he gave on great occasions, the two others for his eldest son and his grandson, his future successors). Returning to the hotel where we were staying until our Legation should be ready, I said to my wife: "I consider my career now complete; I have followed it without any break from attaché to minister and I have handed credentials to a foreign sovereign. I have nothing more to expect. If by good fortune I am ever appointed an ambassador, well and good, but it will be indeed a lucky chance and no one has a right to expect it." My Italian colleague, Baron Galvagna, a bright Venetian whose drawing-room was adorned with the standard flown on an ancestor's galley, and bearing the image of the Turk's arch-enemy, the winged lion of Saint Mark, fretted himself to death and actually died of regret not to have had that lucky chance. His successor Count Calvi, receiving the news, said to me: " Let us take care not to follow Galvagna's example." I assured him he need have no fear on my account.

No sovereign ever had so brilliant a family as the then King of Denmark, Christian IX, the Father of Europe as he was called. Without speaking of his eldest son, the Prince Royal, who was to be his successor, and his eldest grandson, now on the throne, one of his daughters was Empress of Russia, another was that Princess of Wales welcomed by Tennyson's famous ode:

> Sea-Kings' daughter from over the sea,
> Alexandra!

(March 7, 1863), later Queen of England; a third was married to the Duke of Cumberland, who, but for the unjustified seizure of his realm by Prussia, would have been King of Hanover, and their son and one of their daughters married respectively the only daughter of Emperor William II, and Prince Max of Baden, heir to the Grand Ducal throne and last Chancellor of the German empire. Of King Christian's younger sons, one became King of Greece, the other, Prince Valdemar, was elected Prince of Bulgaria but preferred to quietly remain as an officer in the Danish navy; a grandson later became King of Norway; a great-granddaughter, Princess Astrid of Sweden, is now wife of the heir to the Belgian throne. When we left Denmark, King Christian had thirty great-grandchildren.

He was eighty-one when we arrived and looked fifty:

tall, slight, elegant, agile, a splendid rider, of winning manners, the veriest gentleman in Europe. He was immensely popular; it would not occur even to a brute to do anything which could pain him. On foot or on horseback, in all weathers, in slush or snow he would take his daily exercise. Often, without saying where he was going, he would set forth unescorted by anyone, even a servant, even a dog, which made the members of his family a little nervous. More than once, having met him in the course of our own walks in the snow-covered woods near Copenhagen, we were able to tell some of them of his whereabouts and in what direction he was going. I was speaking to him one day of his frequent lack of company in the streets or the country; he answered: " My poor dog has died; he was a descendant, three generations removed, of one that 'la Reine Victoire' (Queen Victoria), had given me. I cannot take upon myself to replace him; it is an honour I render to his memory." Even in a snow-storm the old King wore no fur, but a light overcoat, and he never carried such a vulgar machine as an umbrella. He still took part in the court balls and loved to dance a quadrille with one of his daughters, the Empress or the Queen. His transparent honesty, sincerity, his good sense and excellent memory gave, in addition to his rank, considerable weight to his opinions in political matters.

The Prince Royal, later King Frederick VIII, remained as a dutiful son, somewhat in the shade, during his father's long reign, but he followed closely what was going on in the realm and beyond it.

The harsh treatment inflicted by Prussia on his compatriots of annexed Slesvig filled him with indignation, but the sense of the impotency of Denmark, with no help to expect from anyone, inclined him to subservience rather than resistance: anything to placate the menace at the door. I used to point out to him that those unwise brutalities were not without their advantages:

"They remind your compatriots of Slesvig that they are not Germans."

He once showed us, in detail, his living-rooms on the ground floor of his palace, full of curious old furniture collected by him, portraits of ancestors, engraved crystals, huge silver mugs, proportionate to the thirsts of former days; but he had especially a large collection of notes, scrap-books, newspaper cuttings concerning Danish politics; each document marked and annotated by himself. An implacable memory, still further fortified by these aids, prevented his forgetting anything, either services rendered or wrongs inflicted, whereas a man in politics should sometimes be able to forget.

The King's brother, Prince Hans of Glücksborg, unmarried, good-humoured, courtesy itself, was welcome everywhere. He was Chancellor of the two orders of chivalry of Denmark, one of the rare countries where decorations have a meaning and give their owners a rank in the kingdom's nobility. For there, everybody has his rank and the State Calendar with due changes is published every year. The King is number one; all the others follow; professors, wholesale merchants, are included, no dispute as to places at table or elsewhere is possible.

The two orders are the Danebrog, and far above it, as famous as the *Saint Esprit* or the Garter, the order of the Elephant. Why the Elephant, in a kingdom that never had any? I made researches and found that its origin was a legendary deed of valour performed in the East by a Danish crusader. Certain it is that André Favyn in his *Théâtre d'Honneur et de Chevalerie, ou l'Histoire des Ordres Militaires*, Paris, 1620, two volumes in 4to, is loud in his praise of this order and of its emblem, the Elephant: "We have already noticed the properties of the Elephant, its devotion, its piety, its equity, and that it was among the Egyptians the hieroglyphic symbol of Justice; we can add to this its prudence, its wisdom, the

greater that, its blood being cold and melancholic, it is
held the wisest of all beasts, according to the well-known
aphorism that cold and dryness produce right minds."
(Do they? some people are inquiring just now in the
United States.) Favyn spoke of the hieroglyphics as if
he had been a forerunner of Champollion, but he spoke
at random, for the symbol of Justice among the Egyptians
was, Prof. Moret tells me, not the elephant but the
goddess Mâat, daughter of the Sun.

Lunching one day in our Legation, Prince Hans told
us of his having once governed for a brief while the
kingdom of Greece, while his nephew, recently elected
King, had gone to Russia in search of a wife. Crete,
still under Turkish rule, was already a cause of trouble.
The Greeks were for an energetic attitude; he was for
prudence; with the result that when he passed in the
streets, his quasi-subjects looked intently into their coffee-
cups so as to avoid bowing to him. A Greek ship sent
by him to Crete with the most pacific instructions came
back with a Turk whom it had somehow captured.
The Prince became instantly so popular that, as he was
returning from a ride, ignorant of the event, everybody
rose on his passage with such gesticulations and shouts
that his frightened Arab horse nearly threw him.

On another occasion he told us that when very young
he had dined in Vienna at the table of the Austrian
Emperor, Ferdinand I, predecessor of Francis-Joseph,
and there had met Empress Marie-Louise who had once
shared the throne of Napoleon, a wrinkled woman, the
tone of her voice vulgar and unpleasant. When she
stood, however, she had "grand air."

He added that he had narrowly missed being the
"Aiglon" or something like it. His grandfather on the
maternal side was the Elector of Hesse, dispossessed by
Napoleon. The daughter of this prince was betrothed
to a cousin of hers. When the news came of the divorce
of Josephine, the Elector immediately ordered his

daughter to break the match, saying: "The Emperor will perhaps ask for your hand; it is even *very probable* that he will, and then he will return me my states." But the Princess was obdurate; she would not marry her cousin against her father's will, but declared she would marry no one else. This family difficulty was easily solved, however, for, as it turned out, Napoleon asked the hand, not of the Elector's daughter, but of the Austrian Emperor's daughter, Marie-Louise. The Princess married her cousin and had several children, among whom King Christian and Prince Hans.

Prince Valdemar, the sailor prince who had declined to be Prince of Bulgaria, had married fair-haired, blue-eyed Princess Marie, granddaughter of Louis-Philippe, "Roi des Français," and daughter of the Duc de Chartres, former aide to General McClellan in the war of secession, and volunteer under the name of Robert le Fort in the war of '70. They had four sons, little boys in those days, bright, laughing, noisy boys of irrepressible activity, and one pretty little daughter, Margaret, the last born. The Princess was herself of irrepressible activity. In everything that went on she took a hand, were it a charity ball, a line of steamships, any work, any business; she was in direct correspondence with the Emperor of Russia, who signed his answers Nicky, with the powerful Russian Minister Witte, President Loubet, Mr. Delcassé, and many others.

As with her manifold interests she was wearing herself out, remaining sometimes at her desk up to four o'clock in the morning, I ventured a word of warning; but she only shrugged her shoulders, saying: "Yes, the wheel chair that my children will push, while Caby" (her dog) "walks alongside. . . ."—"And Prince Valdemar," I added, "will follow, weeping. Better avoid all that. . . ." But try and persuade ardour not to be ardent!

She had joined the company of Copenhagen firemen and wore their uniform. We were once talking with her when the alarm sounded; fire had been detected on board a ship in the harbour; she hurriedly left us, donned her helmet, and ran to take her rank in the rescuing party. A delegation of Paris firemen who came to Copenhagen, having seen at the Legation her photograph in uniform and helmet, expressed the keenest desire to possess the portrait of this unique colleague of theirs. I had no difficulty in securing one and it no doubt hangs at this day in their barracks at Paris. Her début at a court where, with great simplicity of manners, there prevailed a rather stiff, old-fashioned etiquette, had been difficult, but she had overcome all obstacles and was beloved by all, from the King to the populace.

A clever horsewoman, she took pleasure in riding with two horses harnessed tandem ahead of hers; she had one or two bad falls and was so severely bruised once that she fainted by the roadside; she was picked up by workmen who did not know her and called her *froken* (Miss); feeling that her leg was not broken, she insisted on being helped to her saddle and returned to town, suffering terribly; she had to take to her bed, but would not tell the King why, and pretended to have a cold.

Her artistic gifts were of no mean order; she painted with remarkable skill in water-colours and modelled animals, a hippopotamus among others, for which she went to Hamburg in order to have a living model before her eyes. It was reproduced in porcelain at the Royal manufactory. When a strange fish was caught or a strange bird was killed, it was sent for her to use as a model. We both contributed to a calendar with a water-colour for each month, presented to the Dowager Empress of Russia. Other contributors were Madeleine Lemaire, Cazin, Renoir, Dagnan-Bouveret, Gérôme, etc., all of them artists of fame. My offering had in the eyes of King Christian's daughter a very special merit: it represented the castle at Elsinore. She caused her father to convey to me her warm thanks.

At each of the places where Princess Marie lived, her private drawing-room was also a studio. Calling on her at Fredensborg we found her room teeming with birds, dogs, flowers, mushrooms, a pumpkin, a large basket containing branches loaded with apples and which she was painting life size. The dog in chief was the afore-mentioned Caby, for whom I more than once gave letters commending him to the care of the French rail-road authorities; a bulldog he was, of ferocious aspect but of meek disposition.

In spite of being a loyal Dane, Princess Marie had remained very French at heart; a huge tricolour falling from the ceiling and touching the ground adorned her sitting-room at Bernstorff; she went on board any French naval ship stopping at Copenhagen and brought gifts to "her friends the sailors." She did not admit that French royalists should call on her and not on the French Minister at the Legation, where we received among others the visits of her brothers, attractive, cheery, adventurous Prince Henry who died a premature death in Indo-China and left some writings collected by his father under the title of *L'Ame du Voyageur*, and Prince John, the present Duc de Guise, who afterwards married his handsome and gifted cousin, Princess Isabelle of France, and has become the head of the Orleans family. Princess Marie was free-spoken with everybody and prompt at repartee. Witte, who had the haughtiness of a parvenu and who had failed in his attempts to launch a loan in the United States, did not conceal his belief that as for the French, they ought to feel flattered at being allowed to lend their money to Russia. "I shall secure a new loan when I please," he said to the Princess; "the French are like hens; I have only to whistle for them to come."—"Take care," she replied, "that it may some day be the cocks that will answer." (My Journal, Feb. 10, 1901.)

The Boer war had caused the British to be then very un-popular throughout Europe; at a cinema in Copenhagen,

Kruger was every night applauded and the British hissed. My German colleague Kiderlen, later Foreign Secretary, would say with his broad laugh: "The British have just inflicted a new victory on the Boers." [1] Caricaturists in various lands had given free play to their sarcastic dispositions. As the Duke of York (future George V) was visiting his grandfather, King Christian, Princess Marie heard him speak bitterly of the French caricatures; she happened to have made a collection of the British ones against France at the time of the Fashoda incident (1898–99), and she sent it, without a word of comment, to the Duke. She received a courteous answer.

Her four sons were brought up in the Protestant religion, her daughter in the Catholic faith. The latter and the youngest son were taken for the first time to their respective churches on Easter Day 1901. During the lunch which followed at the King's table they had, their father told me, a "religious discussion"; the little Princess proudly said: "In *our* church there was a bishop all in gold." Her little brother, not wanting to be outshone, said: "In *our* church, well, there was a woman who fainted."

They have grown, they have married; the eldest son, Prince Aage, has enlisted in our Foreign Legion, showed conspicuous valour in Morocco, and in a very modest account published by the *Revue des Deux Mondes* of the events he participated in, has drawn one of the best pictures of our efforts to pacify the country.

The "Valkyrien" in Siam and at Saint-Pierre

Owing to the important commercial interests of Denmark in the Far East, and especially in Siam, chief field of action of the Danish East Asiatic Company, Prince Valdemar, in command of the *Valkyrien*, the newest Danish cruiser, was sent to Bangkok in 1899–1900. I had on his return several talks with him about his ex-

---

[1] My notes, Jan. 8, 1900.

periences. In one of them he spoke of the visit he had paid to the French Governor-General of Indo-China; he had been greatly struck by the worth of the man. " A man," he said, " such as to become some day President of the Republic," [1] by which words the Prince did not prove a bad prophet, since this Governor-General was Paul Doumer.

The same *Valkyrien*, under command then of Captain Holm, happened to be at Saint-Thomas in the Danish West Indies in 1902, when the news came of the disaster at Saint-Pierre, Martinique, Saint-Pierre having in an instant by the explosion of Mont Pelé been made a new Pompeii; no one could tell whether the convulsions of the volcano were continuing, nor whether it was possible to approach and bring useful help. The Commander wired to Copenhagen asking his Government's permission to go, and without waiting for an answer, shipped food and medical supplies and started on his hazardous journey. When he neared the island he found himself in a complete darkness caused by smoke, steam and ashes; the compass had gone wild, and instead of reaching Saint-Pierre he found himself at Fort de France. But he started again, taking better aim; when he neared the doomed city he dimly saw what he took for a light showing that he was in the right direction; it was a boat burning in the harbour. A French naval ship was there and signalled to him that nothing could be attempted at Saint-Pierre; everybody was dead; but in the village of le Prêcheur, on the other side of the mountain, the inhabitants were in great danger; these should be helped. The *Valkyrien* anchored before that village and removed six hundred people to a place of safety.

When the ship returned to Copenhagen in June, I paid the captain, his officers and sailors an official visit in uniform, was received with the *Marseillaise*, a salute of guns, the French flag flying at the mainmast, and I

[1] August 15, 1900.

expressed the gratitude of France. I was shown samples
of the impalpable dust emitted by the volcano, that
made the air almost unbreathable and which had covered
the deck of the ship; a little bottle-full of it was given me.
The captain and his officers dined shortly after at the
Legation; Admiral Johnke, Minister of the Navy, was
present and I told him that we had especially appreciated
the pluck with which Captain Holm had risked his ship
without waiting for his Government's answer. " If he had
waited," the admiral replied, " he would have been
dismissed from the Navy."

In a brief speech I announced that the captain would
be made a Commander of the Legion of Honour, a
proper decoration for a sailor, since its form was a star,
and its name was Honour.

A subscription was opened for the victims, the King
heading it with 4,000 francs.

AT COURT

Manners at court were simple and cordial in ordinary
circumstances, and very formal, with the observances
of a stiff old-fashioned etiquette on official occasions.
At the dinners we gave in honour of each of the principal
members of the Royal Family, I had to go to the entrance
door on the street to meet my princely guests, followed
by my personnel and preceded by two servants carrying
candelabras which must have a minimum of three
candles each (no maximum was fixed), because staircases,
unlit in the Middle Ages, were not supposed to be lit
now; we could not fail to notice that they were certainly
still not heated. Dinners at court, which were frequent
and were worth the seeing (and the eating), were served
in great pomp by servants in ancient style, dazzling
liveries that included a sort of tall pasteboard richly
ornamented shako, hollow at the top for a bunch of
paper flowers. When the King intended to drink to you,
he had you notified by the head butler, then raised his

glass; you had then to rise to your feet, glass in hand,
bow, drink in your turn after the King had drunk, bow
again, and before sitting down, and this was a most
important part of the ceremonial, look into the eyes of the
King, who returned the look.

The Royal Family was very united; husbands and wives
were devoted to each other. The King had left untouched
the rooms occupied by the Queen, who had died shortly
before our arrival; he visited them now and then as if
to hold council with the dear departed one. When
Princess Marie died, Prince Valdemar could not, for a
long while, bring himself to have her buried at Roskilde,
but had her coffin kept in the Sailors' Church in Copenhagen, so as to be able to visit it at will.

Princes and Princesses had, most of them, danish
fashion, a keen eye for the humorous side of things and
did not allow any cause for merriment to pass by them
unenjoyed. They were the first to laugh at the congestion
caused in the King's little summer residence, near Copenhagen, by the presence of the Emperor and the two
Empresses of Russia, the English King and Queen, the
King of Greece and other great personages whose
attendants had sometimes to camp in the park. To the
Dowager Empress and her sister, Queen Alexandra
of England, was assigned the one room they had occupied
together when young girls, and the guests thus gained
for their common use a room which they called their club.
Vort Land ("Our Country"), a Conservative paper,
represented Kings and Princes sleeping in hay-stacks with
their head and feet protruding, and a royal crown on the
top of the stack; full-uniformed chamberlains cere-
moniously bringing water for the morning ablutions;
an alarm clock over the head of the King of Greece,
because he was supposed to be always late. *Bloek
Sprutten* ("Ink Splashes") showed princesses talking
cows with cow-herds, a peasant, pipe in hand, giving
confidential advice to Emperor Nicholas, King Edward

superabundantly filling a toy automobile, and blowing a trumpet to frighten away chickens; these, and other like scenes, with the caption: "An Idyl in North-Sjoelland."

"The castle," I wrote to Mr. Delcassé, "is surrounded by very pleasant woods and the princely guests walk or drive there. . . . A tennis court has been arranged and the Russian Emperor exercises on it. Nothing has been altered for what concerns the public; the woods around continue to be open to all; a road bordering the castle is not closed. Some passers-by, more curious than discreet, but whom no one disturbs, do not conceal their intention to secure a souvenir of the illustrious visitors, and watch from the road, kodak in hand, their coming out. Police agents have arrived from Russia, but they perform their service with discretion and do not draw attention." [1]

Royal and imperial personages kept coming and going, the most jovial of all being the Prince of Wales, future Edward VII. On the 5th of April, 1900, as we were leaving the Yellow Palace (place of abode of Princess Marie), we met, on the semi-dark staircase, a pale and thin lady, dressed with the utmost simplicity in black, and who was going up with some trouble, resting both feet on each step. My wife, who was in front of me, luckily recognized her and curtesied to the Dowager Empress of Russia who stopped and talked with us. She had received the previous night a telegram from her sister telling of the attempt by a man called Sipido on the life of the Prince of Wales, then travelling to Copenhagen; the train was stopping at a Belgian station, "the window pane was down; the Princess saw a hand suddenly appear there, a shot was fired, the bullet passing between her and the Prince; it was a wonder that no one was wounded."

The next day, having been prescribed by my Government to offer congratulations to the Prince on his escape,

[1] Sept. 15, 1899.

I was received by him and found him remarkably affable
and gracious; I had not seen him for ten years, but he
was little altered, very big, very red, seeming to be in
excellent health. He spoke of the French newspaper
attacks and anti-English caricatures, but only to remark
that in such matters the Government was helpless and
that, moreover, the same dispositions were noticeable
in every country, especially in Germany. He told me
of the attempt in about the same terms as the Empress.
" I was seated in our car with the Princess when there
was seen at the window a brown-gloved hand. I thought
it was a petition and was about to rise when the shot
was fired. The bullet was found this morning in a
cushion. I had walked for twenty minutes before that
along the train and nothing had happened. The dagger
is the really dangerous weapon."

" We often receive," Princess Marie told me later,
" threatening letters from anarchists; after each out-
rage they increase in number; when the Empress of
Austria was assassinated we got many; some told us
we were wrong to imagine that because we were only
Princesses we should escape. The Prince Royal has a
fine collection of them."

The following year the Prince of Wales was King of
England; Queen Victoria had died in January 1901.
The Princess of Wales had always been on excellent terms
with her, the only cloud having been at the time of the
War of the Duchies in 1863. When the danger to
Denmark was so great, she had begged the Queen in
writing to send the fleet to help her native country.
" Poor child," the Queen had said.

King Christian longed to attend the coronation of his
son-in-law and he intended to follow the cortège, as the
kings of old, on horseback. But Edward VII deprecated
his coming because he wanted on no account his nephew
William II to be present; no sovereign must therefore
be invited. The new King apprehended a repetition

of what had happened at the funeral of Queen Victoria, when the German Emperor had made himself unbearable. " He had wanted," the Danish Foreign Minister told me, " to have the upper hand in everything, to take the lead, be the centre of all. He had brought with him all he might need, as if nothing in England was good enough and Germanic superiority should, even in trifles, be affirmed." Warmly encouraged by his daughter, Christian IX insisted, pointing out that there was for his coming a special reason which other sovereigns could not allege, he was the father of the Queen. But his son-in-law would not yield.

The coronation was very near being abandoned. The new King fell ill and was suddenly and secretly operated on, only the Queen and his son being informed. The Prince Royal of Denmark told us, on his return, that though staying at Buckingham Palace he had known of the operation only after it had been performed. He had spent the previous evening with the King, who had played with his dogs and birds, but who now and then put his hand to his side, saying: " I pay too much attention to this, the usual case with people who have always been in good health." [1]

DANISH POLITICS

The Ministers for Foreign Affairs with whom I had to deal in those years were Admiral Ravn, replaced in May 1900 by Mr. Sehested, himself succeeded in July 1901 by Mr. Deuntzer. The Admiral was probably the dean of all the ministers in Europe, " having begun his service as Minister of the Navy in June 1875; he had been, therefore, some twenty-five years in office, and Denmark offered this peculiar phenomenon, that its navy counted officers who were not yet born when the present Minister

---

[1] The operation was successful and the coronation was only postponed for six weeks; most of the Princes who had come for it had by that time gone home.

o

had assumed his functions.   He had, moreover, been Acting Minister of Foreign Affairs for three years." [1] His popularity was, however, on the wane; all the criticism aimed at his Department touched him and not predecessors unknown to the present generation.   Small-sized, large-headed, he was a confirmed Conservative, averse to the taking of any risk, perfectly honest and conscientious, and of very moderate eloquence.   Just outside of Copenhagen existed a settlement for sailors. Rows of small houses formed streets; at the corner of each was a larger house for an officer, who had to see that order reigned in his street.   This settlement had been founded by the great warrior king, Christian IV, father-in-law of James I of England.   A statue was erected to him near those houses which continued still in use.   The day of the dedication was a great occasion: the King, the court, the diplomatic corps, an enormous crowd, were present.   Admiral Ravn had to make *the* speech of the day.   It was a very long one, conscientious of course, but dull, undoubtedly dull.   In the midst of it a dog, who somehow had passed the serried ranks of the multitude and was sitting at the foot of the pedestal, stretched himself and publicly yawned in the sight of all. It was the best moment of the ceremony; the crowd laughed noisily; the court laughed, the Admiral laughed too, but mercilessly continued to read for half an hour more.

Mr. Sehested, his successor at the Foreign Ministry, also a Conservative and an upright man, was fundamentally an agriculturist; he had mixed very little with foreign affairs, most of his time being devoted to his estate in the island of Fyen.   In my first official visit to him our talk ran on the merits and demerits of the various kinds of ravens.

The progress of Liberal ideas was in the meantime more and more marked at every election and the clamour for

[1] To Mr. Delcassé, January 25, 1900.

a change was louder. In 1901 the 1st of May was celebrated in fifty-two cities or boroughs; fiery speeches
were delivered, but order prevailed everywhere. In
Copenhagen, on one side of a lawn a socialist gathering
was told that "Revolution was moving forth, that
capitalists must be destroyed and that when capitalists
should have been thrown out of windows, universal
fraternity would reign"; at best, one may think, a
limited kind of fraternity. On the other side of the
lawn, the King was seen going to the station with his son
Valdemar for one of his walks in the woods, without any
escort or surveillance by the police.

Most reluctantly the King had to yield. Only his
extraordinary popularity had allowed him to delay so
long. To form a ministry of the Left and be Minister
of Foreign Affairs, he selected Prof. Deuntzer, a jurist
and economist, well versed in social questions, who had
travelled, knew Europe well, spoke five or six languages
fluently, among which French perfectly. It was a good
choice and the country was delighted. But I wrote to
Paris, the political changes will not be considerable for,
while protesting against a Conservative Ministry,
periodically threatened with impeachment, Parliament
out of deference to the King voted taxation; it also
voted a number of laws proposed by that same Ministry
and which had for their object the welfare of the working
classes, such as the great law on workmen's old age
pensions, without any deduction from their wages.
Many other projects, however, concerning the improvement of the army, the navy, the defences of Copenhagen,
were regularly rejected as entailing "unproductive
expenses." The old Ministry declared its regret, but
remained in office.

The foreign policy of those successive Ministries,
whether they belonged to the Right or to the Left, was
the same, and conformed with the more and more marked
tendency of the country: to keep out of trouble and

especially give no pretext for displeasure to the formidable southern neighbour. They wanted to persuade themselves that compliance, submission, innocence were their surest safeguards, while, at the same time, as shown since by the above-quoted documents in Prince Bülow's *Memoirs* (Dec. 2, 1904), William II was coolly considering as a first move in case of a war with England, which he then deemed likely, an occupation of the more important points in Denmark without even an ultimatum.[1]

In spite of her proud past the nation inclined to yield, to count on arbitration, on the good faith of the people next door, to use all her revenue for her welfare and have no longer any army at all, as if the giving up of their dogs by the sheep was a way of securing their safety. "They will allege," the German Emperor said of the Danes on the same occasion, "their neutrality, but as they possess only pitiful means to defend it, its value is nil." This was not known for sure then and could only be suspected; but I frequently pointed out the danger for Denmark of becoming a nation of rich merchants, and not even armed merchants, like the Venetians formerly and the British now.

So long as Alexander III had reigned in Russia, the Danes had counted on him; from his weak successor they expected nothing. "Russia is drifting," Deuntzer would say, "she has no leader, the Emperor does not lead." The extension to Finland of the autocratic system had caused in Denmark a deep and painful emotion. "This," I wrote to Mr. Delcassé, March 31, 1899, "may seem strange: Finland is not Danish; it was not such before becoming Russian; the race living there is not Danish and does not speak Danish.

"This emotion, which has been profound at court as well as throughout the country, and even more in reality

---

[1] Above, pp. 129–130. In a previous letter to Bülow he had said: "To be able to count on Denmark would be equivalent to a doubling of our forces in war-time." (Dec. 27, 1903.) *Correspondance Secrète de Bülow et de Guillaume II*, p. 23.

than outwardly shown, is, however, easy to understand. After centuries of power and glory the Danes rank now among the little nations unable to resist. Any absorption of a small country by a big one is disquieting to them. This general process, which more and more extends the power of the strong and diminishes the lot tolerated in the hands of the weak, revives anxieties which, since the War of the Duchies,[1] have never died out. The present case is the more striking in Denmark that this absorption of a small nation comes from that Russia considered for years as the great friend, the great protectress.

"How could she ever interest herself in the fate of the Danes of Slesvig, how could she say a word in their favour after what she has done in Finland? No one had, to be sure, any great illusions, but people liked to think that with the Russians there was some more or less nebulous possibility. Who knows? people said; they no longer ask themselves; they know.

"The German Government keeps a threatening attitude, oppresses the Danes of Slesvig, declares that it will not participate in the 'Peace Conference' if it meets in Copenhagen;[2] well-coached publicists, those sowers of ideas whom Germany knows so well how to use, show how beautifully bright is the other side of the medal; they talk of a customs union, of a fruitful *zollverein*, they try to so act on the minds, that Denmark may some day be attracted into the orbit of Germany, in which are already gravitating much greater states, one of whom was also vanquished by her."[3]

When such questions arose in my conversations with the Danish Ministers, I alluded to the danger, quite aside from a violent intrusion, of a moral or economic

[1] 1848 and 1863–64, for the possession of the Duchies of Slesvig and Holstein.

[2] Copenhagen had first been considered as the place where should be convened the conference which eventually met at the Hague in 1899.

[3] March 31, 1899.

one; of Denmark, which had played an important part
in the history of the world, losing its individuality;
the individuality of even small civilized nations being,
as history has shown, of importance for mankind. "But
what can we do," Mr. Deuntzer once asked me, "being
so very small?"—"Maintain your position and wait;
small kingdoms have more than once seen the fall of
great empires." [1]

A very influential group, I wrote to our Foreign
Minister (Nov. 7, 1902), "is one which I do not know how
to designate except as the intellectual one. It has for
its organ the *Politiken*, the newspaper of the Brandes
brothers; [2] it is formed of people very liberal, but sceptical,
ironical, disdainful of every ancient belief, thinking above
all of present welfare. They do not cease to preach
renunciation and abdication, to request a reduction of
the army (the normal service is of six months!), the
suppression of expenses for armaments. The idea of
compulsory military service, of a country which should
be defended, were it but for honours' sake, seems to them
an old-fashioned and uncomfortable notion. According
to them, if Denmark had no army at all, declared itself
neutral, whatever might happen, showed that it was
absolutely defenceless, Germany, all smiles, would have
for it only favours and good-will. The credulity of
sceptics is often astounding."

Many members of the Lower House kept harping on
the necessity of a proclaimed neutrality owing to which
there would be no need for an army, a navy, or fortifications; all unproductive expenses would disappear.
Mr. Deuntzer, who knew better, tried "to make them
understand the difference between being neutral, which
is the case of every nation except the belligerents, and
of being neutralized, which does not depend on one's
will nor on a simple statement of pacific intentions. Few

[1] November 7, 1902.
[2] One of whom, Georg, was the well-known Shakespearian scholar.

peoples are neutralized, and precisely those are far from having renounced armaments and the defence of their soil, in the event that they should be attacked in spite of international guarantees." [1]

But the movement was too strong for him and he too considered that the best way to secure survival was to placate neighbours whose tyranny in Slesvig was continuing ever worse. At his request the Prince Royal, in November 1902, visited William II, who greatly desired this compliment and received him with the fullest honours, going to meet him at the station, when the rule was to do so only for crowned heads. The Emperor was so insistent, that the Prince had to prolong his stay longer than he intended. Of favourable results for the Danes of Slesvig there was, however, no trace, and in his inner thoughts the Kaiser, as we have seen before, contemplated in those same years an invasion of Denmark in case he himself went to war with England. " Denmark," he said, " must decide to place itself somehow under a German protectorate, first by a *zollverein*, then by military concessions." [2] This was, it seems, a system with him : he saw nothing wrong in preparing the downfall of his best welcomed guests. After having urged the Tsar to go to war with Japan, his first thought, when the Russians were defeated, was to cable congratulations to the Mikado, which, however, Bülow prevented. [3]

THE DANISH WEST INDIES

The long-pending question of the sale of the Danish West Indies to the United States came again to the front during my years in Copenhagen. A treaty for that sale had been signed in 1867. One of the islands, Sainte-Croix, with the largest population, had been French in

---

[1] To Mr. Delcassé, February 24, 1902.

[2] Schoen's report to Bülow, December 2, 1904, Bülow's *Memoirs*, Vol. II, Chap. VII.

[3] To Bulow, March 11, 1905 : *Correspondance Secrète de Bülow et de Guillaume II*, p. 92.

former times, but we had ceded it to the Danes, in June 1733, for 750,000 francs, with the proviso that, if ever they wanted to sell it, we would have a right to get it back for the same sum, " argent de France." In order not to hamper our Danish friends we had at that time waived our right. But the American Senate, which does not easily ratify treaties, had rejected the 1867 one. Negotiations had been resumed at intervals. Henry White came to Denmark on a secret mission in 1900 and 1901 to settle the matter. " We do not desire to con-strain them," he told me, " but if they want to sell, we want to purchase, and they must say yes or no." [1]   I again gave to the Danes the assurance that we would not interfere nor claim Sainte-Croix; a new treaty was eventually signed in Washington, in January 1902. This time it was the Danish Landsting that refused its rati-fication, greatly influenced by a desire not to pain the old King, who was averse to the transaction and let it be known that he could not suffer having his reign end as it had begun, by a diminution of Danish territory. He told me how pleased he was with what had occurred, " and that the Americans were showing no aggressiveness nor discontent."

The sale took place only after his death, under circum-stances narrated in his Memoirs by Secretary Lansing, who during the World War heightened the Danes' fear of being swallowed by Germany, insisting that the reten-tion by them of such a point of vantage in the west might increase the temptation of their southern neighbours to forcibly acquire sovereignty at one stroke over both the kingdom and its dependencies. He wrote: " In the conversation which I had with Mr. Brun (the Danish Minister) in the latter part of October (1915), when he advised me that his Government was not disposed to negotiate a sale of the islands, I had said to him very bluntly that there was danger that Germany, taking

[1] September 2, 1901.

advantage of the upheaval of Europe, might absorb Denmark and that she might do so in order to obtain a legal title to the Danish West Indies which the German Government coveted for naval uses. The continued possession of the islands by Denmark might therefore become a menace to Danish independence.

" I also said that in the event of an evident intention on the part of Germany to take possession of his country or to compel Denmark to cede the islands to her, the United States would be under the necessity of seizing and annexing them, and though it would be done with the greatest reluctance, it would be necessary to do it in order to avoid a serious dispute with the German Government over the sovereignty of and the title to the islands, as we would never permit the islands to become German.

" This plain-spoken threat of what might occur had the desired effect." [1]

A new treaty was signed in August 1916, and was this time ratified by both Parliaments; the consideration was not, however, seven and a half million dollars as in the one rejected by the American Senate in 1867, but twenty-five, and the sovereignty of Denmark was, moreover, recognized by the United States over the whole of Greenland.

Russia and her Minister to Denmark

The representative of Russia in Copenhagen was Count Benckendorff; none of my colleagues was as free-spoken as this servant of the Tsar. Perfectly loyal to his sovereign and his country, he nevertheless did not conceal in his conversations with me his misgivings as to the future of both. His wife, *née* Schouvaloff, was just the same; the greatest crime in history, she once told me, was the partition of Poland; other countries have been subjugated, but this one was divided into three parts and each part was forced to be the enemy of the other two.

[1] Fragment of Mr. Lansing's Memoirs, written shortly before his death and published by the *New York Times*, July 19, 1931.

Before entering diplomacy the Count had filled several functions at court. As a page, he was on duty one night by the bier of assassinated Alexander II lying in state, and had to witness the operations practised at intervals by the physicians, who injected drugs into the body and repainted the cheeks; the horror and stench were such that he nearly fainted.

One of his secretaries, returning from Russia in March 1901, reported that he had witnessed students' riots and that the reports about them had been greatly exaggerated. "That may be true," said the Count, "for what concerns St. Petersburg, but not Moscow, where new industries have attracted a labouring population which has joined the students. It was easy to foresee, but it was not foreseen; it is not the custom in Russia to foresee.

" But those scuffles are nothing, they are what appears on the outside; the matter for anxiety is what takes place inside, what people think. In this respect there has been no exaggeration; on the contrary, the real truth is worse than has been said. In order to work, an autocratic Government must in a way have public opinion with it. The governed must see and understand whither they are being led; this usually suffices; it is, in any case, indispensable. With the new reign, no one understands. It is obvious and a matter of public knowledge that the personal tendencies of the Emperor are the reverse of what he is advised to do and does. He yields, then turns round and acts in a contrary way: which may be called floundering.

" It began with Finland (about which people have so excited him that he himself has become intractable); then a move in the opposite direction, the Hague Conference. We now have the students put down, the zemstvos suppressed, or nearly so, all the safety-valves shut. This policy of compression would have a meaning if it was really followed up, if the hand of Nicholas I was at the helm, but such is not the case, oh! no. There are attenuations, moves in the opposite direction; we flounder.

" We must or must not have universities; if we have, students should not be treated as dangerous animals." [1]

" The Chinese imbroglio is alarming, we have promised to retire from Manchuria, and we do not; this may have serious results." [2]

The Empress being once more in the family way, I expressed the hope that after four daughters she would now have a son. " What does it matter? " Count Bernstorff answered; " that it be of importance to them is natural, but what difference can it make to us? " —" What of the people? " I asked.—" The people do not care any more than we do. In Russia, according to appearances, on the surface, people are all sentiment; they have a tenderness for the Tsar, etc. It is exactly as in France on the eve of the Revolution."

And he quoted a passage he had read in a book, he " did not remember by whom." I remembered, but did not tell him; it was a book of mine.

" The tendency to uniformity and centralization," he said again, " is such that it ought to open everyone's eyes: our revolutionists are in favour of it. . . .

" This Finland business has made us unpopular, and not only in the Scandinavian countries but in the Balkans too. I have not concealed it from the Tsar." [3]

As for Sweden, the Dutch Minister, Mr. de Heekren, accredited to both Stockholm and Copenhagen, told me a little later (September 12, 1901) that the Swedish sentiment toward Russia was now " terror." All the fortifications and armaments were devised in view of a possible clash; the Swedish Foreign Minister goes periodically *ad audiendum verbum* to Berlin and has long talks with Bülow." Subsequent events showed, during the Great War, the consequences of these dispositions.

[1] Conversation of March 1, 1901.
[2] Conversation of January 10, 1901.   [3] April 25, 1900.

Upon everyone, the Tsar, with his honesty, sense of justice, desire to do well, made the same impression; fate had imposed on him a task to which he was not equal; his case resembled in an ominous way that of Richard II and Charles I of England and Louis XVI of France. Princess Marie, like so many others, was struck by his fatalism, his incapacity to react, to make his honourable intentions prevail; in money matters he preferred to pay out of his own pocket rather than try to uproot ingrained abuses. To his military attaché in Copenhagen, General Sirelius, he stated that personally he was for the Boers, but that his Government was against them. As I write these lines I remember the remark made to me once by a Russian of note: "The Tsar has said yes, but the little dog in the ante-room, by a wag of his head, has said no."

The Tsar was often to be met when in Denmark, sometimes in an open carriage, answering with a tired look the salute of the passers-by, sometimes on a bicycle, with his cousin Princess Victoria of England, or driving a little one-horse trap. His light beard and fair complexion, made him look even younger than he was. He struck everybody by his propensity to silence, chiefly due to timidity. Deuntzer told me that a Danish general attached to his person was eight days without hearing the sound of his voice, not even a good morning when they first met each day.

The Russian Emperor's Second Journey to France

In September 1901 the Tsar and the Empress went for the second time to France. I strongly insisted with my Government that Paris be included in the programme, were it but for a few moments, so that the visit should not seem to be made to the army alone, but to the nation. In a private letter to Mr. Delcassé I said: "The true visit to the President of the Republic is one in the place where he lives; the true visit to the nation is one in its

capital. . . . If the impression is given that only a part
of the nation cares for the alliance: if one part of it feels
it is neglected, if the two peoples do not go with out-
stretched hands to meet each other, this alliance so necessary for the European equilibrium will be compromised.
. . . The call may be of the shortest, a tea at the Presidency with a visit to the Alexander III bridge, and a
return to Compiègne on the same day, but it should be
made." (September 8, 1901.)

I failed; Paris was excluded. The departure took
place from Copenhagen with some solemnity on September 10th, at the yachts' harbour. The only foreign
Minister invited, I arrived early with my wife; the next
comers were the four little Russian Grand Duchesses, all
dressed alike, each carrying a tiny bag, obviously, in their
eyes, the most important part of their luggage; sweet,
pretty children for whom the future reserved a hideous
death in the Ekaterinburg shambles. Then came the
Emperor, the two Empresses, the Kings of Denmark,
England and Greece, and the members of the court.
Nicholas II asked Benckendorff to bring me to him, and
after having visibly inclined to simply shake my hand in
silence, made an effort and said: " I am glad to be
going, people are always so nice to me there." The
Empress, standing apart, unable to conceal her timidity,
often taken for haughtiness (" Don't be so imperial,"
her young British cousins used sometimes to say to her),
gave us her hand to kiss without uttering a word. The
difference was striking with the Kings of Denmark and
of England, who were as usual cheery, kindly, simple-
mannered. Avoiding politics, King Edward highly
praised his new toy, an uncommon one in those days,
his automobile, a vast machine that gave him great
satisfaction.

The imperial family was established at Compiègne,
visited Reims, never appeared in Paris, witnessed the
military manœuvres and the review at Bétheny. My

military attaché, Vicomte de la Panouse of the Cuirassiers, who was there, wrote me, September 20, 1901: " Yesterday was the last day of the manœuvres, which took place in the presence of the Emperor, the Empress, the President and Madame Loubet. One hundred and fifty thousand men had been mustered in the immense plain north of Reims and there was a sham battle, in which they were all engaged, that must have been a superb sight. We were four divisions of cavalry at one wing . . .; we charged furiously, to the terror of hares and partridges; my horse crushed one of each. The Tsar must have had a favourable impression of the troops; the movements were well ordered and spirited. . . . But after fourteen hours of manœuvring or waiting, cuirass on back, we were very weary. The retreat at nightfall, with the moon shining on the cuirasses, was very picturesque and the soldiers sang so as not to fall asleep on their horses."

The Tsar caused a collection to be made of all the articles, drawings and caricatures published on the occasion of his journey. It was sent to his mother in Copenhagen, to be forwarded to him later. One of the photographs represented him receiving explanations on the mechanism of a new piece of artillery which was to become famous, the French '75.

President Loubet's Visit to Copenhagen

In the following spring (1902) the imperial visit was returned by President Loubet accompanied by Foreign Minister Delcassé. It seemed to me that a call at Copenhagen on the return journey would be appropriate. At no period of history had any king or chief of the French State visited Denmark: the compliment would be the more appreciated, I had no doubt, that, on a number of occasions, King Christian had expressed to me his sympathy and consideration for our President, his prudence, his family virtues, the aptness of his public speeches, his

AWAITING THE ARRIVAL OF PRESIDENT LOUBET

face p. 207

wisdom, especially when, indifferent to obloquy and opposition, he had brought to an end the Dreyfus affair. Admiral Johnke, Minister of the Navy, was quite positive that the King would be delighted and the crowd enthusiastic. The bureaus at the Danish Foreign Office were much less cheering and scarcely concealed their apprehension of the effect in Germany. They would have liked the idea to be discarded, or, if the visit took place, that it should draw as little attention as possible and be nothing but a simple nod *en passant*. To which I replied: " If a nod, it must be at least a polite nod; no one in his senses will think that we are courting an alliance." The apprehension went so far in that *milieu* that the Russian Minister of the Interior, Sipiaguine, having been assassinated, Mr. Deuntzer asked me whether Mr. Loubet would not give up his visit to Russia. I made the only possible answer: " Our Presidents are inaccessible to fear." The two visits were decided.

The naval division for the journey to Russia was under command of Admiral Roustan, brother of our former Minister to Tunis, later to Washington, and included the *Montcalm*, the *Guichen*, the *Cassini*, and two small torpedo destroyers, the *Fauconneau* and the *Yatagan*. When, leaving Cronstadt, they reached Copenhagen, the larger ships anchored outside and the *Cassini*, with President Loubet and his suite on board, entered the harbour at eleven a.m. on May 25th. The day before, the King had said to me: " To-morrow will be for me a great day." And it was, from every point of view, a most successful one. Instead of waiting for the President to land, Christian IX, now eighty-four, went out in his launch toward the *Cassini*, lightly climbed the gangplank and welcomed his guest; the cannon boomed, an immense crowd shouted hurrahs, the streets were beflagged; the King, gay, charming, beaming with pleasure, praised the Minister of France to the President as a diplomat, a writer and a husband. " The only pity," he added, " is that you will not leave him long to us."

The gilded coach offered to the King by his subjects on the occasion of his golden wedding, and never used since, was waiting and took the chiefs of State to the Christian VII palace, over which floated the French flag, and a banquet of eighty was served. The King had recommended that it be good rather than long, and that it be such as to please even French palates, which it did. Some decorations were exchanged, the King wanted to bestow one on Mr. Loubet's son, but the President had decided that he should accept none anywhere. As a conclusive reason he stated that he had refused one for him in Russia. " But," said the King, " my grandson does not reign in Denmark," and the cross had to be accepted. Toward the end of the meal the King and the President drew papers from their pockets and exchanged cordial toasts.

Admiral Roustan began to feel nervous as time was passing and he saw that he would have to transfer the President at dusk, from the *Cassini* to the *Montcalm*, in the open sea, but the King was loath to part with his guest, and remarked that Mr. Loubet had said that he would visit his capital. So he took him in his carriage and showed him the chief beauty spots of the place. Reaching the harbour and surrounded by members of his family he accompanied him to the *Cassini*, where tea was served, and he improvised a toast much warmer and coming more truly from the heart than the written one at the banquet which had only come from his pocket. President Loubet was not less felicitous in his answer. When parting had at last to take place the King asked us to return to the quay in his launch and said that he would like to have the text of Mr. Loubet's toast. " But," I answered, " there is no text; Your Majesty caused him to speak and his answer was improvised."—" I nevertheless want to have it; put it in writing, please, what you remember."—" And don't forget," merrily added the Princes, that he said this and also that, " and that we were in the front rank of civilisation."

Back in the Legation, I proposed to my wife that we should each take a sheet of paper and write what we thought had been said; I fused the two into one and sent it to the King, who had it printed in the *Berlingske* (the official Danish paper). The result was that, while the President continued his navigation, a text of a speech of his, with nothing objectionable to be sure, but which he had not seen, had been officially published abroad. I cabled the short document to Paris, and as it was found irreproachable, it was inserted in our official paper as well.

The visit, unique of its kind, had been a success from beginning to end and left on all the people in the street and people at court, a very favourable impression. The King, Prince Hans told us, had been rejuvenated, cheered by the event; he felt no fatigue. He sent a telegram for the President to find on landing at Dunkerque to thank him for having called; the idea of the telegram was his and the text was in his own hand.

Our Every-day Life. The End of our Stay

Those Danish years were quiet, pleasant ones. I was on good terms with my foreign colleagues, some of whom were to play an important part on a larger stage, like the two Germans, von Kiderlen, whose cleverness, jokes and very familiarity pleased the Emperor (but once offended him, and caused a temporary disgrace), and von Schoen; each became Minister for Foreign Affairs; the latter, an amiable man, with nothing fiery in his temperament, was destined by an irony of fate to be, as Ambassador in Paris, the messenger of death to a million and a half Frenchmen when he declared war on us, alleging motives so palpably false that he felt a sense of shame recorded by him in his Memoirs; the British Minister, Sir Edward

P

Göschen, Ambassador to Germany at the time of the
Great War, one of the interlocutors in the famous " scrap
of paper " conversation; Count Calvi of Italy, tall, thin,
agile, ever gay, deeming that most things supposedly
difficult, as the composing of an opera, are easy; who,
being dared to do it, walked on a tight-rope in a drawing-
room, and who was bringing up with the utmost care
his young children, one of whom married later Prince
Aage of Denmark and the other the King of Italy's eldest
daughter, so that the Count was nicknamed " purveyor
to the royal courts "; the American Minister Lauritz
Swenson, who gave me my earliest first-hand information
on the character of President Roosevelt, whom he compared with McKinley very much to the advantage of the
former; the afore-mentioned Count Benckendorff, who
was afterwards Russian Ambassador in London. His
compatriot and colleague at Berlin, Osten-Sacken, often
sent him interesting information on the state of Germany,
the difficulties Bülow had with his sovereign and of which
he made no mystery: some line of conduct had been
agreed upon, such or such speech was to be delivered;
on the sudden, for some incident, some news reaching
him, William II would brusquely improvise the most
imprudent and sonorous harangue, like the one in which
he urged his troops sent to China to make no prisoners
but to kill all the Chinese they could capture. Efforts
had been made to prevent those words from being
reproduced by the papers, but in vain.[1]

At the death of our arch-enemy Crispi, Count Calvi
tried to explain the cause of dispositions which had led
him to ally himself with the most dangerous foe of the
nation which had helped his own to win its independence:
the cause was declared to be that he and some others in
Italy were persuaded that we longed to compensate our
defeats of 1870 by an attack and by victories on the
Italians. I assured him that this was the craziest idea

[1] Visit of Count Benckendorff, July 30, 1900.

and that nothing was further from our thoughts than such meanness.[1] A diffusion of the notion of a French attack on Italy, justified by nothing, and from which we could expect nothing, may seem unbelievable; it has, however, been doing duty again in more recent years without even the ridiculous pretext of defeats to be compensated.

Official correspondence, answering inquiries from France, entertaining and being entertained, ceremonies, dispensing hospitality to visitors who came in numbers during the short summer months, still left time for literary and historical studies and for exercise in the open air. I continued the preparation of Volume II of my *Literary History of the English People* and remodelled and enlarged my essay on French sports in olden days. It had been originally the subject of an address I had made at the Sorbonne in November 1892, when, on the same occasion, Baron de Coubertin launched the idea which was to prove so successful, not only in France but throughout the world, of a revival of the Olympic Games. The book, abundantly illustrated, appeared in 1901 under the title of *Les Sports et Jeux d'Exercice dans l'Ancienne France*. It contributed, I hope, in some slight measure, to the renascence of a taste which our ancestors had carried in their day as far as any, which had, in more recent times, sunk very low, and the reawakening of which was indispensable, as the event has proved, to the well-being of the nation.

In the afternoons of the long winters we often left the city by train and, once out of its suburbs, we walked in the woods, followed frozen roads by the seashore, undeterred by the stormy wind, the driven snow, which made it sometimes difficult to open one's eyes, or the darkness that fell as we left the train. Neither man nor cart was to be met, the solitude was complete. Now and then a dog barked; the glimmering light in a cottage gave us

[1] Conversation of August 1, 1901.

an idea of the comfort we would enjoy when, back in our home, we could sit by our porcelain stove, protected from the wind by double windows. We usually stopped at Vedbaek on the road to Elsinore, had a cup of tea and, at the picturesque little station of Danish style, as they all are, took the train to Copenhagen. There, already, began heat, light, comfort, for the cars are extremely neat and well ordered.

Our life in the Danish capital was now and then interrupted by journeys to more or less distant parts of the country, to southern Sweden, to Italy and especially to France, which after a surfeit of northern snows appeared to us more beautiful than ever; it seemed as if we were discovering our capital and the country around it, with so much gaiety in the atmosphere, a sort of sweetness one breathed with the air, the beauty of the monuments, the friendliness of the trees, the success of the " Exposition Universelle " by which France inaugurated what she thought would be a century of peaceful progress.

During one of those stays, Gaston Paris, then at the head of the Collège de France, invited us to a dinner of great literary interest. The author of *Cyrano*, Rostand, was a candidate to the French Academy, and in spite of his merit and immense success, there was, as happens in that learned body, some opposition for impalpable causes. Gaston Paris had arranged his dinner for possible opponents to meet Rostand and be conquered by his charm. The poet and his wife were there, both on their best behaviour, very pleasant to look at but mute. Such silence was so unexpected that it was impossible not to allude to it, which was laughingly done. Addressing his wife, Rostand said: " Bravo, Rosemonde! let us continue; not a word; it is our best chance." They, however, swerved somewhat from their initial purpose, the doubters lost their doubts and the election was a triumph.

I did not fail, on the occasion of those journeys, to call

on President Loubet; and we talked of what was going on not only in Denmark but in the world. I could not but be struck by what he said in a conversation of November 1, 1901, of the danger resulting from the attitude of the Russians toward Japan, and their progress in Manchuria. "They alienate Japan and push her into the arms of England." The Anglo-Japanese treaties of alliance of 1902 and 1905, the Russo-Japanese war of 1904 with its dire consequences to Tsarism, and a first rehearsal of the subsequent revolution were later to justify these misgivings.

One of our Danish journeys took us to Dragsholm (the castle of the Dragon), property of the Zytphen Adeler family. There, as a prisoner of State, the third husband of Mary Queen of Scots, James Hepburn, Earl of Bothwell, spent his last years and died. He was buried in the church of Faarvejle, which was the parish church of the castle, and a mummy, traditionally considered as his (though there is no absolute proof), is preserved in a vault under the floor of the nave. The skin remains; the nose very prominent and arched is complete; the mouth very large; the jawbone (partly on account of the desiccation of the flesh) is prominent, the chin square and forceful. The arms are folded on the chest, below which the body is still wrapped in its winding sheet, only the feet emerging from it. All about the body is a quantity of vegetable remains, looking like broken sticks; we were told it was hops, supposed to have preservative qualities.[1]

Danish spring was heralded by the return of the storks whom everybody loved. Farmers placed on their roofs wooden disks to serve as a floor on which the birds could build their nests, made of supple little twigs. Storks, swans, hooded crows (a pretty species of crow, black only in part and adorned with a very becoming grey mantle), sea-gulls, were the chief birds in which to be interested.

[1] More details in a letter of mine printed by Andrew Lang as an Appendix to his *Mystery of Mary Stuart*, 1901.

The latter had a remarkable sense of dignity; they never begged unless the sea was frozen and they could not work for their sustenance.

Like the swans, the storks took much trouble in educating their young. Awaiting the end of a storm at Aarhus, we watched on a summer day the behaviour of a family of them established on a roof in the courtyard of our inn. The family consisted of father, mother and not less than four children. Before starting on their chase for the daily frog, the parents looked at their young, and we might almost say that we heard them recommending their progeny to keep quiet, wait patiently, and not attempt to leave the nest. The older birds went, but they were no sooner out of sight than the children looked round, drew one leg, then the other out of the nest, and, unable yet to fly, tried to walk on the sharp ridge of the roof; one slipped, nearly fell into the courtyard, but recovered his equilibrium just in time. This gave a scare to all; they hurriedly returned to the nest, and when, by loud clapping of their beaks, the parents announced their return, they found their young where they should be and having assumed a most innocent air. We never told them what we had seen.

During the summers our walks in the woods, merrily garbed then in the fairest green, or on the roads and paths leading to Elsinore, alternated with tennis, played at the foot of an old windmill, on the tree-lined upper terrace of the Citadel. A tennis club, to which most of the younger diplomats belonged, kept the courts in order; a Dane was President; I, vice-President. Games were sometimes like a tourney of nations. One happened to put in opposition France and Germany, the latter country being represented by Count Quadt, first Secretary, and his pretty Italian wife, *née* de Martino. As the issue was in doubt the Count shouted: "Amedea, if we win this set, I shall take you to the circus to-night!" I immediately echoed: "Elise, if we win this set, I shall take you to the circus to-night!" We won and went to the circus, where the chief entertainment was given by a troupe of young Americans playing polo with their bicycles, the ball being cleverly struck by the hind wheel of their machine. But in the box next to ours, whom did we see if not Count Quadt and his wife? We complimented him on his generosity. "Well," he said, "Amedea had done her best." She had indeed, and her best had been very good.

On the green leaves of summer, on the snows of winter, the steps of Time rapidly passed, inaudible. One afternoon a short telegram was brought me from the Chancery. The first group of figures meant: "Decode yourself," for which reason the text and the code were placed in my hands. I decoded and read: "Would you accept to be appointed eventually Ambassador to ——." My wife, who had been out, entered at that moment and I said: "Here is a telegram of much interest for both of us. What can be the meaning of the last group?" Instead of decoding it we amused ourselves by trying to guess, but guessed wrong; we verified, and found that the word was Washington.

In one of my last journeys to France I had met by chance Jules Cambon in the street and we had had then and there a serious talk on the part he had been playing in America. I had heard that he wanted a change. With all possible earnestness I besought him not to desert a post where he had succeeded so well. The event proved that my eloquence had been spent in vain.

Our departure from the country where we had passed quiet, happy years and where many, great and small, had shown us friendship and affection, could not but be accompanied by sadness. While we were breaking up our establishment and everything was topsy-turvy at the Legation, the King, indifferent to etiquette, called on us. There was luckily one armchair still available for him to be seated. He asked who was making our removal. The custom among diplomats was to entrust that all-important operation to a Hamburg firm, under the belief that its method was the best. But it had seemed to me being accredited to Denmark that it was appropriate to have recourse to Danes; so I was able to answer: " Sire, your subjects." The King rose and addressed the workmen in a little speech exhorting them to use their best skill. They did, and with the single exception of one solitary finger-bowl broken, the whole of my possessions reached Washington in perfect condition, not a plate chipped.

Ingversen, who had accomplished this deed, had henceforth his business paper embellished with freight trains and cargo-boats inscribed as carrying the furniture of Ambassador Jusserand.

The King gave us a farewell dinner (November 13, 1902) at which his daughter the Russian Empress, the Prime Minister and others were present. He had caused the rarest historical porcelain preserved in the family museum at Rosenborg to be brought out and used for the occasion, which some old stickler for etiquette considered going a little far. The Empress spoke with feeling of her two countries, of Paris where she had spent only two weeks some twenty-five years before, of the Montebellos, whose recall she deplored, a recall brought about by trifles of the utmost insignificance. The King proposed our health in a charming little speech and, as we were leaving, took our hands and said: " Promise me to return, if I live."

We promised. " But," he said, " some imagine that they will return, and do not."—" With us," we answered, " it will be otherwise," and two years later, during our first leave of absence from America, we visited Denmark again, and saw with the most pleasant emotion the old King, now eighty-six, as straight as ever, awaiting us on the steps of his country seat with a bouquet made up of all the varieties of roses in his rose garden, destined for Madame l'Ambassadrice.

For a few days we resumed then our old Danish life, dining with the King, with the Prince Royal, taking tea with Princess Marie, enjoying once more our walks in the woods, playing tennis at the Citadel, seeing again our friends, among whom the birds, hooded crows, swans, storks and sea-gulls did not pass unnoticed. The chief subject of conversation with the King and his eldest son was the Russo-Japanese war, which saddened everybody in Denmark. "That war," said the King, "which should have been avoided, which peace will not really end, and in which not one Grand Duke is taking part," a circumstance that could not fail to displease a sovereign who in 1848, when a young officer, had fought for his country.

Many questions were put to me on the United States, on that extraordinary President Roosevelt, "more powerful than a King," on the causes of the intense unpopularity of the Russians in America. Why such animosity? I answered: "Finland, the persecuted Jews who emigrate to the States and do not remain mute, the suppression of the local liberties at the very time when, on the contrary and without loss of time, they should have been increased. It is through a development of local liberties granted not all at once, but ceaselessly and by degrees, that a revolution might be avoided. Discontent, moreover, is rife among the Finns, the Poles, the Jews, the Armenians. The Emperor is insufficiently kept informed by Ministers whom he does not call together in his presence, but sees separately, each blaming and gainsaying the other who does not know and cannot rectify."

"More liberty should be granted," said the King. "My Liberal Ministry is moderate and gives me every satisfaction. My daughter did everything to enlighten her son, but in vain."

His last words were the same as previously: "You promise to return, if I live."

We visited Denmark once more, in 1911, but the old King had been laid among his ancestors by the side of his loved wife Queen Louise in Roskilde Cathedral. We placed on his tomb a wreath of red and white flowers, the colours of Denmark, and, on the tomb of Princess Marie, in the Sailors' Church, one of tuberose, her favourite flower.

When we had left Denmark and, two or three months after our return to France had sailed for the first time to America, the Prince Royal, as he was then, had kept informed of our movements and had written us a letter so timed as to be given to us on landing, his desire being that his greeting should be the first welcome we would receive on those distant shores. He too expressed the courteous wish that we might visit Copenhagen again, and we decided to see him in his glory as King Frederick VIII. We remained a whole day with him at Fredensborg, the last day, and a very pleasant one, that we were to spend in Denmark. A full account of it was given, in the merry style that was his, by the then American Minister to Copenhagen, the poet, writer and charming conversationalist, Maurice Egan.

CHAPTER X

MEETING THE STATUE OF LIBERTY AND MR. ROOSEVELT

I HAD received, on the occasion of my appointment, abundant congratulations, emphasizing the importance of my new post. Mr. Paul Cambon, our Ambassador at London, had written me that he would have liked his son, just arrived from Tangier and assigned to Tokio, to be included in my personnel. "The history of the century now beginning will be filled with the affairs of the Extreme East and with the growth of the United States, which will become before fifty years the arbiters of the world. Young men should henceforth familiarize themselves with men whose power is constantly growing." From Mr. Ribot, "There is no post more considerable to-day than Washington." From Mr. Georges Picot, of the Institute : "I do not know whether I am mistaken, but our diplomatic mission to the United States seems to me, at the beginning of the twentieth century, one of the most important on our small planet. No illusion is possible; the equilibrium of the world is moving west-wards. . . . You will no longer decipher manuscripts, but men, so as to obtain from them a revelation of the manners, the ideas, the politics of to-morrow."

Late in January 1903, after a rough wintry passage, on the good ship *Lorraine*, then quite young, that I saw for the last time when she brought Marshal Joffre to America in 1917, before she was dismantled for old age, we beheld, on the horizon, that grand statue presented to a liberty-

loving country by another liberty-loving country : our
first glimpse of a land, a President, a nation known to us
only by hearsay.

A number of young reporters flocked on board, asked
what we thought of all those unknowns, and plied us with
bewildering questions. My wife was requested to say
what she thought of the respective merits of Racine and
Shakespeare, and I whether I did not think that the
threatening attitude assumed by three monarchical
Powers (England, Italy, Germany) toward Venezuela
betokened an intention on their part to establish a monarchy at Caracas. We answered to the best of our ability
queries which it would be as absurd to take amiss as it
would to be offended by jokes when crossing the line.
The British Ambassadress, who had arrived shortly
before us, told my wife that she was delighted at her
coming. My wife felt flattered. Lady Herbert added :
" Because I am no longer the last landed, and it will be
your turn now to answer questions."

On Saturday, the 7th of February, I presented my
credentials. Accompanied by Col. Bingham and followed
by my personnel, like myself in uniform, I was met at the
White House by Secretary Hay. I had then, in the oval
blue room, my first glimpse of President Roosevelt, whom
I found very young for a President, the picture of health,
with ruddy cheeks, overflowing spirits, a man to enjoy
life in all its aspects, to enjoy its pleasures and to enjoy
even its troubles.

The interview began as it behove, in a grave and solemn
tone. I solemnly read a little speech prepared in advance,
and the President solemnly read a little speech probably
written by Adee, both texts very friendly and courteous,
but not without resemblance to others delivered in similar
circumstances for over a century.

Then solemnity vanished, the visage of the President
beamed, his eyes sparkled and a conversation began on all
sorts of subjects, far and near, ancient and modern. " I

AT WORK, FIRST YEAR IN WASHINGTON

face p. 221

have bought," he had said to one who had repeated it to me, " the works of the new French Ambassador, and I am ready to pass an examination on them." He compared wayfaring life in the Middle Ages with wayfaring life in present-day Colorado. We discussed Chaucer, Piers Plowman, Petrarch, Venezuela, the Hague tribunal, its usefulness and limitations. Disarmament should not be thought of, he said, and would not be, especially by him, who above all things wanted Congress to vote a considerable increase of the American navy. His slightest gesture, the twinkle of his eye, the movement of his lips, the tone of his voice, gave the same impression of force, of will to do things, of cheery optimism.

The first reception we witnessed at the White House was in honour of the Army and Navy (February 12). It was particularly remarkable by the presence of the famous chief Joseph of the *Nez Percés*, who had distinguished himself as a military leader in the war against the Americans. He stood, surrounded by his warriors, in their native costume, with their impressive head-dress of eagle feathers trailing to the ground. Chief Joseph's features were strongly marked; the nose was prominent, the mouth large with thin lips, the complexion brownish, wrinkles were many. Immobile, impassible, he wore an expression of profound sadness which inspired sympathy.

The first public speeches by President Roosevelt that I heard or read were of the same stamp as our first conversation : one at the laying of the corner-stone of the new war college, when Mr. Elihu Root, then Secretary of War, also spoke. I noticed the vigour, the insistence on the important words, the peremptory gestures of the President, his bitter condemnation of limp individuals, of " weaklings " averse to effort, his praise of energetic minds and his picture of that world power of the United States which now gives them responsibilities East and West and duties which they are not free not to fulfil, but which they can fulfil well or not. The attitude they should observe is that of the armed just man.[1]

In an address at Chicago, April 2nd, President Roosevelt spoke on a variety of subjects, but especially on the Monroe doctrine, whose elastic and extensive character was put by him in full light. The acquisition of territory is not alone barred to foreign Powers : this doctrine " not only forbids us to acquiesce in such territorial acquisition, but also causes us to object to the acquirement of a control which would in its effect be equal to territorial aggrandizement."

In the same speech he quoted a proverbial saying that custom has caused to be attributed to him, and the first part of which is usually forgotten, the whole meaning being thereby altered : " Speak softly and carry a big stick, and you will go far."

We dined for the first time at the White House on the 24th of February. My wife sat next to the President; I, next to Mrs. Roosevelt, gentle, refined, distinguished, with, as I noticed later, a will of her own, never forcefully exerted, but which, however, was felt. The President said to my wife : " I am not learnéd. I know about some subjects which have interested me and which I have studied. Between them are immense gaps. Mrs. Roosevelt is much more literary than I am; she can read Spenser, which is for me impossible."

He had been of late keenly interested in the Mongols and their invasions in Europe, but he could not remember where they had stopped ; he asked some senators who were present, but they did not know. The French Ambassador could say, Trieste, and the French Ambassadress, by a special grace from heaven, was also able to say a few words on the Mongols. To these tribes we owe, she and I, a debt of gratitude for the increased esteem in which we were held, from that moment, by the President. He asked the senators : " Is there any one of you whose wife

[1] February 21, 1903.

would know something about the Mongols?" Some
senators whose wives were not present laughingly answered: "Ours certainly would."

In the smoking-room the talk was about present-day
politics. The President, exuberant, full-blooded, joyful,
shrewd, "enfant terrible," accompanying his talk with
forceful gesticulation, was a delight to look at and listen
to. In a burst of joy he had a sonorous laugh; he struck
the table, exclaiming Hoo! Hoo! He said he would
ask us to come and visit him *tête-à-tête*.

A Doctor's Degree at Chicago

I was still in Denmark when I had received a cable-
gram from the University of Chicago asking me to come
to their next Commencement, and saying they wanted
to be the first to confer a degree on the new-comer in
America. It had seemed to me impossible to make an
engagement so far ahead and at such a distance. I had
expressed my thanks and declined.

Shortly after our arrival, being still in the midst of
unopened packing-cases, and having to superintend the
deeds and misdeeds of a small army of workmen, I received the visit of Dean Judson, who had come all the way
from Chicago to renew the request. My first impulse
was to decline again, but I thought: Here is this visitor,
a man of importance and of many duties, no longer
young, who has travelled so far in such an uninviting
season: to refuse is impossible. So we started for Chigago
on March 13, crossing a large part of the country, our
eyes wide open so as to lose as little as possible of the
sights. What struck us most was that there were no
villages, but only incipient cities.

A warm reception was awarded us, a large banquet
was offered with a double-columned menu: in one
column the food, in the other the speeches, with a mention
of the subject. I headed the list, the subject allotted me
being: A message from France; so that the first after-

dinner speech I heard in America was one by myself. What touched me very much was the immense applause which greeted me when I rose, before I had said a word ; the applause obviously went to dear France.

Listening to the other speeches, witty and good-humoured most of them, I noticed the importance on such occasions of the funny anecdote. Dr. Henry Van Dyke, famous as a poet and novelist, later as a diplomat and a defender of the good cause during the war, feared he had taken too much time and spoke of the young lady seated in a train passing under a tunnel. A young man sitting next her pushed his hand into her muff. The indignant young person said : " Well, sir, what do you mean ? I give you just . . . twenty minutes to with-draw your hand." The speaker was afraid his twenty minutes had elapsed.

I could never bring myself to use an anecdote heard before. It chanced sometimes that I could raise a laugh or, on the contrary, cause the audience to become pensive, but it was by some remark or narrated fact. When an anecdote came to my mind, it was always accompanied by the remembrance of the orator whom I heard using it, and to repeat it seemed to me a theft, though many such witticisms are, in fact, common property. More than once I remembered, but abstained from repeating, the remarks of the Governor of New Hampshire at a triennial meeting of the Cincinnati who, fearing like Dr. Van Dyke that his time had elapsed, spoke of Holger taking Christine for a drive in his sleigh. They moved noiselessly over the Norwegian snow, crossed frozen fiords, white hills and white dales, keeping silent. At length Holger said :

" Christine, will you marry me ?

" Christine answered : Yes.

" They drove on, evening came, then they turned, again crossed hills and dales and frozen fiords, and when they were near the city, Christine said :

" Holger, have you nothing more to say to me ?

" Holger answered: I am afraid I have said too much already."

Another anecdote which now and then recurred to my mind, but which I never used because I considered it as the property of President Angell, now of Yale, was the story of the traveller who reaches the inn exhausted. He falls helpless on a chair and says: " I want two fried eggs and a few kind words."—" Yes, Sir," said the waitress. She returned after a while with the eggs. The traveller said: " Have you not forgotten the kind words? " —" No," she answered, and leaning toward him she added in a low voice: " Do not eat them."

A man unique for his store of anecdotes was Jacob Dickinson, Secretary of War under President Taft. His fund was inexhaustible. On a long railway journey he kept us laughing most of the time with his funny stories. But I could never get rid of my shyness on this score nor conform to the classical technique for an after-dinner speech thus summed up: " Lead to your anecdote— Your anecdote—Recede from your anecdote."

The President of the University on whose behalf I had been invited, Wm. R. Harper, a typical American, cheery, resourceful, never dismayed at any mishap, who with the help of the Rockefellers had brought the Chicago University to an extraordinary degree of prosperity, was not present at the banquet. He had gone some time before to Arizona for a rest, but on the way out had been snowed up for three days, and on the return journey his train had been delayed fifteen hours by a collision. He was one of the nine passengers who escaped without a scratch. He arrived the following day, worked till late at night, rose at five o'clock for more work and suddenly decided to go with us to New York. But then nature had its due and he slept for seventeen consecutive hours.

He told us once of his beginnings in life and how he had in his youth equal dispositions for music and for literature, with a preference for music. His parents'

Q

resources were very modest and it seemed to him that he
would more easily provide for his own wants by becoming
a musician. If he could enlist in a travelling circus he
would satisfy his desire to roam the country and be self-
supporting. The great circus of those days, the one
before Barnum's, having come to the little north-western
city where he lived, he signed an engagement as key-
bugle player in the company's orchestra. He was filled
with joy, but his father not at all; he had the engagement
cancelled and the young stroller was sent to Yale. He
again tried to avoid a literary career, saying that the
expense was too great and that it would be the ruin of his
family. The family insisted that he should wait until
that sad event happened. He therefore continued his
studies, was ordained a minister, obtained his doctor's
degree and subsequently became President of Chicago
University.

He still had his key-bugle and sometimes played on it,
accompanied on the piano by Mrs. Harper.

During our stay in Chicago we saw with lively interest
the museums in which French art is remarkably well
represented, the park with that masterpiece, the statue of
Lincoln by Saint-Gaudens, the Viking's bark that came
all the way from Norway for the Chicago Exhibition, of
exactly the same build and rig as in Viking days and
which, though it encountered bad weather, was never in
danger. We visited at great length the harvesting machine
manufactory of Deering and MacCormick, where the
ingenuity of the machinery, the intelligent labour of
high-salaried workmen, the large payments bestowed on
inventors and the good example given by the employer
who, rich though he was, arrived every morning between
seven and eight, lunched on the spot, did not leave before
five, and rarely went out at night so as to keep in good
condition for work, resulted in products without peer
throughout the world.

At night there was a dinner and reception given in our

honour by Mr. and Mrs. Cyrus MacCormick in their charming home full of works of art selected with the best possible taste by these real connoisseurs, a place of honour being reserved for French art. After the dinner a very good-looking young lady came to me and said: " Sir, allow me to place myself under your protection."— " Certainly, you may count on it, but to what do I owe such an honour? "—" In this assembly there are only you and I who are not MacCormicks."

We were still in Chicago when former Senator Thurston called. He had travelled from Saint-Louis to Washington, and finding that I was not there had turned toward Chicago (what are one or two days of rail more or less?) to bring me in person an invitation to speak on the second day of the ceremonies for the inauguration of the Saint-Louis Exhibition. That second day (the first of the coming month of May) was under his management and he considered it important that in a city founded by the French, the French Ambassador should be heard.

But the latter, so recently arrived, trammelled by the thousand and one details unexpectedly coming up when one begins a new life, unable as yet to gauge what time his official duties would allow him to spend on such journeys, politely, but clearly, refused. Former Senator would not be refused and at last said: " What could we do that would make you yield? "—" Let the President of the United States ask me," was the jocose answer. But the answer was taken seriously: " He will ask you " (and he did, even seconded by the Secretary of State).

" If I went," I said, not knowing Saint-Louis, and only remembering Papin, La Clede and the others, " what language should I use? French or English? "

" Oh," Mr. Thurston answered, " it does not matter, the hall where you will speak is of such dimensions that whatever be the power of your voice, you will not be heard."

" This is indeed very strange. You go to Washington,

that is some distance, then to Chicago, that is some distance, to ask one whom you do not know, to visit your city and make an address not a word of which will be heard."

" You are a new-comer," the former Senator remarked. " You will not be long to observe that we Americans love to be in a place where speeches are being delivered."

We returned by way of New York, where I had to preside over the yearly meeting of the important and ever-growing association the " Alliance Française," which has for its object no " Alliance " at all, but a study of things French. We had a first glimpse of the museums and park of the vast city and went for a general view of it to Brooklyn bridge at sunset: to my mind one of the grandest sights in the world. Beheld separately, the enormous skyscrapers, of cubic shape most of them, are not things of beauty; looked at in their ensemble, with the numerous white vapours fluttering from their summits, the red sky as a background, the huge river at their feet, they assume an air of majesty and seem the work of giants. The same thought occurs as before the Pyramids : " Mere men could do that ! "

April 14.—The President and Mrs. Roosevelt ask us to dine at the White House and to go afterwards to the play with them. At table, besides ourselves, Justice and Mrs. Holmes, Miss Alice and two young men; a very simple, very merry dinner. The play called *The Crisis* was being performed at the Lafayette Theatre close by the White House. When we arrived the orchestra was playing a succession of pieces and there was no play. But now an announcement was made: " The troupe comes from New York and the railroad company has sent by mistake part of the luggage in various directions, two actors have no costumes; the audience must be patient." Some more music is offered. Then a new announcement: " Luggage continues to travel to unknown parts. Actors will do their best in their travelling clothes."

Then the play begins; generous and patriotic melo-
drama, full of over-good sentiments, dealing with the
civil war; the handsome young hero, a northerner,
pardons his enemies, fights the southerners, kills or tames
the wicked, saves the good, frees the negroes, or in any
case a negress, and in the end marries the handsome
southern girl who, out of love for him, gives up her cousin
and her slaves. And the war continues, for the crisis
was the struggle in the heart of the young lady and not
the one on the battle-fields.

I expressed my surprise that such a comparatively
recent event, which had rent the country, could thus be
made the subject of plays. With us, apparently more
nervous, *Thermidor*, which promised to be a triumph for
Coquelin and Bartet, was stopped after the first performance. Justice Holmes who, as a northerner, had
been wounded in the outskirts of Washington, replied
that the events in the play seemed to him as remote as
the wars of the Romans.

SAINT-LOUIS

To the Saint-Louis celebration all Ambassadors had
been asked. Only three went, representing France,
Italy, and Mexico. The occasion was the cession of
Louisiana to the United States, after negotiations terminated on Easter Day, 1803, and in which took part, on
the French side, Bonaparte first Consul, Barbé-Marbois,
former Secretary of Embassy in America during the War
of Independence, and Berthier, former officer in Rochambeau's army and future Prince of Wagram. The Americans wanted only to secure from us New Orleans; we
decided to yield the whole of the immense territories
called Louisiana. The sentiment that dominated the
negotiation was: we have helped them to be free, let us
help them to be great. Not a word was said in the treaty
signed " au nom du peuple Français " on April 30, 1803,
" eleventh year of the French Republic," of any sum being

paid to us. But, in two additional conventions, sixty
million francs (barely representing public property
transferred to the States),[1] were provided in our favour,
while about twenty million for the payment of certain
French debts were set apart in favour of the United
States. We knew better than the Americans themselves
the value of those inland territories, owing to the reports
of some of our recent explorers, and the event has shown
that we were not mistaken in our estimate. At the time
of the Saint-Louis ceremonies, Colorado alone was yielding
more revenue in one year than the total sum inscribed in
the convention. To call a purchase (as in the words the
" Louisiana Purchase Exhibition ") a transaction signed
by us in order " to give to the United States a strong
proof of friendship " was a misnomer.

To Saint-Louis I went alone; my wife had not been
well since our Chicago journey, and this was very unpleasant to us both, not having been separated for one
day since our marriage: a very frequent case in France
where novels are one thing and usual lives another. A
sister of mine shortly before her marriage received a
letter from her betrothed saying: " I hope this is the
last letter I shall ever have occasion to write you," and so
it was for over twenty years.

The Exhibition was only sketched on the ground, to be
opened the following year, and the ceremonies were
preliminary. They lasted two days and were presided
over by former Governor Francis, future Ambassador to
Russia. President Roosevelt, former President Grover
Cleveland, Cardinal Gibbons, Secretary Root, had come.
On the first day, April 30, there was a reception for President Roosevelt attended by an immense crowd. When
I passed before him, forgetful of the immense crowd he
stopped me for a talk on various subjects, among which

---

[1] " In the cession are included . . . all public lots and squares,
vacant lands, and all public buildings, fortifications, barracks and
other edifices which are not public property." Art. II.

the Mongols; we mongolized for just a few minutes, but they seemed ages to those who were waiting. He ended, saying: " You must come, with your wife, on my return, to the White House. I have five hundred questions I want to talk with you about."

After a military parade, under command of General Corbin, the grand meeting took place for the chief speeches. The hall was exactly what Mr. Thurston had announced; nothing had been neglected to prevent anyone from hearing anything. The place, hastily constructed in boards, thick-packed with people, to the number, we were told, of thirty-five thousand or more, was of vast immensity; it had many doors, some of which remained open all the time; a quantity of broad strips of bunting, stretched from one side of the hall to the other, efficiently stopped the sound of the speakers' voices and prevented their reaching anywhere.

Mr. Francis called the assembly to order. He had been given a beautiful gavel for the occasion; he used it with such a masterly hand that he broke at one stroke the gavel and the desk. Cardinal Gibbons rose to pronounce the invocation, his emaciated face, pale blue eyes, austere yet kindly expression, won the sympathy of all who could see him, but no one heard a word of his prayer. Then came the turn of President Roosevelt; his stentorian voice was of no avail; he asked that the ruins of the desk be removed, and leaped upon the table where it had been; thunderous applause greeted this feat of agility. From that place of vantage he renewed his efforts, but in vain, he remained inaudible. Now and then a ray of sun piercing the overcast sky lighted the hall for a brief moment; it was received with prolonged cheers and applause, in which the orator good-humouredly joined.

After him spoke former President Grover Cleveland, lustily cheered by an assembly in which the democratic element predominated. He did not jump on the table;

he did not force his voice, but read low and quickly, as if for himself, a long paper prepared for the occasion. The hearers, who heard nothing, continued to show that good will characteristic of American audiences, no one moved, no one left, no one showed any expression of boredom; just a few people in the remotest corners apparently cracked jokes among themselves, some few quarrelled, but without causing any real trouble.

As he resumed his seat, the former President turned to me and said: " When your turn comes, don't make a fool of yourself, and do not strain your voice." I was not as yet americanized enough to reply " You bet," but I answered something to that effect.

In the evening, a banquet. The Italian Ambassador, Mayor des Planches, having fallen ill, only two Ambassadors remained, the French and the Mexican, who were asked to dine at the table of the two Presidents. During the meal, in the clatter of plates, forks and conversation, I had a long talk, in loudest voice, across the table with Mr. Roosevelt on a number of moral, literary and historical problems. He loves Scott, likes Mérimée, especially his *Enlèvement de la Redoute*, hates Zola, enjoys Marbot, considering as true the general impression given by him, although many of his smaller facts are obviously fanciful; a certain sabre stroke is materially impossible. The President spoke thereupon of the difficulty in our days of using the sabre, now practically useless; he had suppressed it for his roughriders in Cuba, giving them only carbines and revolvers. He highly praised our continuing to fight in 1871 when all hope of victory was gone: " Battles like those of Chanzy and his army are enough for the glory of a nation."

Toward the end of the meal, toasts and speeches. As the Mexican Ambassador was the dean and I the last arrived, I sat at ease, curious to hear what my colleague would say, and this is what I heard: " As I do not know your beautiful language, I ask my friend Jusserand to speak in my stead." I had to cease sitting at ease, and to make as unprepared an address as ever I delivered. The subject luckily was not difficult, and when I sat down President Roosevelt proposed my health.

The chief event the next day, May 1st, was the second series of speeches in the great hall, the presiding officer being former Senator Thurston. Mr. Roosevelt had gone, continuing his political journey, but Mr. Grover Cleveland remained, and I again sat next to him. I intended to follow his advice, but seeing that the crowd had considerably dwindled, not more than four or five thousand being left, I thought that by dint of speaking slowly, very loud, scanning every syllable, I might make myself heard. So it happened. Pt. Harper, who had come from Chicago, went purposely to sit in the last ranks and told me that my voice reached even there. Frequent applause, in which Mr. Cleveland several times joined, and his warm congratulations when I had finished, were my recompense. At a reception in the evening I was assured by several of those who shook my hand that the new French Ambassador had " made a hit " and that his speech " was the talk of the town." The Cuban Minister, M. de Quesada, was loud in his praise and gave me a copy of a book of his, which he inscribed to M. J. " Gloire Latine."

It would perhaps be appropriate to quote some samples of this " masterpiece," the subject of which was the French pioneers of the region in early days and the fate of Louisiana; I must possess a text somewhere; I have just interrupted my writing in order to find it, but failed. It is probably better so.

The papers were not quite as favourable; one said that being French I gesticulated of course too much; another, on the contrary, that I unceremoniously kept my hands in my pockets. Only in their disapproval of my hands did they agree.

June 10.—Arrived yesterday evening in New York. Columbia University has voted me a doctor's degree. Prof. Brander Matthews, famous for his works and teaching on dramatic art, comes in the morning to fetch me. We cross that lovely place, Central Park, full of squirrels. The University, formerly King's College, founded by a royal charter, which may be seen handsomely framed in the principal hall, has a huge, constantly increasing population of students. To-day is Commencement Day, what was called in the Middle Ages, Inception, the day when the student, having secured a degree, could begin to teach (*incipere*—to begin). Nine hundred degrees of bachelor, master of arts and doctor are to be conferred; eight or ten honorary degrees of Doctor in Laws will be bestowed, one on the Governor of New York, an influential member of the Republican party, Mr. Odell.

We meet in the University Library, a solid building of fine material to last for ages, given, in honour of his father, by Mr. Seth Low, Mayor of New York, who is there, gay, kindly, rotund, with sparkling eyes and a pleasant smile.

A long procession is formed of students of both sexes; the professors and doctors follow; Governor Odell is vociferously acclaimed.

We go down to the gymnasium, transformed for the day into a theatre. On the stage the dignitaries; in front of them three arm-chairs, for the President of the University, Nicholas Murray Butler, so young that I had at first taken him for one of the undergraduates; on his right for the French Ambassador, on his left for the Governor.

Prayer, music, a speech by the President, practical and sensible on the actual value of optimism. The honorary degrees are announced, each being justified by a member of the University, Brander Matthews in my case: if I thought myself unworthy before, I could not after having heard him. I was favoured with the students' yell; the difficulty of pronouncing my name was such that every-body laughed at their well-intentioned, but fruitless, exertions.

Another prayer, and again formed into a procession which allows us to have a glance at the imposing University buildings, in fine stone, meant like the library to last. Gifts are piled upon gifts; five hundred thousand dollars is a nice but moderate one, causing no wonder. Columbia has its eye on an adjoining piece of ground worth two million dollars, not very large, but commodious for dormitories, in order that students be not scattered anywhere in the town; some benefactor or other is sure to give it to the University, which without waiting, and though having presently no money for that particular purpose, has come forth as a purchaser, and thus prevents anyone else from capturing it. There is a virtue in optimism, said President Butler.

Lunch is served under the presidency of Dean Van Amringe, an old, kindly man, very cheery, with a stentorian voice, red cheeks, and white moustache. Toasts and speeches. All the recipients of an honorary degree are called upon to speak. They say good things, each reading a carefully prepared paper, rather the tone of a professional lecture. The students politely applaud.

I had an easy success in speaking without notes, on their future life, telling them how they should continue to educate their minds, perfecting the teaching of the University in the midst of even a strictly business career, and how they should eschew a success for themselves, even though honourably reached, if it meant a disaster for their neighbour. I was favoured with a much better yell than the first time.

Governor Odell, looking serious and peremptory, a man not to be trifled with, smiling but rarely and faintly, talked politics, explained how one could succeed in them, roundly blamed the Democrats, ever ready, according to him, to put spokes in the wheels; he had a wonderful

success and was granted yells of a superior kind. Having
a train to take, I could not remain for President Butler's
concluding speech, not the least interesting of all, for in
it was to be announced the last crop of gifts gathered in
by the University.

June 12, 1903.—A dinner at Secretary Hay's, only six
people—the two Hays, President and Mrs. Roosevelt, we
two. The President is beaming, delighted with his
political journey around the United States, undertaken
in view of his candidacy to the Presidential nomination
next year. He is very grateful to Senator Hanna, a
great friend of McKinley and the most powerful member
of the Republican party, who showed no jealousy and
did nothing to diminish the rising man's success.

Another object of Mr. Roosevelt's journey had been to
impress people with the importance of certain points of
his programme, above all the necessity for a powerful
navy. With possessions as far removed as the Philippines
and with the firm resolve that the Panama Canal must
be American, and that the States should be able and
ready to defend it, the having of a strong fleet was now
of prime importance. The more so that the recurrence
of the Germans' ambitions bobbing up, now on one and
now on another point of the globe, what they called their
Welt Politik, suspected when not positively known, were
a serious cause of anxiety. They had contemplated the
acquisition of some of the Spanish possessions, " at least
one of the Philippines (Mindanao) " [1] a partition with
England of the Portuguese colonies [2] and of Morocco.
" We must decide without waiting," wrote Count
Hatzfeldt to Bülow, " what parts of Morocco and what
points on the coast would be especially valuable for us." [3]
" The possession of the Samoa Islands," wrote Tirpitz,
" would have even now a great importance for the

---

[1] Bülow to Hatzfeldt, June 8, 1898: *Grosse Politik.*
[2] Text of the Treaty of Partition, *ibid.*, August 30, 1898.
[3] A personal letter of February 8, 1899: *Grosse Politik.*

German fleet in order to have there a port of call on the
way to Kiao-Chow" (occupied in November 1897);
the opening of the Panama Canal will greatly increase
their value; " our objective must be a German possession
of the whole group." [1] They also had an eye on Saint-
Thomas and the Danish West Indies [2] and other places.

After the trouble in Manila, the Venezuelan affair had
brought the United States and Germany to the verge of
a break. A number of nations had claims against
President Cipriano Castro and his country; England
and Germany had sent war-ships to blockade the Venezuelan coast, and Germany was scarcely concealing her
intention to seize some harbour and make there a settlement, not " permanent," she said, but for how long?
The President had thereupon ordered the whole American
fleet under Dewey to Porto Rico, prescribing that " the
ships be kept in fighting trim and ready to sail at an
hour's notice " (December 1902). He told the German
Ambassador Holleben that his Government should
within a certain number of days accept a settlement by
arbitration and give up all thought of any seizure of
territory, permanent or otherwise, failing which Dewey
and his fleet would enter into action. Holleben thought
the President was bluffing and did not take the matter
seriously. Finding, after a brief while, that the answer
was not forthcoming, the President saw Holleben again
and insisted upon an answer within twenty-four hours;
this time the answer came; Holleben, who had such
mistaken ideas as to bluff, was recalled and dismissed
from the Service.[3] Far from showing a resentment which

[1] In *Grosse Politik*. A note of Oct. 21, 1899.
[2] See further, p. 308.
[3] Mr. Roosevelt's account of those events, and Dewey's confirm-
atory letter, are in Bishop, *Roosevelt and his Times*, I. 221. In his
book on *Theodore Roosevelt* (preface 1931), Mr. Pringle states that this
version " is inaccurate and prejudiced " (p. 283) : that the President's
" subsequent version of what occurred was romantic to the point of
absurdity " (p. 284).
But reading further in the same work, one finds that all the facts of

he felt would be dangerous, given the kind of person he had to deal with, Emperor William multiplied, on the contrary, signs of good-will toward Americans: a man ready to threaten is no match for one ready to act. When Governor Francis went to Berlin the following March to request the participation of Germany in the Saint-Louis Exhibition, he was received with marked favour by the Emperor, who promised an important contribution and duly kept his promise. When an American squadron visited Kiel in June, the Emperor was profuse in his

---

any importance in the said version are corroborated by independent evidence. The instructions received by Admiral Dewey are vouched for by himself. Holleben's two successive visits and the strong language used by the President " are demonstrable by a witness who was present " (Mr. Loeb) and who felt convinced that the Ambassador would abstain from giving his Government " a correct picture of ' Mr. Roosevelt's attitude ' " (p. 288). Whether the German Government decided to yield after, as Mr. Roosevelt thought, a more explicit telegram from Holleben, or after oral statements of Speck von Sternburg, who had returned to Germany after a private visit to Washington, and as he wrote to the President, " told them the truth every bit of it," Dec. 15, 1902 (p. 288), certain it is that Mr. Roosevelt's " attitude " was the determining factor, that thenceforth there were no threats of territories being occupied, and that acquiescence was secured to arbitration unaccompanied by those " definite limitations " which had been attached to a previous acceptance (p. 287).

That when drawing up at the request of Mr. Thayer, in August 1916, a written account of what took place, Mr. Roosevelt was influenced " by the current conception of the nature of the Hun," the World War having " poisoned his mind against Germany " (pp. 287, 288), can scarcely be admitted. The texts quoted by Mr. Pringle himself show that such " poisoning " had taken place long before the war and had been due to Germany herself, who, among other causes of irritation, " had been the one important neutral to exhibit overt hostility during the Spanish war " (p. 281). Mr. Roosevelt had early come to the conclusion that he ought to be, whenever possible, as courteous and complimentary to the Kaiser as the interest of the United States should require, but that, whatever might be Emperor William's words and pledges, he must never be trusted. Bishop, on his part, quotes a number of characteristic texts dating back to 1897–98. In a letter of February 5, 1898, Mr. Roosevelt, certainly uninfluenced by the Great War, wrote: " Of all the nations of Europe it seems to me Germany is by far the most hostile to us. With Germany under the Kaiser, we may at any time have trouble if she seeks to acquire territory in South America " (I. 79).

attentions toward the admiral and his officers. The local authorities followed suit.

During all the years he was President, Mr. Roosevelt never relaxed in his exertions to have his country possess a considerable navy, tirelessly appealing from Congress, who shied at the expense, to the nation. "The yards," I wrote to my Government, May 30, 1903, "increase their exertions to fulfil the programme dear to the President. His ideal is that, for a certain period, five ships be added every year to the American navy. Six are presently building in the Chesapeake, two are almost finished. In the course of his long journey, Mr. Roosevelt has missed no occasion to insist on the necessity of rapidly increasing the national fleet, and the Secretary of the Navy (Moody) has also been travelling to promote the same cause. The Venezuelan trouble is one of the most telling arguments. . . . There is no doubt that in a few years a fleet of high value will be at the disposal of the United States, especially if new incidents keep public attention aroused and facilitate the vote of appropriations."

This same summer the President reviewed the naval forces of his country at Oyster Bay, twenty-one ships in all; he minutely inspected the chief ones, extolled the merits not only of Admiral Dewey but of the gunners who were the best shots. He asked for their names, insisted on the necessity of favouring them and they were awarded higher pay. To Mr. Roosevelt personally is due, without the possibility of a doubt, the present position of the United States as a first-class naval Power.

The talk, during the Hay dinner, fell on Russia and the massacre of the Jews at Kishinev. It had created a profound impression in the United States, where Jews are numerous, many being rich and powerful. It is alleged that New York contains more of them than did Palestine in Biblical days. Petitions for remonstrances to be made at St. Petersburg, and even for diplomatic relations to be broken, are circulated everywhere and signed by many men of standing who are not Jews. Former President Cleveland has consented to preside at an indignation meeting. The storm which, on account of the Venezuelan affair, had recently burst over England and especially over Germany, now breaks over Russia, considered until recently as the best of friends. The Russian Ambassador, Count Cassini, receives quantities of letters threatening his life; he told me that he had complained to the President himself, who pleaded the custom of the country and said that he too frequently received such letters; some were sent to his daughter Alice, and even to his eldest son, aged fourteen.

In the course of the dinner, Mr. Roosevelt spoke of those petitions, of the newspaper articles in which he is described as a vile toady to the Russian tyrant, of a Jewish delegation he is to receive on Monday. What language should be used? " If only you say the wrong thing," Mr. Hay answered, " your success will be enormous; better, however, say the right thing." The more so, I ventured to add, alluding to the massacre of some Italians at New Orleans and to a few horrible lynchings which had recently occurred, that it is a very delicate matter to remonstrate about other people's sins when the like are committed in one's own country.

Mr. Hay showed us after dinner some of the rarities of his library—the first volume published by Tennyson, the poet's own copy, with corrections in his hand; the autograph manuscript of Lincoln's Gettysburg address, and some proofs revised by him, for, far from being an improvisation, every word had been carefully weighed. Famous now throughout the world, it produced on the hearers very little effect. As the conversation passed to other subjects, President Roosevelt, still holding one of the precious printed sheets, shook it unconsciously but strenuously, to the unexpressed dismay of the owner, much too polite to show his feelings. Fortunately no havoc resulted.

Our host spoke also of a lady (I have known since for sure that the lady was a man) who had once said to him: "It is a shame, Mr. Hay; you, who knew Lincoln so well, should really write something about him." One of my own bibliographical treasures consists of a finely bound copy of the ten-volume history of Lincoln by Hay and Nicolay, with a letter from the giver in his inimitably graceful style: "DEAR EXCELLENCY—I send you, for my own pleasure more than for yours, a copy of a book which occupied the best fifteen years of my life. I cannot ask you to read a book which has no merit except that of veracity, and which lacks completely actuality; but it will fill so large a place on the shelves of your library that I hope it may occasionally recall me to your kind remembrance. Yours faithfully—JOHN HAY." Since the work was given me twenty-eight years ago, it has never been out of my sight, and is before me as I write, a constant reminder of one of the rare minds it was my good fortune to know.

June 24.—Another small dinner, this time at the White House. Mrs. Roosevelt has gone, the furniture has its summer coverings; the only guests are Mr. and Mrs. Hay, former Attorney-General and Ambassador, Wayne MacVeagh, shrewd-witted, as sharp-featured as Voltaire, and Mr. Wheeler, President of the University of California.

The President is in his best mood; he is always in his best mood. He discusses with me, perhaps at greater length than the other guests would have liked, the authenticity of the *Kingis Quhair* and recurs with delight to his experiences during his Western trip. It will be very interesting in California, he says, to watch the effect of a Mediterranean climate on the development of Americans growing up under a blue sky, in front of a blue sea. The great amphitheatre of the University is an exact replica of that of Epidaurus: the French school at Athens has supplied the plans and measurements. Lectures are

R

delivered there in the open; it is known in advance that during three-fourths of the year there will be no rain.

All sorts of gifts were offered him during his journey, especially live animals, for he is known to love them. He has had to send most of them to the Zoo, but he has kept the excellent horse Wyoming, whom we saw him ride yesterday in Rock Creek Park, and the badger Josiah. We asked to know Josiah and the President ordered him to be brought; he took him in his arms, and walking round the dining-table, offered him to be caressed by us. Josiah looked well; he was as large as a big angora cat, grey-coated, with a black-lined sharp nose. He allowed us to pet him and did not bite.

We ourselves once increased the White House *ménagerie*. A servant of ours had brought to us one of those little tortoises that used to roam the lovely woods around Washington, where wild life still prospered, with tortoises, rabbits (we called them hares because it flattered them), quails, partridges, woodpeckers, birds of every plumage and song, chipmunks, squirrels, some snakes but which never proved troublesome, the whole transformed since into rows of brick houses. We offered the tortoise to the President; it was adorned with a tricolour ribbon and was carried by him in great solemnity to the gardens. " It will be shown in future years," he said, " as being a descendant of the one presented to Washington by Lafayette."

The conversation touched as usual on all sorts of subjects, past and future wars, Prince Eugene, about whom the King of Italy has sent a fine recent work to the President, Turenne, Villars and others. " If the United States were involved in a war," Mr. Roosevelt said, " I would have my son enlist at once, and so would Root have his."

American politics cause Mr. Roosevelt unmixed delight. Something unexpected, impossible to foresee, constantly happens. Unaccountable ideas, incidents and people have to be dealt with, and it is a pleasure. In the midst of so many whimsicalities you cannot doze away your days.

The President speaks with glee of his war against the trusts: those combinations are too powerful; unchecked power begets tyranny. He highly praises J. J. Hill, a man of pluck and sense, who began transportation in the North-West with dog sledges, and has finally opened up immense territories to progress and civilization with his railways, boldly built across a desert country, now, thanks to him, no longer a desert. " He detests me, but I admire him; he will detest me much more before I have done with him."

A silence; no one approves nor ventures a remark. The selection of Hill, perfectly honest, to whom so much is due, as the typical trust builder who should be destroyed, seemed to many unaccountable.

Mr. Hay was thoroughly averse to that policy. " Where will it begin," he said to me afterwards, " and where will it stop? Where is the limit, the line of demarcation? I know of two barbers who have decided to join forces, having only one shop instead of two: a great saving and advantage for both; will they be prosecuted?

" The judicial award concerning the Hill lines is indefensible; it gives no reason, and simply refers to an *idiotic* law (the Sherman law) which had been wisely allowed to remain dormant. People speak of monopolies, but there are none and there cannot be any here. Former monopolies granted by royal charter forbade certain kinds of trade or industry to be practised by any but the holders of the charters. Such a danger does not exist among us."

The fight, however, continued; the Supreme Court sided with the President; a certain number of mergers were broken up. A movement in a contrary sense has developed since and railroads, shipping lines, etc. are presently encouraged by appropriate commissions and by the Government to combine and cease a competition detrimental to all.

On one point, however, Mr. Roosevelt's policy has prevailed, as it should, namely, the question of the *secret* rebates: an unjustifiable abuse. Secret advantages granted by transportation companies allowed a firm to so compete with rivals that it could kill them unawares. This, owing to his exertions, is no longer possible.

The Jewish petition, which the President had decided at first not to forward, was on second thoughts sent to Russia; but, as was to be foreseen, the Imperial Government refused to receive it.

July 4.—To-day is the first time, strange as it may seem, that Independence Day will be officially celebrated in the national capital. For the reason doubtless that they do not vote, the patriotism of the inhabitants of the District of Columbia has been of a more dormitive disposition than elsewhere. Mr. Macfarland, President of the Commissioners of the District, had come some time before to invite me to the intended celebration; because of the unique part played in former days by France I should be expected to make an address, no other Ambassador was to be asked; Admiral Dewey would read the Declaration of Independence.

We joined forces, the Admiral and I, and adopted some rules of strategy. The heat was terrific; sleep at night was almost impossible. We made it known that if a platform was not provided under which our heads would be in the shade, we should strike. We got our platform, on the lawn to the left of the White House; in front of it were an orchestra and a chorus, then chairs, then under the tall trees, vacant space for the crowd.

After an invocation by a Catholic priest, Mr. Macfarland spoke of the event we were commemorating and in graceful terms of France and her representative. He presented " Admiral Dewey, the most illustrious admiral

in the world." The applause was prodigious, enthusiastic, endlessly renewed; it was a pleasure to see so
many beaming, happy faces. The Admiral rose, beaming
too, red-faced with white moustaches; all pricked up
their ears to listen to such an authoritative voice denounce
the misdeeds of the unspeakable George III. But what
they heard was this: "As my voice is not very good, I
have asked a young friend of mine to read to you the
Declaration of Independence." The announcement was
followed by a thunder of applause, more cheaply won, we
told the recipient thereof, than any we had ever heard.
The Admiral was too popular for anything done by him
to be taken amiss. When the applause, which was
mixed with some good-humoured laughter, subsided, he
sat down, his young friend came forth, and shouted in a
tone which reached the limits of the Park: "When in
the course of human events . . ."

It was then my turn; my address was well received,
the *Marseillaise* was played. I had taken my cue from
one rarely quoted in American public speeches, Bossuet,
who had condensed in a brief sentence the ideal of
freedom that citizens should try to attain: "a state
where people are subject to nothing except the law, and
where the law is more powerful than men." Secretary
Hay kindly wrote congratulations.

Then spoke Secretary of the Navy Moody, later a
member of the Supreme Court. He was as a speaker the
success of the day; his eloquence, warmth, good grace,
courage, his energy and obvious sincerity drew all hearts
to him. After an impassioned praise of France, "our
friend in the days of our weakness, who, alone among
the nations of the world, brought decisive help to the
insurgents," he delivered to an audience, which he felt
he held in the hollow of his hand, some home truths,
unusual on such festive occasions, denouncing various
scandals, lynchings and other violations of the law.
He knew that in so doing he was following the same line

as his chief, the President, who, addressing soon after a considerable crowd at Syracuse on " Labour Day," was as severe on capitalists only concerned with their personal profits, as on workmen blinded by hatred and by the teachings of the sowers of hatred. Neither of the two classes according to him can prosper if the other is miserable; to try and persuade them of this is not to preach to them the difficult doctrine of disinterestedness, but the more accessible one of their own undoubted interest; a people is just as unworthy of liberty, whether it tends toward anarchy or toward tyranny. " Rich people complain," Mr. Roosevelt said to me a little later, " that I harrass them. Maybe, but I save their children."

To a member of Congress he wrote: " The statement alleged to have been made by the inspector that I ' ordered ' the indictment of —— ——, or anyone else, is a lie, just as much a lie as if it had been stated that I ordered that anyone should not be indicted. My directions have been explicit. Anyone who is guilty is to be prosecuted with the utmost rigour of the law and no one who is not guilty is to be touched. I care not a rap for the political or social influence of any human being when the question is one of his guilt or innocence in such a matter as the corruption of the Government service.

" I note what you say, that the circulation of this report about me may alienate the support of many of ——'s friends from my administration. Frankly, I feel that anyone who would believe such a story must be either lacking in intelligence or else possessed of malignant credulity. If anyone is to be alienated from me by the fact that I direct the prosecution of Republican or Democrat, without regard to his political or social standing, when it appears that he is guilty of gross wrongdoing—why, all I can say is, let him be alienated."

Team work was done by the President and his Secretaries.

Manchester by the Sea

We spent the summer at Manchester by the sea, having selected a modest wooden house in a quiet street, not far from the famous " singing beach." Those were charming restful months; we had in Boston, or along the coast, relatives whom it was a pleasure to visit in their fine homes and gardens, Justice and Mrs. Loring, the Misses Loring, Bishop Lawrence, Amory A. Lawrence and other Lawrences as agreeable as they were numerous. The sea was not a dull sleepy sea, but sometimes a roaring sea, dotted on ordinary days with sail-boats, while big steamers passed in the distance. The hills were green with luxuriant foliage, the slopes covered with flowers, and no individualistic walls prevented the passers-by from enjoying the sight; the whole region was almost too beautiful, and one brought up in the country, seeing so much mere pleasure-ground, would now and then long for a tilled field or even a little dunghill.

Every morning the " singing beach " had a visit from us, even in bad weather, when the surf sang somewhat loudly and its caresses were rather rude.

Agreeable society assembled at the Essex County Club and we went there every other day to play tennis. The rest of the time we took walks, usually to Gloucester, sometimes, for part of the distance, following the railroad track and jumping aside with alacrity when we saw a train coming. But we discovered paths which in a round-about way took us to our goal, keeping us all the time in the shade, a very important boon in that season. Now and then the blue sea with its white sails appeared between the trees.

Quiet charming days, with sufficient time left for official routine work and for study, facilitated by the Boston Public Library's tireless generosity in supplying books. I was able to finish then Volume II of my

Literary History of the English People, carrying it as far as the civil war.

The active life of the country was represented by manufacturing cities of which we visited several; Lawrence for weaving, Lynn for shoes, Gloucester for cod-fishing, Boston for various industries, among which elegant printing.

At Lawrence we saw in detail the Pacific Mills founded fifty-five years before by the Lawrence family; the country was swampy, but the Merrimac river could put in motion the wheels of a mill. The attempt was a great success; others came and a fine, prosperous city grew up. The Pacific Mills turn out woollen cloth, some silk and wool, but above all cotton cloth. An incredible quantity of ingenious machines do most of the work, wash, comb and dry the raw product, transform it into thread and into cloth, and print the ornamental designs, so obviously French that, entering the room, I could not help remarking on it. "Certainly they are French," was the answer; "we trace them from silk patterns that we buy in your country. In this we are no match for you." Workmen overlook the machines and see that their intelligent iron slave makes no mistake: the task is not an unpleasantly hard one; none of them looks harassed.

Some thirty years ago there was not a single foreigner among them; the first introduced was an Alsatian, brought over because of his experience in cloth printing. He was looked at as a curiosity. Now the proportion of real Americans, that is of those whose parents and grand-parents were born in America, is 10 per cent. Many of the new-comers get naturalized, but most of the Canadians, who are very numerous, go home after having made some money.

There were at the time of our visit about five or six thousand workmen employed, their average salary was $8.50 a week, the stokers receiving $9.50; they worked from 6.30 to 12 and from 1 to 6; there had been no strike for the last twenty years. All the philanthropic foundations established by the present Lawrences had, just as in Chicago, disappeared. Workmen no longer wanted them; they wanted their due, no more, no less; the hospital, the library and the rest had been fused with the city's. We noticed at one place elegant gothic arches: this had been the library. A sense of dignity causes this rejection of all show of kindliness; but it blunts that feeling of brotherhood and that understanding of a similitude of interests, the spread of which can alone solve the social problem.

We visited one of the boarding-houses that have accepted the rules devised by the firm, which, to that extent at least, protects its workmen as regards cleanliness, moderate prices not to be increased, etc. It was kept by an old Canadian woman and her daughter, who beamed at the thought of receiving the Ambassador of the old country. They did not allow us to go before we had seen every room, nook and corner of their house. " One does not so very often see one's Ambassador," as they were pleased to call their visitor. All was tidy and well-kept. In the dining-room, each guest had his napkin, and it was clean; in the sitting-room, a piano, as some work-women play; the kitchen very neat; in the bedrooms, not a piece of clothing left haphazard anywhere; some obviously inhabited by fervent Catholics were adorned with crucifixes and pious engravings.

Lynn and its neighbourhood is a shoe manufacturing country. Modest, scattered houses of the region had in former times a sort of annex, now empty, which served for home shoe-making. The invasion of giants, that is of machines, has destroyed here as elsewhere those tiny manufactories. In one of the chief establishments we were shown every phase of the work, from the arrival of the skins—goat from Argentina, colt from Russia, kangaroo from Australia—to the exit of the finished boot, of which 1,200 pairs are turned out each day. No cleverer machines can be imagined : the promptitude and perfection with which they cut, nail, burnish a heel, or embroider button-holes along the festooned line of a woman's boot is a wonder. Workmen must, however, be proportionately attentive, the slightest absentmindedness on the part of a machinist can ruin a boot.

Men and women employed there seemed kindly and contented. They worked steadily, did not talk; not a minute was lost; the shop was well lit, not unpleasant to be in; no disagreeable smell, but at certain places much noise. Men received between ten and fifteen dollars a week. Women eight to ten. Those exceptionally talented received more. Foreigners, especially Irish, were numerous. Drunkenness was rare. No philanthropic works were connected with the manufactory; employers and employees were, however, on good terms.

The manager, who had shown us with great kindness every detail, asked me for my opinion. " I have admired everything," I said, " although keeping some slight doubt as to the efficiency of the soles."—" Soles," he answered with a wink, " should not last too long." Pleased with the interest we had taken in every particular, he asked permission to offer my wife a pair of shoes. Knowing that they sold for $3.50 I thought I could without remorse accept the gift. He removed my wife's boot and inspected it with care, turning it one way, then another, looking at the seams. " This," he said, " is what we cannot do." They were hand-sewn boots, made to order in France. He valued them at seven dollars, but they had only cost twenty-eight francs, at that time $5.60.

At Gloucester, the capital city of the " Sacred Cod," we were guided by Mr. Dustin, of John Pew and Sons, 331 Main Street, ship-owners, ship-chandlers, cod merchants; they possessed sixteen boats; the Gloucester fleet was of about five hundred. These boats are much smaller than ours and are supposed to be more seaworthy; usually manned by twelve to twenty men who receive in many cases half their catch as pay. The cod is piled up in compartments and covered with layers of broken ice. It is salted on land (with salt coming from Trapani) and stretched on " flakes " to dry.

The number of fishermen was about 5,000 for Gloucester and 20,000 for the whole coast. Fifty years before they were all Americans; now there is a large mixture of Irish, Canadians, English and above all Portuguese. In former times they continued fishing all their lives. Now, after a while, they retire, open a shop and ply some small trade in the city. Anyone considered clever, plucky, with sufficient knowledge of the sea, may become a master. Some of these retire on a little fortune of twenty to thirty thousand dollars.

All their catch, which includes some herring and mackerel, is sold in America; a few of their boats, not many, had tried to find a market in Ireland. One sees in railway stations neat little wooden boxes, with a statement of the weight of the contents, which are boneless cod.

Sailors were well fed; some added to their fare delicacies, such as preserved milk or California fruit. They drank tea, coffee, water, no alcohol being allowed; they observed the rule without difficulty. Some when they came home indulged more than they should, but when they sailed again they conformed to the rule, knowing that it was for their own good.

They have heard of our bonuses to those of our ships kept the cleanest and think that it is a good notion. We visited a boat just arrived. No hammocks, but narrow bunks, two rows of them in the fore-part of the craft; the intermediary space was used as a kitchen. The central part of the ship was reserved for the fish and the layers of ice. On the deck, plenty of troughs into which

the cod is thrown as soon as caught; a good deal of
fishing takes place from the deck itself, and at intervals
in the sides are grooves for the lines. Six or eight
diminutive dories are lined up on the deck.

An all-pervading smell of cod permeates this part of
the town.

We remained at Manchester until late in the season.
The fine houses had their shutters up, brilliant society
had gone; autumn had arrived and her magic wand had
transformed mere foliage into the richest purple mantles;
the " singing beach," whose waves had become icy cold,
sometimes sang for us alone. Tempests arose, dashing
with such spray the rockbound coast that we took train
to Rockport the better to enjoy a sight more impressive
there than anywhere else. By the beginning of November
we returned to Washington.

PANAMA

Confirming despatches sent to my Government in the
spring, I had written them on September 22, 1903:
" I am still persuaded that the President will do all he
possibly can to have the canal at Panama and not elsewhere. I know, for having heard him say so, how in-
tensely he wants it; he will neglect nothing that may
enable his country to perfect this work and be the master
thereof. He will certainly never allow any European
combination to step in and resume it." I doubt that
Nicaragua will be seriously thought of. " One of the
hypotheses most openly considered of late months by the
Press, is a rebellion of the States of Panama and Cauca,
which would form themselves into an independent
republic and come to an immediate agreement with the
United States. A conversation I had some time ago with
the Columbian Chargé d'Affaires has shown me that
such a contingency does not seem to him unlikely, but on
the contrary threatening and probable."

The revolution, in which the chief part was played by the French engineer Mr. Bunau-Varilla, who has published a full account of it,[1] and who became the first Panamanian Minister in Washington, took place on November 3, the State of Cauca remaining, however, aloof.

On November 11, President Roosevelt asked us to lunch with him at the White House. In the absence of Mrs. Roosevelt, Miss Alice presided. The other guests were Robert R. Hitt, President of the Committee of Foreign Affairs of Congress, Justice Day and Mr. and Mrs. Lucy. I heard only afterwards that the short-sized latter gentleman with dishevelled white hair, who remained silent most of the time, was the famous Toby M.P. of *Punch*. This was one of Mr. Roosevelt's characteristics; no one out of the common could visit the shores of the United States or grow up within its bounds, whatever be the turn of his mind or the colour of his skin, without the President's wishing to make his acquaintance and trying to bring out what was in him. He had granted, the day before, an interview to the deviser of a new religion, J. A. Dowie, the founder of Zion City, who pretended to be the reincarnate prophet Elijah, and had travelled East announcing that he would convert New York, but this miracle proved somehow beyond his powers.

During the lunch the President, whose policy was founded on the Treaty of 1846 with New Granada, giving the United States the right and obligation to prevent any obstruction to a free transit across the isthmus, spoke of Panama: " Everything goes on there," he said, " as we would wish; I am about to receive Mr. Bunau-Varilla. It is reported that we have made the revolution; it is not so, but for months such an occurrence was probable and I was ready for it. It is all for the best; such a revolution is quicker and not more bloody than

[1] *Panama, la Création, la Destruction, la Résurrection*, Paris, 1913.

our arbitration. If the Columbians try to send troops by sea against Panama, the American squadron has for its instructions to divert those ships to some place where they can do no mischief. Our own ships will avoid with the utmost care any action which might look like actual war against Coiumbia."

Literature had as usual its part in the conversation. Addressing my wife, who was his neighbour, Mr. Roosevelt said: " The *Iliad* bores me. Those Greeks, those Trojans who run after one another around the walls, talk away and never reach any result except with the help of the gods, are in my eyes of no interest. Speak to me of the Sagas and the *Nibelungen*; there you see real heroes; death is in their eyes and they continue to fight, making the best of it, until the last minute."

The French Ambassadress asked him whether he had read the *Song of Roland*. He had not. " There," she said, " you would find as much valour and more poetry." —" Have you a copy? " the President said, turning to me, " the original text and a translation? "—" Yes, I have." —" Then send it to me please to-morrow morning without fail."

I sent the book and for a while Charlemagne and his peers replaced the Mongols in the non-political preoccupations of the President. The slightest details had fixed themselves in his mind; he knew every personage, even the secondary ones, and as they became for him a frequent subject of conversation, the *Song of Roland* was read by quantities of people and enjoyed more popularity in Washington society than it ever did before, or ever has since.

NEW ORLEANS; THE ANNIVERSARY OF THE CESSION

The transfer from France to the United States of French-founded New Orleans and French-discovered Louisiana had taken place in December 1803. I was earnestly invited by the local authorities and the French Creoles to visit them on the centennial of the transfer.

My wife was not well, so I started alone, on December 16. What is to be seen now from the windows of a railway car is different, certainly, from what I saw and thus described in my travelling notes:—" An abundance of reddish, monotonous, dreary plains, some pretty wooded hills, then the reddish plain again; few inhabitants, the majority of those who can be seen, negroes; the houses are far apart, wooden boxes whose logs and boards, often unpainted, have been blackened by the weather, a sorry sight. When a few have been formed into a group, there is a station; the train stops in the midst of Main Street, opposite the store, a sort of bazaar where every kind of thing is sold and the inhabitants congregate to talk together, see the train pass, ask travellers what goes on. No touch of colour except the glaring, large bills of a circus that has been, or will be, here. So long as the rain has not washed them away, the bills continue to glare.

" No stone edifice; the church, when there is one, is a wooden box like the houses. The street is nothing but a road, and roads are nothing but tracks, muddy and deep-rutted.

" Long before reaching an inhabited spot, and long after, the eye is saddened by an abundance of refuse, the droppings of civilization, empty cans, broken saucepans, old newspapers. Nothing gives the impression of settled lives. Why take care, sweep, put things in order? We leave to-morrow."

Same sight the next day; the ground is of an intense red; the ill-kept tracks, bordered by no ditches, are red too and look like open wounds, unhealed, inflicted on the fields. Same blackened wooden houses, same dumpings, same stops in the midst of defenceless Main Streets; but vast cotton plantations, on some of which negroes are gathering the crop that at the end of the leafless twigs looks like large flakes of dazzling white snow. A movement has been started to weave it on the spot, and the rare towns, or incipient towns, that we pass through, have such manufactories. They think they will rival Massachusetts, for they have the product at hand and labour is cheaper, but Massachusetts hopes to retain its supremacy owing to the better quality of its labour.

As we approach the sea, the flatness of the country is still more complete—no tunnels, many rivers and swamps; on immense spaces the railroad line is perfectly straight.

At the table where I take my meals, usually sits a greybearded gentleman who proves very interesting. He had first addressed me in Italian, then in English. He had hunted the elk with President Roosevelt, crossed Siberia, visited South Africa with Cecil Rhodes; he knew most of the people and countries I knew, and many more besides. Looking at the plains we were crossing, he said he had not seen them since the civil war, and that he had belonged to the same body of troops as Comte de Paris (who with his brother the Duc de Chartres was aide to General MacClellan). Both were tall, but the Count had the bad habit of stooping, which he never lost; I saw him once in England at the Ascot races, he was stooping. In the course of a bloody fight he was entrusted, my companion said, with an order, to carry to the other end of the firing line. He had to cross a large open space where plenty of bullets were whistling. He rose on his stirrups, his head perfectly erect, crossed the space under fire, returned perfectly erect, and then resumed his stoop.

When we reached New Orleans, my companion handed me his card and I learned that he was the Rev. Mr. Nevin, Chaplain to the American colony in Rome.

I was the guest at New Orleans of Mr. Walter Denègre, of an old French family every member of which speaks French without the slightest trace of an accent. In the garden of his fine house were enormous magnolias rising higher than the roof. My first day was spent visiting

the French institutions, which I found numerous, prosperous and a great credit to the men of our race; Tulane
University, founded and endowed by a French Creole
of that name, where our literature was zealously taught
by Prof. Fortier; the French hospital; the Society of the
14th of July which had a school for boys, the French
Union which had a school for girls; a special Ear, Eye
and Throat hospital founded by Dr. de Roaldès, who
had spent his whole life and fortune trying to be useful,
and who continued to be so, not letting his native cheer-
fulness be in any way abated by the terrible calamity that
had befallen him; he was ataxic and blind.

At each place, champagne was served and speeches
were delivered, which I had to answer. None was on the
programme for that day; but, before noon, I had been
made to deliver nine.

I visited also, in company with the Governor of
Louisiana, Mr. Heard, the battleships sent for the ceremonies, an American one, the *Minneapolis* with Admiral
Wise, and a new French one, the *Jurien de la Gravière*:
23 knots at the trial, which was then considered a
remarkable performance.

The French of New Orleans had their market, where
the names Dupont, Dupuis, Durand abounded over the
stalls, a newspaper, *l'Abeille*, and an Opera House of their
own, where, that evening, a ball was given, one with a
touching historical significance. The hall was handsomely decorated with wreathes of foliage, and the
festivity began with a parade of the local authorities,
headed by the Governor and myself; when we reached
our places we stoppped and all the couples marched past
us curtseying very low in the ancient graceful style; very
low too did we bow in return. What was unique and
moving on this occasion was that the ball reproduced the
last one given under the French flag by the last French
Governor of Louisiana, Laussat, one hundred years
before. The dances were gavottes and minuets; the

S

young ladies with sparkling eyes were the descendants of the young ladies whose eyes had sparkled a century ago and who had been the guests of Governor Laussat. Several of those of to-day had on the very dresses worn on that occasion by their great-grandmothers. There was, however, one difference: as it was known, on the first occasion, that the fête once ended, so would be the rule of France over Louisiana, the dancers were loth to give the signal, and the ball lasted until nine o'clock the next morning.

Saturday the 19th was the day for the official speeches, delivered under the presidency of Governor Francis, who had come on purpose from Saint-Louis. At the City Hall, a speech by the mayor, Mr. Capdevielle, a tall, lean Creole with a white moustache, a fluent speaker, able to use both languages without any accent, and whose good-humour was catching.

At the old Archbishopric, where an interesting historical exhibition had been arranged, a learnéd, and perhaps a trifle long, speech by Prof. Fortier.

In the big square in front of the Cabildo and of the Cathedral, adorned with a statue of Andrew Jackson, winner over the British of the battle of New Orleans, 8th of January, 1815 (a replica of the one in Washington), not far from the muddy Mississippi, broad as an arm of the sea, a large platform had been built for the authorities; and a vast crowd surrounded it. Governor Francis introduced me to the public and I came forward, in doubt as to what language I should use. Looking around it seemed to me that, in those earnest faces of men of the people, the French element predominated, so I used my native tongue. The joy of the listeners was exuberant; each sentence was applauded, and with such warmth that even those who obviously did not understand, applauded for company's sake. When I returned to my seat, Governor Francis loudly congratulated me: "Your speech was excellent," he said, adding, "I did

not understand a word, but I saw quite well from the
expression of those who did, that it must have been
excellent."

Later in the afternoon a military review took place; a
thrill suddenly ran among the semi-French multitude,
and the cry arose: "Voilà les Français!" as there
appeared in the distance a detachment of sailors from the
Jurien de la Gravière, with the red *pompon* on their caps.

I was able, during the rest of my stay, to visit the
tropical trees, plants, flowers, squirrels, birds and hot-
houses of Audubon Park, listen to a very creditable performance of *Carmen* at the French Opera, attend with
Governor Heard a solemn pontifical mass in the Cathedral
at which Monseigneur Chapelle, a son of Auvergne, offici-
ated, a replica mass of one celebrated a hundred
years before, when was sung in New Orleans for the
last time the *Domine Salvam fac Rempublican ; Domine
Salvos fac Consules*, take part in a banquet offered by the
French colony in the great hall of a house belonging to
the "Union Française." More speeches were exchanged,
a piece of music, unknown to me then, was performed;
everybody rose. I asked my neighbour what it was.
"Don't you know?" he answered; "it is the hymn of
Secession, *Dixie ;* we always rise when it is played." The
health of the absent Ambassadress was proposed, and to
my surprise, the President of the meeting, M. Vergnolle,
suddenly produced, as by a conjuror's trick, a loving cup
with a beautiful inscription, which I was asked to take
to her. It has never left her table to this day.

I parted with regret from them all, and from Walter
Denègre, who had been such an excellent guide, wise
adviser and clever contriver of moments of rest in the
midst of manifold obligations.

CHAPTER XI

OUR FIRST TREATY OF ARBITRATION—MR. HAY AND MR. ROOSEVELT

As our Republic was strongly in favour of a pacific settlement of international disputes and we had recently concluded an arbitration treaty with England (October 14, 1903), I took the initiative, January 18, 1904, of proposing to my Government that we approach the United States in view of a similar agreement. The English, it is true, had signed one called the Olney Pauncefote treaty which the American Senate had rejected in 1897, but time had passed; in his message to Congress of December 1903, President Roosevelt had praised the procedure of arbitration. We might propose, I thought, an agreement so modest that the Senate would perhaps accept it; it would be better than nothing, and we should thus continue our tradition of concluding with the States the first treaties of every kind duly put in force by them: first and only treaty of alliance, 1778; first treaty of commerce, 1778; first consular convention, 1788; first treaty for the increase of American territory, 1803. We never had any occasion to conclude a treaty of peace.

My suggestion was agreed to and I signed with Secretary Hay, on the 2nd of November, a treaty of arbitration which, it seemed to us, would meet the Senate's approval, as it excluded from its action all the chief causes of possible trouble, what concerned " the vital interests, the independence or the honour of the two contracting Parties," the term honour being of undoubted elasticity. This was a beginning, and it might be improved later. The Press was very favourable; the *New York Herald* declared that the prestige of France as a friend of peace, recently manifested by the part she had played in the Anglo-Russian crisis,[1] was, according to general opinion, greatly increased by the early negotiation of the treaty just concluded.

The example was at once followed and similar treaties were signed by England, Germany, Italy, Spain and other countries.

But while peace associations were loud in their denunciation of the treaties as insignificant, the Senate found them much too significant and refused its approval. " A treaty entering the Senate," said Mr. Hay in his irritation, " is like a bull going into the arena: no one can say just how or when the final blow will fall, but one thing is certain, it will never leave the arena alive."[2]

This, and other rebuffs from the same assembly, which now found him too pacific and rejected his treaties, and now too bellicose and haggled about his battleships, did not abate in any way the President's optimism and cheeriness. As I complimented him on his wisdom in preserving his good-humour, he said: " McClellan, in the civil war, was a man who would always have succeeded—he knew it and said so—if only the instruments in his hands had been perfect. But one never has perfect instruments in hand; they turn, they twist, they break, they cut your finger. One must act for the best, avoid being impeded by irritation or despondency, and move forward to the extent possible. The Senate will not give me all I want, but I shall snatch some part of it."[3]

[1] We had succeeded in securing a peaceful settlement of the trouble when Russian battleships had sunk English fishing boats in the North Sea, taking them for Japanese war vessels.

[2] Thayer, *Life and Letters of John Hay*, II, 263.

[3] Conversation of February 19, 1905.

I signed in fact, three years later, February 10, 1908, with Secretary Root, France again taking the lead, an even weaker treaty which, " with the advice and consent of the Senate," was actually ratified.

Mr. Hay was a rare mind, a wide intelligence with windows open on all the avenues of life, a large acquaint-ance with men and books, a gifted writer in prose and verse; modest withal, never trying to push himself to the front, speaking in subdued tones, and scarcely opening his lips when uttering a memorable saying or a shrewd, humorous remark. President Roosevelt and he delighted in each other's company in those intimate conversations in which we sometimes took part; the President called his secretary John, and the secretary called his chief Theodore.

Mr. Hay, who in his youth had been Lincoln's secre-tary, bridged, as it were, the years between the living generation and that of Mr. Roosevelt's favourite hero. Having discovered in the huge *History of the Second Empire* in seven volumes by La Gorce, that young Hay figured there and was described as " cet ombrageux Américain " (this touchy American), the President took pleasure in teasing him and calling him so. In our talks at the White House, " L'ombrageux Américain " was a usual periphrase to designate the Secretary of State.

Sensitive and reticent, Hay was unable to take rebuffs and checks cheerily. The Press was not parsimonious in its praise of his policy, but the slightest blame or obloquy, unavoidable though it be in a democracy, gave him more pain than any praise gave him pleasure. Very different in this from his chief, who scarcely knew what it was to worry, he knew only too well, to the injury of his health; even a speech which he had written, and written perfectly well, in advance, and which he would only have to read, caused him to worry and lose sleep. He, almost blush-ingly, more than once confessed as much to me.

He brought to the fulfilling of his all-important functions, besides his other qualities, a knowledge of foreign countries and a long practice of affairs rare in America. In one respect, and an important one, given the rules and customs of his country, he was deficient: he failed to be in touch with those whom, for the realization of the policies he favoured, it would have been well to exchange ideas with, and, while performing all his duties, his ingrained disposition to live apart and avoid familiarity, especially with the members of the Senate, whose approval was none the less indispensable for the success of his plans, served him ill. Jealous of their prerogatives, anxious not to lose the slightest particle of them, uneasy about the self-willed dispositions of the chief of the State, Senators were the more exacting toward his Minister. And the Minister took no trouble about them. " The Constitution," I wrote to my Government, " drawn up at a time when the United States had, so to say, no neighbours, and when their leaders, beginning with Washington, desired to be bound to other countries by as few treaties as possible, has placed the main power in those matters in the hands of the Senate. This assembly, of course, does not negotiate treaties, but what is of more import, when these reach it ready negotiated, it remodels them as it pleases. It thus happens that, acting without any check, it devises another text which cannot fail to please the electorate, since other people's advantages are diminished and their own increased, but which may prove unacceptable to the other contracting party and becomes a dead letter. A striking example is the Newfoundland treaty.[1]

" The indispensable check to the action of the Senatorial Committee of Foreign Relations was usually supplied by the Secretary of State, who did not disdain to haunt the Capitol, to give explanations, plead the cause of the

---

[1] Signed November 8, 1902, by Mr. Hay and Sir Michael Herbert; the Senate remodelled it entirely, suppressed the chief advantage reserved for Newfoundland, and killed it.

treaties under discussion, in a word to perform with
patience and good-humour a task not always agreeable,
but indispensable, given the precedents and the Constitution.   Mr. Olney, for example, did so with great success.
Mr. Hay considers such interference unworthy of himself;
hence misunderstandings, and an ill-will which, instead of
suggesting to the Secretary a change in his ways, inspire
him with epigrams which always end by reaching the
ears of the wittily ridiculed senators.

"The final result is that the latter, left to themselves,
and little enough inclined by their position to restraint,
give free play to their own criticisms, ask for something
different, and thus arrangements of international importance fail one after the other.

"If this continues, foreign Governments will wish that,
in spite of obvious inconveniences of all sorts, their
Ambassadors be admitted to explain and discuss the
proposed texts with the Senatorial Committee, so that,
since to it belongs the final say, its decisions be not rendered *motu proprio* without any explanation from the most
interested party." [1]

At the time when I was writing thus, the health of Mr.
Hay, worn out by his functions, the most important part
of which he fulfilled admirably, and by his capacity for
worrying, began to give way.   Going to Bad Nauheim
in the hope of recuperating (March 1905), he met Henry
White at Genoa and told him that "there was nothing
the matter with him, except old age, the Senate, and two
or three mortal maladies." [2]

Mr. Hay was passably well disposed then toward
France, extremely well toward England, very averse to
Germany.   During his cure at Bad Nauheim he refused,
alleging his health, to arrange an interview greatly
desired by William II, who was the more irritated that,
in spite of that same health, the Secretary managed to

[1] March 21, 1905.
[2] Henry White, *Thirty Years of American Diplomacy*, p. 244.

pay a visit to King Edward. He saw also M. Delcassé, "an incident," he said to me on his return, "which history should ignore," but it has become known since. He died on July 1, 1905, mourned from the depth of his heart by President Roosevelt, who wrote me, July 3: "I thank you for your kind and friendly note, and I know how sincere your sympathy is. John Hay's loss is one which I feel most deeply, not only for the sake of the country, but because of my strong personal affection for him. I mourn him as a friend as well as a public man."

Some time later, after a dinner at the White House, the President led me to his study upstairs and had a box brought to him, full of letters from Hay. He had been requested by Henry Adams to give them for publication. He inspected them one by one; great and small questions were dealt with in perfect familiarity and confidence. Many began "My dear Theodore." It was striking to find how quickly incidents which had dazzled onlookers, for a while in full limelight, sink into obscurity: for many, explanatory notes would already be necessary; in more than one case we had difficulty in remembering what was alluded to.

The letters were full of wit, with more vivacity than force. Hay was better able to banter than to decide. His banter was of the best sort, seasoned with a distant, detached good-humour, sometimes tinged with melancholy.

I suggested reserve; there were not many letters in which the Secretary did not ridicule somebody; the rule should be, as it seemed to me, not to print any letter which the author himself would not have liked to have published.

In the course of the year 1904, an event which did not draw much attention in America, but which was of great importance for us and even for the world, had taken place. The chief points of friction still remaining between France and England had been satisfactorily settled, thanks to the wise diplomacy of M. Delcassé, M. Cambon and the favourable influence of King Edward, who, while the negotiations were going on, had said: " More than ever now, we must have ' no bone of contention ' between ourselves and the French Government."[1] Three conventions were signed on the 8th of April, 1904, one settling the two countries' differences in Egypt and Morocco; another concerning Newfoundland and West Africa; the third Madagascar, Siam and the New Hebrides. More impervious than ever became the two nations to the Kaiser's threats or blandishments. We were less and less isolated in the world and the force of attraction of our strengthened group became greater. I was thrilled at the news and wrote to M. Delcassé who, during President Loubet's journey to London in July 1903, had, with Lord Lansdowne, laid the foundations of the closer understanding: " The papers have not yet published the text of the memorable treaties just concluded, and the French papers giving it have not yet arrived. But all that is said of them is so well calculated to please a French heart that I cannot help adding my congratulations to so many more already received by you. It must be a very delightful consolation for you in the midst of so many difficulties that confront you every day, to think of those services of a permanent character rendered one after the other to our country, and to be able to consider that the unique duration of the Ministry is the least of the reasons that will perpetuate the remembrance thereof." (April 20, 1904).

As time went on we saw more and more of the President and his family, and a friendship developed to last until one of us should die. We were constantly invited to meals at which only the family or some especially in-

[1] March 1, 1904, Sidney Lee, *King Edward VII*, II, 248.

timate friends were present. At the end of a musicale at
the White House where the Diplomatic Corps was present,
Mr. Roosevelt asked me confidentially, but in his usual
sonorous voice, to lunch with him the next day. Count
Cassini, dean of the Corps, with whom I was on excellent
terms, though I knew that he described me as " a Petrar-
quist, not a diplomat," overheard the invitation and said:
" My dear friend, you beat us all," and he added in a
sour tone, " but I do not envy you."

" Then," I thought, " there is no cloud to darken my
pleasure."

Talk never failed to be on those occasions *de omni re
scibili*, past, present, and even future, distant and near
by, peace, war, literature, the races of men, the bad
manners (pointed out by myself) of a White House dog,
worrying the White House squirrels, social problems, the
possible improvement of mankind, the short-sightedness of labour, the short-sightedness of milliardaires, a
possible reform of orthography on which he was for some
years very keen (should one write *through* or *thru*?); the
German Kaiser, " for whom," said our host, " I had an
inclination for a year or two; but nothing is left of that;
it is passed, adjudicated; he cannot in any way be
trusted " (May 20, 1905); Admiral Dewey, who had
spoken disparagingly of the Germans, but publicly, and
who being reprimanded had replied, publicly also:
" I was perhaps wrong, but what I said was just what I
think." Asked privately by the President to explain, the
admiral had called, and all he had said by way of an
apology had been: " Well, you know, I am like you;
I cannot help saying what I have on my mind."

Sports were not forgotten; the President, whose study
upstairs was adorned with a variety of boxing gloves,
fencing swords and masks, was keen then about the
Japanese wrestling, *Jiu-Jitsu*, and was taking lessons;
he invited a few of his men friends to a performance by
a little group of noted Japanese experts in the great

ball-room at the White House, which some papers described as a desecration. The chief champion, famous in his country, Mr. Hitachyiama, a man of considerable size, kindly, courteous, all smiles, was presented to Mr. Roosevelt by the Japanese Ambassador. Then there was a solemn entry of the large man, two ordinary wrestlers and a sort of umpire, dressed in brilliant but very much abbreviated costumes. Some ceremonies resembling prayers take place; the two wrestlers crouch on the ground on all-fours; the umpire wielding a species of lacquer caduceus gives a signal: the two rush forward; there are convulsions, upheavals; one seems to have suffered a bad fall, but rises again and makes the other fall heavily on the mat. No strokes; they only try by strength of arm to throw their opponent to the ground. At each stop they drink a mouthful of water. During the fight, which is ardent but brief, the umpire emits guttural sounds to encourage the wrestlers.

The champion in his turn appears; he does not wrestle; that is beneath him. But he gives their lesson to the ordinary wrestlers. They rush against his mass, which remains immovable. In a turn of the hand he throws them to the ground. We are asked to feel his pectorals, which are of remarkable hardness.

Ordinary boxing was practised by the President with renowned Mike Donovan, who said of him: " If anyone tells you he is an easy mark, don't believe it. . . . I never saw a pleasanter man or one who gets more enjoyment out of a thing. He's a fighter and knows how to give and take blows."

His enthusiasm for sport was not, however, limitless. In one of those sayings which, if collected, would form a new *Poor Richard's Almanack* well worth preserving, he declared: "Nothing better for a man than to have excelled at football when he is twenty; nothing worse if he has nothing else to show when he is forty."

His readings were the occasion of endless discussions.

Time and again the Mongols reappeared, the *Nibelungen*, the *Song of Roland*; he teased my wife, who was responsible for his having read the song, with the emotiveness of Charlemagne's army, stopping to weep over Roland's disaster instead of running after the Saracens. The answer was: " This was, for the poet, a way of speaking, and, moreover, if they wept it was not out of fear."

Books dealing with great deeds and men of action were those that especially delighted him; the stories of the most intrepid, the boldest, the proudest went to his heart. He was immersed at one time in the story of Giovanni delle Bande Nere. He had read Morley's three volumes on Gladstone and told me that, if they seemed to him a good biography, the hero thereof did not please him at all. No more did Balfour, who, at the time of the North Sea incident, when British fishing craft were sunk by Russian cruisers, had had recourse to noisy verbosity: " The reverse of the system I am for: to speak softly and carry a big stick."—" What," I said, " if by chance a recourse to strong words prevents a recourse to strong knocks? Occasions vary."

In war his admiration went to those who do not yield. He admired Stoessel at Port Arthur, so long as he had not surrendered; one should never surrender. As I quoted to him Galliffet, charging again at Sedan, and replying, when asked whether he was ready to try once more: " As long as there is one left," he said: " That is what moves me and gives me a thrill, more than all the stories about Port Arthur." He added : " What I like in France is, that with all her literature and fine arts, when the hour for fighting comes she is always ready."

As the Mongols continued to hold now and then a place in his thoughts I lent him Cahun's *Turcs et Mongols, des Origines à 1405*, a stitched copy which came back splendid, in full binding, with a letter saying: " I have read Cahun's *Turks and Mongols* with such thoroughness and assiduity that at the end it was dangling out of the covers, and I have sent it to Washington to have it bound, with instructions to deliver it to you.

" . . . I have been immensely interested in it. It is extraordinary how little the average European historian has understood the real significance of the immense Mongol movement of the thirteenth century and its connection with the previous history of the Turks, Mongols and similar people. Until I read Cahun, I never understood the sequence of cause and effect and never appreciated the historic importance of the existence of the vast, loosely bound Turkish power of the fifth and sixth centuries and of its proposition to unite with the Byzantines for the overthrow of the Persians. . . . For a Frenchman Cahun is dry; but the dryness of writers of your race, if they are good at all, is miles asunder from the hopeless aridity of similar writers among our people."

He ended saying: " I wish you could get down here to see me some time. Now under no circumstances must you permit Madame Jusserand to take a trip that would be tiresome, but if you and she happen to be passing through New York I shall arrange to have the *Sylph* take you out here for lunch and then take you back in the afternoon, and you would have an enjoyable sail, while Mrs. Roosevelt and I would have an enjoyable lunch! "

A P.S. was added: " Since writing this your telegram has come. I hope you both will enjoy your summer to the full. If you see de La Gorce, tell him how much I like his work, and that I read every word and was at times painfully struck by certain essential similarities in political human nature whether in an Empire or a Republic, cisatlantic or transatlantic."[1]

He far preferred, all things equal, the way in which a book was written in France to the way it was elsewhere, and ridiculed people who gave themselves learned airs, showing contempt for any work pleasant to read: " readable, they think, therefore superficial." I reminded him

[1] Oyster Bay, July 11, 1905.

of Guizot's remark which sounds like an " Irish bull "
and is of unquestionable truth : " Unless a book is readable it won't be read."

His own reading included many other works besides
his favourite histories, biographies and mediæval epics,
his favourites because tinged with heroism.   He praised
Aucassin and Nicolette, was full of admiration for Mistral,
with whom he exchanged letters, was enthusiastic over
Pastor Wagner's *Simple Life,* which was for a while his
great hobby, delighted in Owen Wister's works because
they were of such excellent literary quality and so true to
nature.   He sent me a copy of *The Virginian,* a poor one,
for which he apologized, the only one he had been able
to find where he was.   I thanked him, saying : " True
the ' setting ' is poor, but I shall see to that ; a book with
such a word from such a hand should be better dressed
than Cinderella was after the fairy Godmother's visit.
Now it looks too much like Cinderella *before* the visit."

After an intimate dinner at the White House, Mr.
Longworth and Miss Carlisle play in pleasant fashion on
the violin and the piano.   Owen Wister sits in his turn at
the piano and sings some bantering popular ballads.   We
are all standing about him ; merry and laughing, the
President takes the chief part in the amusement and even
cuts a few capers on the polished floor to the accompani-
ment of Wister's music.

When grave matters were at stake, Venezuela, Morocco
or the Russo-Japanese war, I was sometimes asked by the
President to call on him after dinner for a serious private
talk.   Late as might be the hour when it ended, three or
four newspaper men, keeping watch like sentries, would
emerge from behind the columns of the porch and ask
what I had said, to which query the answer, agreed to by
the President, was that " a conversation belonged by right
to the principal interlocutor ; and he alone could dispose
of it as he thought fit."

On one occasion the interview took place on a Sunday

evening, and the fact having been mentioned in the papers, I received from a Sabbatarian association, which took for granted that this foreign Ambassador must have forced his presence on the Chief of State, a very disagreeable letter remonstrating with me for having violated the Sabbath and the constitution of the United States, "which protects our Chief Executive in his Sabbath, from any official duties," as well as from "social amenities." I was offered a chance to explain how I could have acted in a way so little in conformity "with the Christian character and church membership of our beloved President Roosevelt."

I had prepared a brief answer simply stating that I was sure I had in no way violated the Sabbath nor the constitution of the United States, but the President did not allow me to send it, and asked to consult with Secretary Hay. The result was his writing me a letter of his own, expressing in his most vigorous style his opinion of the incident. He had read it at a Cabinet council, and the amusement created was such, that the Ministers declared all the documents ought to be published. They were not and shall not be; the matter stopped there.

I had frequent occasions to write to my Government about the Chief of State to whom I was accredited, telling, for example, of his enormous success in November 1904 when he polled more than double the votes registered by his predecessor McKinley, who then held the record. The White House was flooded with congratulations; among the earliest came those from the Kaiser, who, not averse to being spectacular, sent his in Latin. The President's power could not fail to be proportionate to his success; the event had shown that his favourite policies were his country's favourite policies. "I would far rather," he told me, "be a full President for four years than half a President for eight." He published on that occasion his famous letter ending: "On the fourth of March next, I shall have served three and a half years . . . and this constitutes my first term. The wise custom which limits the President to two terms, regards the substance and not the form, and under no circumstances will I be a candidate for or accept another nomination."

"This," I wrote to my Government, "is surely a courageous determination, hard to take for a man who, when his powers come to an end, will be fifty. One could not swear that some means will not be found, in a distant future, to break such a vow. . . . Agile minds are in any case already busy, and Mr. Taft, Secretary of War, quite popular and greatly loved, who has borne the principal weight of the campaign of speeches, is spoken of as the next republican candidate."

As for Mr. Roosevelt, what would he do at the end of four years? "Perhaps," he told me, "think of the Senate, though it cannot be an easy matter in my State" (New York).

One particular trait of Mr. Roosevelt's personality was not long to come to the fore. Immediately after his election, he caused an increase of the American fleet so dear to his heart to be announced: the building of twenty-five units, among which three battleships, to be begun at once. In his annual message to Congress, December 6, 1904, he bestowed on "the great battleships, heavily armoured and heavily gunned," praises which recent inventions no longer justify. But he wisely insisted on men and ships never remaining idle: "Our great fighting ships and torpedo boats must be ceaselessly trained and manœuvred in squadrons. The officers and men can only learn their trade thoroughly by ceaseless practice on the high seas. In the event of war it would be far better to have no ships at all than to have ships of a poor and ineffective type, or ships which, however good, were yet manned by untrained and unskilled crews. . . . The marksmanship in our navy has improved in an extraordinary degree during the last

T

three years . . . No effort must be spared to make the service attractive to the enlisted men." This was a point to which he attached extreme importance: that men in the most modest condition, were they coal-miners, canal-diggers at Panama, enlisted men in the army and navy, or western farmers, should lead as much as circumstances could allow, pleasant, hygienic, contented lives.

Still impressed by the grave turn that the Venezuelan question had taken shortly before, he bluntly insisted in the same message on the Monroe doctrine being a double-edged instrument. " It is not true," he said, " that the United States feels any land hunger or entertains any projects as regards the other nations of the Western Hemisphere. . . . If a nation shows that it knows how to act with reasonable efficiency and decency in social and political matters, if it keeps order and pays its obliga-tions, it need fear no interference from the United States. Chronic wrong-doing or an impotence which results in a general loosening of the ties of civilized society may, in America, as elsewhere, ultimately require intervention by some civilized nation, and in the Western Hemisphere the Monroe doctrine may force the United States, how-ever reluctantly, in flagrant cases of such wrongdoing or impotence, to the exercise of an international police power." [1]

The idea of a settlement of all quarrels, not by " police power," but by arbitration, was in the air, but there, at that time, it remained suspended.

He recurred, with even more insistance, to those same questions in his message of the following year, in which he also again attacked plutocrats and men whom, in one of his striking phrases, he described as "just legally honest." His paper was chiefly remarkable, however, for the energy with which he put forward his views, inherited by his party from Washington, Hamilton and

[1] December 6, 1904.

the " federalists " of the early days, as to the importance
of centralizing, unifying and solidifying, to the advantage
of the Federal Government, and the weakening of the
local State Governments, the forces and laws of the
country: the main point which even now, when the
programmes of the two parties somewhat overlap, continues to separate Democrats and Republicans.

Washington indeed had written to Governor Harrison
of Virginia: " The disinclination of the individual States
to yield competent powers to Congress for the Federal
Government, their unreasonable jealousy of that body
and of one another, and the disposition which seems to
pervade each of being all-wise and all-powerful within
itself, will, if there is not a change in the system, be our
downfall as a nation. This is as clear to me as the
A.B.C."

He feared " the worst consequences from a half-
starved, limping Government that appears to be always
moving upon crutches and tottering at every step "
(January 18, 1784).

In the course of an official dinner at the White House,
I had a long conversation with the President, across the
table, because he had on his right Prince Fushimi, who
spoke only Japanese, and on his left the Mexican Ambassador, who spoke only Spanish. He talked of his election
with joy, but also with modesty, saying that " such a
wave of popularity could not fail to be followed by a
reflux, and that his mind was prepared for it, but that
in any case he remained, after his success, free from any
engagement that was not public and from any promise
he could not keep."

He spoke of France with much sympathy, saying that
there was no foreign colony in the United States more
reputable and orderly than ours. Its members organize,
care for their own poor and their sick (in New York and
several other cities they have hospitals of their own),
and they show the best qualities of the citizen. He

pointed out the large numbers of illustrious Americans who had French blood in their veins. He ridiculed the opinion according to which the French are not colonizers, and at the risk of being overheard by the German Ambassador, he quoted, as an example of how we make ourselves loved, Alsace-Lorraine. He knew the book of that valiant Miss Kingsley, recently dead,[1] so favourable regarding our action in Western Africa.

According to American customs and parlance his Ministers are his secretaries. " He sees in them men of experience and of sound judgment who are there to instruct him, not to direct him. He visibly wants to be his own Minister."

Either inherited from McKinley or selected by himself, those same Ministers formed a remarkable group of patriotic men, well informed, hard-working, and wise in their counsels. They were or became, most of them, personal friends. He wanted them to be as much as possible representative, not only of his party but to some extent of the nation. He desired to have a Catholic among them and to replace Moody, appointed Charles Joseph Bonaparte, grandson of Jerome former King of Westphalia, and owner of a valuable collection of Bonaparte letters and relics. " I must also have a Jew," he said, and he chose Oscar Strauss of a family famous, not only for its wealth but for its charities; both proved excellent choices.

" He works ceaselessly," I wrote, " for the increase of the strength of his country, so that it may be feared everywhere and have nothing to give up which it is in its interest to possess." Alluding to those augmented forces, he said to me once: " When I think of the future, I can imagine possibilities of war with Germany, with England, with Russia, with Japan; I cannot foresee one with France." [2]

In his brief inauguration speech he insisted especially

[1] November 16, 1904.   [2] January 25, 1905.

on the necessity of being strong, and of course just and generous, but strong because for nations as for individuals justice and generosity, if without strength, are of little avail. Pascal had said the same thing in even more pregnant words. The President expressed his fear lest, with the increase of "industrialism," his country should become less and less interested in military matters.

I saw him on April 4, 1905, as he was leaving for the west in the hope of enjoying a six-weeks or two-months holiday and of having to think less for a while about the Russo-Japanese war, Morocco, Panama, Venezuela, San Domingo, Congress and other sources of trouble. I found him as gay and happy as a schoolboy, rejoicing at the prospect of crossing much country, seeing masses of people, delivering a quantity of speeches and killing a number of wolves. He was taking with him a lot of books, among which the afore-mentioned seven volumes of La Gorce and *La Guerre des Français en Espagne* by Rocca, the second husband of Madame de Staël. He would return having classified the facts in his mind and engraved them in his memory. As regards historical synchronisms he was extraordinary and could have given points to Macaulay himself.

Wolves, bears and books did not make him neglect speech-making. On his return he stopped at Chicago, where there were labour troubles and workmen had asked him to receive them, to which he had assented with alacrity. They complained of his known intention to have recourse to force in case of disturbances. He answered that he most certainly would; that he had nothing against the unions, being even an honorary member of one, but the unions as well as the companies must obey the laws. The next time I saw him, he told me how glad he was to have had such a good opportunity to say what he thought, and that the words attributed to him were those he had used: " I war on plutocrats and Trusts who violate the law, I shall war with as much zest on workmen acting alike. I war on no men as rich or poor, but only as law-breakers."

At one of the parties in the East Room, artistically remodelled by McKim, in his youth one of the most brilliant pupils of our Ecole des Beaux-Arts, I pointed out to the President that something was lacking for the White House to be quite complete. We had always been interested in that building, the earliest plan for which had been drawn by Major L'Enfant; could we not give the finishing touch? The four mantelpieces in the great room were empty; two candelabras on each side, nothing in the middle. I suggested that the busts of some famous Americans, accompanied by Sèvres vases, be placed there. The President heartily welcomed the idea and my Government cabled that the next time I came to France I could go to Sèvres and choose what I pleased.

I proposed to the President Houdon's busts of Washington and Franklin, already in existence at Sèvres. Then there must be a Lincoln; Jefferson must not be omitted; for if it were, what would the democrats say? There was a bust of him, also by Houdon; the whereabouts of the original were not known, but there existed plaster casts. For Lincoln I should have liked Sèvres to use a reduction of the head of the statue by Saint-Gaudens at Chicago; but I had difficulty in securing the necessary permission. I knew, however, of a bust by Volk, a Dutch sculptor, made before Lincoln grew a beard, and I asked Robert Lincoln his opinion of it. He answered that there was no better likeness of his father and that the copy in his possession was at my disposal.

The four busts were made, I chose four pairs of vases to accompany them and a huge case containing them arrived; I asked permission to supervise the unpacking. The Sèvres Manufactory takes pride in its packing, and asserts that you can play football with their parcels without injuring the contents, but, for the unpacking, you must proceed in orderly fashion and follow strictly the instructions on every partition inside the cases. In the packing was found a piece of cardboard on which was written in pencil : " Salut de cœur au Président de la grand République Américaine.—A. B. ouvrier emballeur." [1] I handed it to the President, whom it obviously pleased more than the perfunctory telegrams from royal and imperial hands he receives for his birthday. He wrote me : " I think those busts are beautiful, above all Houdon's Washington, which always seems to me to give Washington's strength as no other bust or picture that I know does. They are the very nicest ornaments for the White House that could be imagined ; and, my dear Mr. Ambassador, such a gift makes me understand why we naturally turn to your country to teach us how to do those things which need in the doing the perfection of good taste."

I replied that I would forward his letter to France, but that it would not be published for fear that mounds of porcelain be sent him from various States.

" This," he said, " cannot be altogether prevented ; an imperial correspondent has already sent me a bronze bust, not, it is true, of Washington, but of himself. I did not presume to keep it for my own use and I have presented it to the Corcoran Gallery."

The same sovereign who, since the Venezuelan clash, had found that American friendship was worth the having and American enmity worth the avoiding, was on the watch for occasions to please, and selected them sometimes cleverly, sometimes less so. He not only multiplied congratulatory telegrams, but printed them, " which gives me the appearance in the eyes of some," said Mr. Roosevelt, " of courting them. For just an inaugural lesson by Mr. Peabody in Berlin, a telegram

---

[1] " Heartfelt salutations to the President of the great American Republic.—A. B., workman packer."

and I must answer it! When Mr. Barrett Wendell
began his remarkable lectures at the Sorbonne, you did
not cable."

Besides another bust of himself, bestowed on the
Museum at Saint-Louis, the same imperial giver offered
to the President a statue, not of Washington either, but
of Frederick II, which greatly puzzled Mr. Roosevelt
and the American Government. What could be done
with it, and what inspiration could be drawn from it
in a Republican State? A long time passed before it
was formally accepted, and the delay caused irritation
at Berlin. Secretary Root, who was peerless in the
unknotting of the knottiest knots, suggested its being
placed in the central yard of the unborn military college,
just sketched on the ground and not yet built. As there
would be other pedestals, other statues not less appropriate for a Republican State were proposed in the
President's entourage, such as Genghis Khan and Tamerlane, worthy Mongols both of them.

At the unsolicited gift, the principal newspapers showed
irritation rather than pleasure; letters were published
denouncing that tyrant, that " butcher," a bad son, a
bad husband, an ungodly man; sarcastic articles were
numerous; shortly before the inauguration which took
place on the 19th of November, 1904, more than two
years after the offer, the *Washington Post* still protested
against the acceptance of the statue of a king who was
no more at one with the heroes of American independence than Tamerlane; and no more sympathized with
the American fight for liberty than George III himself.

On the occasion of the ceremony a special mission
had been sent from Germany; the " Wacht am Rhein "
was played, and the President having risen by mistake,
everybody else rose except the French Ambassador and
his personnel, who remained seated and covered. The
dean of the corps, Count Cassini, remonstrated: " How
did you presume to remain seated when the President

stood up? "—" The President stood because he did not
see that I was seated." Baron Speck Sternburg, who
was an upright man, explained that the musical programme had not been submitted to him; else he would
have had this piece omitted. The answer was: " The
air is not the German national air, at the performing
of which we always rise. If, on the other hand, we
object to the *Watch* it is less on account of the words,
for we do not object to the Germans keeping watch on
the Rhine, than of the spirit of animosity with which
custom has clothed it." The incident left no trace.

VISITORS, JOURNEYS AND MEETINGS

A number of happenings prevented our lives from
being in any way monotonous: journeys to more or less
distant cities, speeches to deliver, Doctors' degrees to
receive (" The French Ambassador is becoming American
by degrees," said Chief Commissioner Macfarland), congresses to attend, visitors of note to entertain; Mrs.
Green the historian, a woman of heart and wit, an Irish
heart and Irish wit, Pastor Wagner, John Morley, who
told us, and has repeated in his memoirs, that the two
things which had struck him most in America were very
much alike, namely Niagara and President Roosevelt.
He also said (November 1904) that the Liberals were
sure to return to office at the next election, that the
Prime Minister, unless his health forbade (and it did),
would be Lord Spencer. As for himself, he would ask
to be Foreign Secretary " so as to be able to declare
war on France if you are not sent Ambassador to London."

Quakers from Philadelphia called one day, real Quakers
who addressed my wife in the words: " Friend, how
doest thou? " which seemed to us touching. Even more
so the remark of the Little Sisters of the Poor, who,
admiring on their first visit the very modest magnificence
of our Embassy, exclaimed: " How beautiful Paradise
will be," which gave us an idea of the poverty of their

own surroundings, and of the gentle and naïve character
of their faith.

I visited, or revisited, a number of cities, attended
many congresses and delivered a quantity of speeches.

Nothing flattered and touched me more than to be
asked, alone of the diplomatic corps, to take part in
meetings where purely American questions were to be
discussed. The Ambassador from France was not considered to be really a foreigner. On those occasions I
always accepted and studied in advance, to the best of
my ability, the subject to be treated, so as not to be
limited to generalities and banalities. I thus spoke on
the reforesting of mountains, the rivalry between railroads and waterways, the merits and demerits of the
sky-scraper (and was in consequence made an honorary
American architect), on the reform of the code of procedure of the State of New York (and was made an
honorary member of the Bar Association), on infantile
mortality and barely escaped being made an honorary
obstetrician. On that occasion a delegation had come
from Baltimore with an invitation. I apologized, pointing out that the subject was really too far removed from
my usual line of studies. They replied, " We shall be
quite frank with you, we are doing a good work, useful
for the country ; if we had your name on our list of speakers
it would advertise it." The argument was decisive and
I accepted.

On the appointed day I went to Baltimore and found
that besides the speech-making, there was an exhibition
showing how to tend new-born children. Before a recess
I saw Cardinal Gibbons standing by a cradle containing
a new-born pasteboard babe. I complimented him on
the good example he was giving, apparently rocking the
cradle. " I did not come here," he said, " for that
purpose, but to give my blessing. I usually retire after
having given it, but having heard that you will speak, I
shall remain and hear what you have to say."

He pronounced the blessing and I was asked to open the series of speeches: I did my best, with the help of Budin and other French celebrities, to show what we were doing to prevent conditions unsatisfactory enough from becoming worse. I spoke also of such good work as the *Consultations Gratuites pour les Mères Nourrices* and the *Repas Gratuits* for the same, any nursing mother receiving a meal free of cost, no questions asked.

My *brother-accoucheurs* who filled the platform granted me the warmest reception, and their dean, the famous Jacobi, threw me kisses.

On the anniversaries of Washington, Lincoln and every fourth of July, I always had a speech to make, sometimes several on the same day, and in the same city, and it was not an easy matter to avoid repetitions.

Knowing that the President would speak at the Congress of Forestry I asked him what his particular line would be. He answered: " I do not know, but Pinchot knows, ask him." Pinchot, Chief Forester of the United States, a former student at the Nancy and Frankfort forestry schools, an enthusiastic admirer of Mr. Roosevelt, and staunch defender, with his bosom friend Garfield, of the preservation of Natural Resources, was present and told me. The President and I spoke on the same day, January 5, 1905; our speeches did not overlap. I laid stress especially on what was being done in France and on how, while in America recourse was still had to the cruel method of burning a forest to clear the ground, we carefully preserved what was left of our trees, those friends of man. We " thought much about to-morrows because we had known so many yesterdays."

The numerous addresses delivered on that occasion were gathered together in a volume, but a few were printed separately, and widely circulated over the country. Mine was one of those happy few, and the consequence was that some took me for a great expert

and, sending an analysis of their soil, asked my advice.
I did better than risk an opinion, and sent such requests
to our School of Forestry in Nancy, whose recommendations received in due time were worth following.

Journeys were made to near or distant places, always
on interesting occasions: Saint-Louis, to inaugurate the
French pavilion, see the International Exhibition, now
complete, and address the French participants; to
Canada, and as we were rolling through a flat banal
country, suddenly a trifling sight gave us a thrill: a
sign-post on which were the words: "Traverse du
Chemin de Fer"—France again! The ever-expanding
city of Montreal was visited; also Quebec, whose glorious,
tragic events were described to us on the spot by Judge
Routier, a Canadian writer of note, speaking so vividly
and knowingly that it seemed the fight was of to-day
and we were witnessing it. We saw the tomb of Montcalm, on which the noblest inscription was placed by
Lord Aylmer, then Governor of Canada: "Honneur
à Montcalm; le Destin en le privant de la victoire,
l'a récompensé par une mort glorieuse."[1] A noble inscription indeed, with its conception of that death which
is a reward; an honour to Montcalm and a credit to
Lord Aylmer.

A visit also to Charlottesville, Monticello, the tomb
of Jefferson and the University of Virginia, on the invitation of the same President Alderman, the most per-
suasive of men, previously met at Tulane, and who, no
less eloquent a writer than a speaker, had sent me a
letter saying that the very walls of the University bore
witness to the merits of France, the merits of her hands,
the quality of her thoughts, her brotherly generosity.
"The France of Lafayette has not altered; she has
lived."

Led to West Point by Secretary Taft, I was asked to

[1] "Honour to Montcalm; Destiny in depriving him of victory,
recompensed him by a glorious death."

review the cadets in their becoming old-time uniforms
and to see them the next day receive their commissions,
after addresses by Mr. Taft, General Chaffee and myself.
I wrote to my Government: "I brought back from
this brief visit a most favourable impression. The fine
bearing of those young men, their modest and yet reso-
lute air, the fact that they belong to a *milieu* in which
money is not of primary importance and in which people
deem there is something better to do in life than merely
to get rich, the marks of sympathy they gave to our
country, all that I could observe, contributed to leave
with me a delightful remembrance of the occasion." [1]

I went again to Chicago in December 1905, and delivered the University convocation address, taking for
my subject "Some Maxims of Life," and I saw then
for the last time President Harper, who, afflicted with
an inexorable disease, knowing full well that there was
no escape, remained the same as in his happier days, as
brave, as smiling, his mind busy thinking of others, of
his University, of what was going on in the world, not
of his own fate. In his misery, almost unable to move,
he offered a grand, a memorable sight, there is no other
word.

On March 23, 1906, a memorial ceremony, in most
imposing style, was held at Annapolis for John Paul
Jones, whose remains, recovered by General Porter, then
Ambassador to France, had been sent on an American
battleship to the United States. The search for his body
had been a terrible task; he had been laid in the Protestant
cemetery, a narrow one, with coffins piled on top of one
another, long disused, with houses built over it, Rue de
la Grange aux Belles, on the outskirts of Paris. The
French engineer entrusted with the work told me of
its extreme difficulty, tunnels having to be dug under
the buildings, coffin after coffin to be examined, pesti-
lential exhalations causing the search to be most un-

[1] June 15, 1905.

wholesome. One coffin was at last found, the dimensions of which tallied with those of the sailor's body. There was no inscription; no one, therefore, could be sure that those were *not* his remains. The lid having been scraped, one word, however, appeared, the word ".' Anglois," which was not surprising, many English people having been buried in this Protestant cemetery. In his zeal to get rid of an uncongenial task, the engineer would not accept this explanation, but suggested that if the complete inscription were visible it would read: "John Paul Jones, terreur des Anglois." General Porter, however, remained adamant; work had to be continued until another coffin was found, with no inscription either, but the contents of which seemed really to be what had long been sought.

After having died in such poverty and so neglected that the commissioner of his district in Paris had had to pay for his burial, John Paul Jones had now the honours of a triumph. Nothing was too good or too expensive; a squadron under command of Admiral Campion was sent by France. In the largest hall of the Naval Academy French and American sailors mounted guard around the coffin, on which had been placed the gold-hilted sword presented to Paul Jones by King Louis XVI. President Roosevelt delivered the principal oration, warm in his eulogy of the country which had given the dead hero the means of winning his battles and which had herself produced such sailors as Tourville, Duquesne and Suffren, " second to no sailor in any navy." Their history was familiar to the President, for they were men after his own heart. " You have read a good deal," he once told me, " but on that chapter I could give you points."

He did not miss such a favourable opportunity for insisting on the necessity of his country's possessing a strong navy, with officers determined, whatever the event, never to surrender. " It is well for every American

officer to remember that, while a surrender may or may
not be defensible, the man who refuses to surrender
need never make a defence. The one fact must always
be explained, the other needs no explanation. Moreover, he who would win glory or honour for the nation
and for himself must not too closely count the odds."

Other addresses were delivered by General Porter,
deeply moved and with tears in his eyes, Governor
Warfield of Maryland, who claimed so much for his
State that we were wondering what in the meantime the
twelve others had been doing, by the Secretary of the
Navy and myself.

Another ceremony, also inspired by a sentiment uniting
the navies of the two countries, took place three days
later on the campus of Saint John's College, Annapolis.
It has been wondered, since the Great War, who first
had the idea of raising a monument to the unknown
soldier, whether French, English or others; the first idea
was in fact American, and long preceded that war.
Some unknown French soldiers and sailors, who had
lost their lives during the War of Independence, had been
buried in what is now the college campus. It occurred
to the Society of the Sons of the Revolution that, while
all the leaders had their monuments, of these plain
soldiers who had nothing to offer but their lives, and
who had offered and lost them, there was no reminder,
and they decided to erect a monument to them. The
presence of a French squadron made the occasion particularly auspicious. At the laying of the corner-stone
the Governor of Maryland and Admiral Campion were
the chief speakers; the monument, a beautiful one, was
erected some years later, unveiled by my military attaché,
Captain de Chambrun, a descendant of Lafayette, and
Miss De Grasse Fowler, a descendant of Admiral De
Grasse. The chief address was delivered by Mr. Taft,
then President of the United States. The memorial
consists of a huge block of granite on the face of which

a bronze bas-relief represents, passing as in a dream, the French Army of former days; in the foreground a figure of Memory lays the palms of remembrance on two small tombs, of the style usual for plain soldiers, on which are engraved the words: "Ci-gît un soldat de France— Ci-gît un marin de France."

On the 6th of June, 1606, had been born at Rouen the famous dramatist Pierre Corneille. All over France his three hundredth anniversary was being celebrated. Yale University decided to take part and asked us to be present. Received by Mr. Farnam, we could once more appreciate the charm of American hospitality. Led by our host we visited the well-appointed lecture halls, dormitories and museums of the vast place, built of excellent material, in Old English style. We met President Hadley, also Professor Sanderson who had arranged the celebration, which consisted mainly (after, of course, speeches by him and by me) in an abbreviated performance of the *Cid* by College students. Given the extreme difficulty for them of playing such a play in a foreign tongue the result was remarkable; they had been rehearsing every day for weeks; the prompter had almost nothing to do. The Don Diègue (young W. E. Mac-Come) was excellent; all were creditable; the heroine, Chimène, was a tall young man, evidently trying to imitate Sarah Bernhardt. Alas, when, with gesticulations in the heroical style, he demanded the head of Rodrigue, the clasp on his shoulder broke and there, in full view of the audience, was bared the well-muscled back of a baseball player. The audience roared. "Such," said a student sitting next me, "is our sad fate; the utmost we aspire to when we play a tragedy is to give no occasion for laughter; but to-day, as usual, we have had the laughter."

Extracts from Massenet's music for the *Cid* were, after that, very pleasantly rendered on the piano by a student.

Of all these visits, and there were many more, the

most important, and worthiest for us of lasting remembrance, was one to Philadelphia on the anniversary of Franklin's birth. Two years before, a joint resolution voted by Congress had decided that a single gold medal should be struck for the occasion and presented, in token of gratitude, to France who had taken to her heart the philosopher when he came asking help for a struggling new-born State, not yet recognized by any nation.

The order was given to the most famous sculptor America had produced, Saint-Gaudens, and his brother the medallist. A first attempt was not very satisfactory; a wreath of foliage had been placed upon the sage's brow with strange effect. It looked like an old woman's cap. Secretary Root, in charge of the work, asked me what I thought of it; I replied: " This does not seem a bad likeness of Madame de Maintenon." The wreath was removed and the medal appeared what it really was, as good a moral and physical portrait of Franklin as Houdon's bust, by which it was obviously inspired.

An assembly, in which abounded illustrious men and elegant women, filled, on the 20th of April, 1906, the Philadelphia auditorium to the roof; we on the stage had before us thousands of brilliant, happy faces, smiling a welcome to each of the orators, selected for the purpose by the President; Mr. Root, then Secretary of State, made the presentation of the medal, and to show that he was addressing France, faced her Ambassador and not the audience: his was the most eloquent and touching five-minutes speech I ever heard, each word pregnant with meaning, warm with the same sentiments that had animated the ancestors, of the men and women now listening, continuity being thus evidenced. " The medal," he said, " is American gold, as was Franklin." In itself it is not much; " it is not appreciable even as a gift when one sees in historical perspective the great share of France in securing American independence,

U

looming always larger from our own point of view, in comparison with what we did for ourselves.

" But take it for your country as a token that with all the changing manners of the passing years, with all the vast and welcome influx of new citizens from all the countries of the earth, Americans have not forgotten their fathers and their fathers' friends.

" Know by it that we have in America a sentiment for France; and a sentiment enduring among a people is a great and substantial fact to be reckoned with."

I clasped the Secretary's hand and said to him: " What a wonderful address! " He replied: " I spoke what should be spoken, and it is time it were said."

Eleven years later, Mr. Root and I meeting in Washington, he said to me: " Do you remember what I said in Philadelphia of a sentiment enduring among the American people being a fact when reckoned with? Now we see it in action." America had entered the war.

In replying to the presentation address, I expressed the thought that I would have " two golden gifts to forward to my Government, the medal and the speech of Mr. Root, one of those rare men who prove the right man whatever be the place." And as I was speaking, I was struck by the thought that while we were together, happy and smiling in a pleasant atmosphere of friendship, on the other side of the continent San Francisco was burning. Having recalled what medals had been struck in France at each forward step in the War of Independence, beginning with the relief of Boston in 1776, I added: " My earnest hope is that one of the next medals to be struck at our Mint and added to the series, will be one to commemorate the resurrection of that great town which now, at this present hour, agonizes by the shores of the Pacific. The disaster of San Francisco has awakened a feeling of deepest grief in every

French heart, and a feeling of admiration, too, for the manliness displayed by the population during this awful trial."

The audience was deeply moved, and though this address could not compare with that of the Secretary, the earnestness with which it had been delivered won the speaker much applause and approbation. The great Shakespearian scholar H. H. Furness, who had himself given a noteworthy oration on Franklin earlier in the day, wrote: "After the first three or four sentences you took the audience captive; you must have felt how entirely you held them in your hand. Your happy phrases and attractive accent completed the charm.

"Pray remember that I am merely reporting what was said to me on all sides; for my confounded deafness (I always have to use a bad adjective when mentioning it) kept me from hearing a single word."

There was a banquet, with many other speeches; one by Senator Lodge whom the President had chosen to represent him and who made one of those bitter-sweet addresses in which he excelled. Being nothing if not a Massachusetter, he remarked that the selection of himself was not inappropriate, "for if we trust history and believe what we read in books, after all, Franklin was born in Boston, Mass."

The chairman, Dr. Weir Mitchell, well known as a neurologist, a novelist and a poet, a Philadelphian to the core, was equal to the occasion and rising to his feet said: "No, Sir, he was not, he was born in Philadelphia —at the age of seventeen."

Reports received shortly after from our military attaché, Captain Fournier, and from M. Thouroude, an agent of the French S.S. Line, the *Chargeurs Réunis*, who, returning from Yokohama, happened to be in San Francisco at the time of the earthquake, had confirmed my first impressions as to the behaviour of the population. In a letter to my Government on the different forecasts of

experts, or so-called experts, concerning the future of
the United States, I paralleled the qualities of the inhabitants, the resources of their soil, the advantages of
their geographical position, the absence of any powerful
and hostile neighbour, and on the other hand their
defects, their temptations, their social problems, that
mosaic of all sorts of races, already in the country, like
the negroes, or brought by an ever-increasing immigration taken, not wisely, as a compliment. Which will
prevail, Ormazd or Ahriman?

" To form an opinion as to the future of the country,"
I wrote, " a most important element of appreciation is
supplied by any violent cataclysm that may cause those
weak ramparts, the habits of life, the police and administrative barriers, to crumble, allowing the population to
appear, as it were, in the state of nature, left to itself,
following at will its good or bad instincts, so that it
becomes possible to ascertain by actual experience whether
the good or the evil predominates.

" Such an experience, extremely telling, has just taken
place at San Francisco. Here is a great city, with a
mixed population, a great merchant-city, a great sea-
port, with much wealth and much poverty, the inhabitants of which suddenly find themselves, one morning,
without any premonition, reduced all of them to a similar
state of complete destitution. Police is no more, the
number of troops is insignificant. Left to itself, this
population, made up of rich people little accustomed to
help themselves and poor ones whom great temptations
might incline to plunder, could not fail to show what
was its mettle: what would be the outcome of such a
crisis, order or disorder?

" The experience was wholly favourable to the United
States. Disorders, cases of plundering or banditry were,
given the circumstances, remarkably rare. The population resumed its equilibrium, organized itself in comparative calm, even good-humouredly. It showed that

what predominated in it was the civic instinct, a longing for well-ordered lives." [1]

I had spoken at Philadelphia without instructions. My Government took me at my word, ordered the medal from Bottée, one of our best medallists, and a former "Prix de Rome," who, understanding the beauty of the occasion, worked at it with a passionate desire to surpass himself. When it was ready, instead of sending it, my wife and I, as will be seen, took it to San Francisco.

Pastor Wagner, of "simple life" fame, an Alsatian, lunches at the Embassy, a tall, well-built man, with a ruddy face and almost white hair and moustache. He delivers in the afternoon a lecture on his favourite subject, at the Lafayette theatre, being presented to the audience by the President, a very rare honour, and he speaks in the evening at the White House before Mr. Roosevelt, his family, his Cabinet Ministers and some intimate friends, among whom we were. His subject was "Unknown France," the France that works, the France or the *braves gens*. He spoke extremely well and his address, in French, had great effect on those (not the majority) who could understand. He has very just reproofs for those who cannot bear contradiction and who are therefore "lost for truth." He has also an appropriate word for those who, visiting a country, choose to see only what may be shocking or repugnant and have no look but for the "rubbish box." Such travellers have not, however, ceased to travel.

At a dinner at the Embassy, March 5, 1905, Baron Mayor des Planches, Italian Ambassador, speaks of the first visit to Berlin in March 1899, of King Humbert, accompanied by Crispi, who had with him Mayor as secretary. A banquet was offered by the Reichstag to Crispi, while the King was dining at the Palace.

[1] June 10, 1906.

As he was starting for the banquet a coded telegram arrived signed Menabrea, Italian Ambassador in France. Mayor asked his chief not to wait; he would take to him the uncoded text with all speed.

The telegram told of a rumour according to which King Humbert would return by way of Strasbourg and of the very bad effect produced in Paris.

Mayor knew that, according to the original plan, the return was to be by way of Baden. He therefore took upon himself to reply to Menabrea that he should deny this report, and considering the occurrence as grave, he telegraphed to the same effect to all Italian Envoys in Europe, signing all those despatches: Crispi.

He reached the dining-hall half an hour late and was reprimanded for his delay. He showed the Menabrea telegram to Crispi, who did not stir, then his own, and Crispi remained apparently unmoved.

Both learned later that the idea was one of the Emperor's own; he had not mentioned it even to Bismarck, who, when he learned of it, showed great irritation and said: " This would have been a provocation." The Emperor had planned a grandiose entry into Strasbourg and had given orders for trees to be taken from the Black Forest to form a sort of triumphal avenue leading to the Palace. Those preparations had apparently caused word of the project to get about and it was given up.

Did William II come to know of the part played then by Mayor des Planches? Certain it is that when Mayor was later appointed Councillor of Embassy at Berlin, the Kaiser refused to receive him, which was without example for a diplomat of that rank. What a great man you are! his comrades at the " Consulta " said to him.

M. Bunau Varilla of Panama and Quellenec of Suez, both members of the Commission instituted by President Roosevelt to discuss the best way of building the Panama Canal, dined with us, tête-à-tête at the Embassy in November 1905. They had brought their blue prints, and after dinner gave us a captivating account of what they considered the most practical plan. If the Americans are in a hurry, and they are of course in a hurry, a lock canal should be built which will take some fifteen years, unless, as time passes, better machinery is devised; but built in such a way that work may constantly go on to reach the definitive goal, which should be a sea-level canal. This would take a long time, but nations do not die, and the work can be continued for any number of years, the number being increased or diminished according to the amount of money available.

The President decided for a lock canal, and discarded the system which would eventually have transformed it into the Straits of Panama. Machinery having improved from year to year, and the work having been ultimately put into the hands of Colonel Goethals, the wise and firm autocrat of the Canal, before nine years had passed the new waterway was at the disposal of international shipping. I had several talks with the colonel, and always found him full of praise for the work done by the French, and for their methods. When any surveying had been done by them, he found it was needless to verify, the work had been well done and the calculations were sure to be absolutely accurate. He confirmed to me the story I had heard about the French dredge abandoned in the jungle; such machinery considered as being " of course " inadequate had been usually thrown into the excavations dug for foundations, and filled in with cement so as to form reinforced concrete. Out of curiosity, that one was repaired, the wooden parts which had become rotten were replaced, the machinery was oiled and, to the astonishment of all, the dredge began to work as if nothing had happened. A hunt was instituted in order to recover as many such as possible and the result was the same. " The houses in corrugated iron, we received from the French," he said, " are in better condition now

(1908) than those we have recently built. Graft, about which so much has been said, must have been inconsiderable, given the importance of the work done."

Representative Mann told me that before going to Panama he thought the United States had never made a worse bargain; he now considers that they have never made a more advantageous one.

A visit from the famous railroad pioneer of the West, J. J. Hill (December 9, 1906), ardent, lively, expressing in a gentle voice peremptory propositions, with a multiplicity of figures to back them. He does not believe in the development of American trade in the Pacific. The Philippines are, he thinks, of small commercial value. The President is, in his eyes, generous, warm-hearted, but too impulsive, and sometimes reaching too quickly decisions of grave import.

Referring to the terrible death in his private car of Mr. Spencer, Director of the Southern Railway, he spoke of the quantity of accidents. "Yes," said he, "they are awful, and their number will grow, there is no doubt as to that. The transporting power of the railroads increases 7 per cent. while the goods they have to carry increase 100 per cent. The Block system exists only in theory; it is not observed. Freight trains follow each other, happy-go-lucky, the engineer keeping his eye on the light of the train ahead of him. No sufficient remedy has been found."

He added that since September he had been four times from Saint Paul to New York. Accustomed as he and his people are to such trips, he never fails to wire to his wife that he has arrived, so that she may be certain there has been no mishap.

I suggested that as usual in human affairs, when they went too far to the wrong, an improvement was sure somehow to occur. My father had told me that in his youth, when one took the stage coach to go from Lyons to Paris, it was a customary precaution to draw up one's will. This precaution is no longer customary.

THE RUSSO-JAPANESE WAR. THE JAPANESE QUESTION

At the extreme end of the Asiatic continent, Corea, the Hermit Kingdom, self-centred, self-satisfied, resolved to preserve as far as possible its isolation from the rest of the world, and to shape alone, for better or worse, its own destinies; and next to it Manchuria, one of the outer provinces of the huge unwieldy Chinese Empire, a province rich in fertile lands, mines and natural resources, the cradle of the last Chinese dynasty, whose emperors had been on the throne for three hundred years.

As neighbours, they had, on land, Russia, and on the other side of the narrow sea, Japan. Between these empires a keen rivalry had been growing up for years, each striving for the mastery of those other two countries which did not belong to either of them. Negotiations had taken place, promises had been made, so as to avoid a clash, the ultimate results of which it was impossible to foresee. The Russians, who had sent troops to Manchuria, had promised to evacuate it by the 8th of October, 1903, but they had not evacuated.

Secretive and smiling, avoiding high talk, negotiating leisurely, the Japanese had in the meantime brought their army and navy to a maximum of efficiency. Some ominous remarks had occasionally escaped them, as when they had told our officers at the time of the relief of the Legations at Pekin, that they had defeated China in their previous war and must defeat a European country in the next, so as to show what they were worth.

Deeming now that the moment was propitious and that their forces were well in hand, fortified by their agreement of 1902 with England, which recognized their special interests in Corea, they moved forth with decision and promptitude; no delay, no hesitation in their plans. On the 4th of February, 1904, they broke relations with

Russia; on the 8th they fired the first shot of the war, sinking some ill-guarded Russian ships in Port Arthur.

Before the break had occurred, when it merely seemed a possibility and the Tsar inclined to avoid it, William II had not concealed his indignation at such pusillanimity: Nicholas should go to war, push it to the extreme, be uninfluenced by early reverses; " by his weakness the Tsar endangered the monarchical principle; " if the Russians continued to withdraw before the Japanese, within twenty years the yellow race would be established in Moscow and Posen." [1] He proposed to the Tsar, later in the year, an agreement " to put an end to the arrogancy of England and Japan," but as France was to be left out of it, Nicholas II, in his honesty, refused. Nothing dismayed, the Emperor wrote to Bülow: " We must cultivate the more our relations with America and Japan." [2] Japan's arrogancy was no longer a deterrent.

Obliged to fight on the defensive at the farthest bounds of their immense Empire, connected with their base only by a single-track, inadequate railway, the Russians showed their usual magnificent bravery. But led by generals of very unequal merit, trammelled by the incoherence, to say the least, of their administrative services, although they won a few partial successes, and were more than once within grasp of a sweeping victory, it all ended in defeat; defeat on land, defeat on sea, losing the battle of the Yalu in May 1904, of Telissu in June, of Liaoyang in August. The following year, between January and May, Port Arthur surrendered, the Russians were definitively beaten at Mukden and their fleet destroyed at Tsushima.

Neglecting nothing in order to show their superiority even in details, the Russians having notified in the first

---

[1] 4th and 8th of January, 14th February, 1904. *Correspondance Secrète de Bülow et de Guillaume II*, pp. 28, 32, 35.

[2] October 29, 1904, *Correspondance Secrète de Bülow et de Guillaume II*, pp. 72, 87.

month of the war that, owing to circumstances, they would not take part in the Saint-Louis Exhibition, the Japanese asked that the ground thus vacated be added to their section.

During all this time American public opinion was enthusiastically favourable to Japan. Each of the ethnic groups which had reason to complain of Russia fanned this sentiment, Poles, Jews, Finns, as well as the Scandinavians, friends of the Finns. The successes of the Japanese, their care, their method, their spirit excited admiration; from the man in the Senate to the man in the street, the feeling was the same; some clergymen preached from their pulpits against Russia. At a Presbyterian meeting a resolution was passed in favour of Japan, whose predominance would be more favourable for the diffusion of the Gospel, Russia being but nominally Christian.

At a meeting of the Asiatic Society in which the Assistant-Secretary of State took part, an address to the Mikado was voted, expressing the hope that the efforts of His Majesty would have a decisive influence for the regeneration of Asia, as it had had for the regeneration of his own country.

According to several of the most influential newspapers, Russia represented barbarism, and Japan civilization. Secretary Hay told me in June that Gordon Bennett now and then caused the insertion in his own paper, the *New York Herald*, of a note favourable to Russia, which he cabled from Paris, influenced as he was by his pro-Russian surroundings, but that the next day this same paper would resume its anti-Russian campaign.

Dining at the Embassy, Senator Lodge spoke of the ardent propaganda of the anti-Russian ethnic groups and expressed the darkest misgivings as to the future of Russia, with her class wars, " The more dangerous that they were not now apparent on the surface."

Insufficiently informed by his Government, the Russian

Ambassador Cassini was in a difficult position to react, given especially that the President detested to have to do with an Ambassador left ill-informed. He considered it a poor compliment to himself. The high deeds of the Japanese filled Mr. Roosevelt with admiration, and as a former Assistant-Secretary of the Navy, he was indignant at the clumsiness of the Russians, who, neglecting to be on their guard, had had at the very outset several of their ships sunk at Port Arthur. " It is all right to say that the Japanese note was not a real declaration of war : that is a matter for diplomats to argue about. But in such tense moments a fleet with anyone at its head who is not a fool, knows how to guard itself. How can the Russians have allowed the Japanese torpedo ships to come so near? Did they take them for their own? Then they did not know where their own were. Long before we came to blows with Spain our coasts were under constant surveillance." [1]

Secretary Hay, who had early proposed to me that our two countries should offer their good offices, was from the first in favour of peace: " Such a war cannot profit anyone. There have rarely been cases where such a result was so evident. If it is for a market that they are fighting, what will be the state of that market when they have finished? "[2]

As I was leaving for my usual visit to France, the President told me that " he did not think anything could be done before I returned, to bring about the cessation of those deplorable hostilities, but that he would be quite ready then to act in agreement with us if there was the slightest chance to usefully intervene " (June 20).

I found him, on my return in October, as severe as before on the Russian leaders, but with his admiration for the Japanese perceptibly toned down by the consideration of what too sweeping a victory by them might entail to

[1] Conversation of February 15, 1904.
[2] Conversation of June 9, 1904.

the detriment of other Powers. " From my point of view," he said, " the best would be that the Russians and the Japanese should remain face to face, balancing each other, both weakened. And such is the most prob-　able result." He added : " France is one of the Powers who have least reason to feel anxious about Japan. Your navy is too strong for the Japanese to be able to hurt you ; you would too easily remain masters of the sea."

In a later conversation he said : " We shall have to considerably increase our navy." [1]

As the war developed he was confirmed in these dispositions. During the following winter he spoke to me several times of the advisability of a prompt peace. He recommended the Japanese to think of it and to consider moderate terms ; the Russians ought also to think of peace ; if they should lose Mukden (which they did in March), their enemy would be more exacting. I pointed out that the Press, which was for peace, was ill advised in using an abusive tone toward Russia : this made it more difficult for her to yield. [2] On May 15 the President spoke again on the same subject and of his efforts with the Japanese. " Would you perhaps," he said, " try something with the Russians ? The difficulty is, of course, increased by the fact that the belligerent whom one addresses is at once prone to infer that his enemy must be exhausted, has perhaps suggested the *démarche* and that it is therefore not the time to yield."

He reverted to this later with more insistence, and I cabled to M. Delcassé : " Mr. Roosevelt is aware of the great credit you enjoy at the Russian court and would be glad if you would ask our Ambassador in Russia to speak also to the Tsar in favour of peace. He attaches much importance to your intervention " (June 6, 1905).

The British were for an immediate peace and Lord Lansdowne had made it known to the President. Return-

---

[1] Conversation of October 17, 1904.
[2] Conversations of February 17 and 19, 1905.

ing from London the British Ambassador, Sir Mortimer Durand, told me (June 9) that his Government had not been consulted by Japan and was afraid the victors would propose hard conditions, but was desirous this should not be. "A peace," he said, "which would push west-ward the immense bulk and weight of the Russian people would be deplorable for us. Instead of finding the Russians weaker than we expected, we found them stronger. We would never have believed that they could have maintained so long, and so far, forces of such magnitude. We are considering an improvement of our defences in the Afghan region."

The Kaiser, who had been still encouraging the Tsar, in March, to carry on the war to a finish, now, doubtless fearing troubles in Russia and the bad effect a shaky throne would have on " the monarchical principle," was in favour of peace and of the chief rôle being played by Mr. Roosevelt as having the best chance of succeeding.

Early on the morning of June 8th, a telephonic message came to the Embassy from the White House. Mr. Roosevelt wanted to see me at once. As I entered he said: " I have not Mr. Hay by me " (very ill, he died shortly after); " you must give me your opinion, which will replace his for me. A proposal for peace, forwarded through Cassini, has failed, but one through Meyer " (American Ambassador at St. Petersburg) " has succeeded. The Tsar is consenting. I must send now an official appeal to both Russia and Japan. Here is my cable, read it, and see whether you have any suggestions to make."

I proposed a few changes, meant to better safeguard the susceptibilities of Russia. They were accepted and the cable was sent. During the brief interval between the cessation of Mr. Hay's functions and the assuming of them by Mr. Root, the President continued to use me as a friendly adviser *amicus curiæ*, calling me John Hay. Some time afterwards, as he was discussing confidential matters with a Senator, he thought he noticed a little surprise on his visitor's face at the presence, among a few intimate friends, of the French Ambassador. "Never mind," said the President, "he has taken the oath of Secretary of State."

The Japanese minister, Takahira, asked Mr. Roosevelt whether he thought that, owing to our Russian alliance, I would object to his coming to see me. I said: certainly not, saw him a number of times and ever found him sensible and trustworthy, the burden of my talks being: Do not try to impose conditions impossible to condone or to forget; if they are harder than war, the Russians will, of course, prefer war and you will arouse against you the whole nation, part of which has remained up to now dormant. Do not make a peace barring all possibility of friendship in the future with your present enemy."

In one of those talks, Mr. Takahira said with much insistence: "My country's sentiments toward yours are quite friendly. The delicate situation resulting from your alliance with Russia is well understood. Japan has no ambition whatsoever from which you can take umbrage; it is very different as regards Russia, with whom a conflict had, for a long time, been unavoidable. None can be conceived between France and Japan."

I cabled to my Government: "Mr. Roosevelt is only too well aware of the difficulties of his undertaking and he will do his best not to wound Russian susceptibilities. But he finds no less acute ones on the Japanese side and he has much to do to attain a result, given that at every step, each of the belligerents wants the other to speak first, and makes it a point of honour to be more exacting about minutiæ that seem indeed scarcely perceptible when compared with the realities at stake, foremost among which thousands of human lives to be saved." [1]

After difficult negotiations, more than once near a rupture, Russia and Japan accepted the suggestion of the

[1] June 16, 1905.

President, who, desirous not to be mixed up in it more than was strictly necessary, proposed as a place of meeting for the delegates some spot between Mukden and Kharbin; failing which, the Hague. The Russians proposed Paris, that the Japanese discarded as well as London; they insisted on Washington, or, if the summer climate made this city too uncomfortable, another American one, more to the north, which was agreed to.

From France, where I went for a while in the course of the summer, the conversation continued by cable with Mr. Roosevelt. He strongly insisted on my Government's seconding his efforts at St. Petersburg for peace, which was done and for which he thanked us. The Kaiser, now all for peace, was active in the same direction.

We had some days of complete rest at Saint-Haon. In a long letter to the President about the war, Morocco and other thorny questions, I said: " Where I write peace is profound; the rumours of the world do not reach so far; our peasants till their fields, easily contented, using ploughs which would make Chicago shudder and even the Egyptian Pharaohs laugh. They don't complain, they sing their usual songs and manage to rear their families; one of seven or eight is growing on my little strip of land. From the open window I hear one of my sisters teaching a young nephew orthography and hinting that the proper spelling for toad in French is not *crapeau*."

Meanwhile no such pastoral rest for the poor President. On August 21 he wrote me: " I have just sent you a cable about the peace matters. Dealing with senators is at times excellent training for the temper; but upon my word, dealing with these peace envoys has been an even tougher job. To be polite and sympathetic and patient in explaining for the hundredth time something perfectly obvious, when what I really want to do is to give utterance to whoops of rage and jump up and knock their heads together—well, all I can hope is that the self-repression will be ultimately helpful for my character.

AT PEACE IN ST. HAON. AUGUST, 1905

face p. 304

When they drive me too nearly mad, I take refuge in Maspero and study the treaty between Ramses II and the Hittites, comparing it with Ramses' preposterous boastings over his previous victories, and feel that after all we are not so far behind the people who lived a few thousand years ago as I am sometimes tempted to think."

Controlling himself, showing as much dexterity as forcefulness, the President succeeded and a peace, which has been observed ever since, and owing to which Russia and Japan were able to fight on the same side in the Great War, was signed at Portsmouth, New Hampshire, on September 5, 1905.

The most striking testimony as to the part played in it by Mr. Roosevelt came from a Russian of rare experience in international matters, Professor de Martens, who had been a member of the Russian delegation at Portsmouth, his words showing how meritoriously and completely the President had been able to check his temper during the conference: " We Russians had come to Portsmouth without taking anything that he had said seriously, and yet when we left the United States it was with the knowledge that, all through our stay there, we had been brought into close proximity with one of the most powerful personalities now alive in the whole world. . . . The man who had been represented to us as impetuous to the point of rudeness, displayed a gentleness, a kindness, a tactfulness mixed with self-control, that only a truly great man can command." [1]

Though decidedly swerving from Washington's recommendations in his celebrated " Farewell address," best fitted maybe for his times than for later ones, this American intervention in the world's affairs shed a new lustre on America herself and her President. Both belligerents expressed their gratitude, the world applauded and the Nobel prize was awarded to Mr. Roosevelt.

[1] An article by him in the *Outlook*. Bishop, *Roosevelt and His Time*, I, 422.

x

Unwilling to apply the money to his own use, he had at first decided to make the workmen employed on the Panama Canal benefit by it. One of his cherished ideas, and one which cannot be too much followed, was to help every category of people to lead a life which, although circumstances might cause it to be more or less hard, should nevertheless be enjoyable. To this intent he once appointed a commission to study the means of making the farmer's life more attractive: the best of all ways to prevent the overcrowding of cities. Now he proposed that his Nobel prize should go to make more pleasant, hygienic and comfortable the life of those men of various colours and nationalities fulfilling, in a depressing climate, a difficult task, important for the whole world.

The little group of his intimate friends warmly approved of his plans. Other suggestions were, however, made and prevailed; they looked more grandiose, but were not of easy realization; for years the money remained stagnant and was finally applied to the relief of the victims of the Great War.

After a few days in London where we had found Count Benckendorff sadder than ever at the lack of forcefulness of the autocrat of all the Russias and at the damageable influence of the reigning Empress with her "pedantic imperialism," having had a charming time with John Morley, greatly admiring his library and taking note, as I wrote to the President, himself very keen about such matters, of "several good points in view of our own definitive house, which we shall never build, but which we improve constantly in our minds," we returned to the United States and found on alighting at Washington (September 30, 1905) that we had travelled from New York on the same train as Mr. Roosevelt. He cheerily welcomed us, an ovation was given him by the crowd, he asked us to dine the next day at the White House and he left us, saying: "I must now go to my carriage, where there are already my wife, three children, three dogs and a cat."

The dinner was a merry family party where the latest events and many other topics were discussed : the Russo-Japanese peace, the rôle of the chief Russian delegate Witte, " who had proved useful because peace was in the interest of Witte," Venezuela, Carnegie, Morley, Maspero's Ancient History (warmly praised), the embarrassment of Baron Rosen, the new Russian Ambassador, when he came to say that the Tsar wanted to take " the initiative " of a second Hague Peace Conference, to which the President had courteously assented, choosing to forget his own " initiative " of the previous year, the question of Constantinople and of the Bulgarian ambitions, the Kaiser's fitful politics. " There were moments," the President said in his cheery way, " when I would have given a month's salary to have you with me for one hour."—His spendthrift propensities, I thought.

His telegram to the Tsar, he explained, had been forwarded through Ambassador Meyer, both using a very simple code easily deciphered by the Russians, to which there was no objection. But one day a ludicrous incident happened : in a conversation with the Ambassador, the Tsar answered a paragraph which had not been forwarded to him.

Concerning the German Kaiser the President's sentiments were the same as before. One fault, an irredeemable one, marred such good qualities as he possessed : " He is not to be trusted." I spoke of his unattainable desire to have us side with him, in other words to have us accept his hegemony, which could not be. " You are quite right," Mr. Roosevelt answered, " no oath could restrain him if he found it in his interest to violate it."

I said that his periodical outbursts were enough to keep us on our guard, as when, inaugurating a new bridge at Mainz, he had declared : " I hope to cross this bridge one day at the head of my brave army, leading it against France." By order, the papers had not reported these words, but I knew of them from a witness.

The President continued the most courteous exchange
of polite compliments with the Kaiser, but always kept
his eyes open, ever fearing some new flash of that omnivorous ambition which had been so near having the
gravest consequences at Manilla and in Venezuela. He
now suspected unholy views of the Kaiser's concerning
Holland, and recently published documents have shown
that all was not vain in that suspicion. "If the Germans
did anything to Holland or tried to capture Saint-Thomas
from the Danes," he told me, "I would occupy the
Dutch colonies and would get to Saint-Thomas before
them." [1]

The change I had noticed some time before in the
President's views concerning Japan had gradually increased and had spread by degrees throughout the
country itself. Admiration was now qualified by misgivings as to what the Japanese might be tempted to do
next. The restrictions put on them in California and all
along the Pacific Coast galled their increasing pride.
The questions of the prohibited future immigration and
of separate schools for Japanese children seemed inextric-
able. The West showed no disposition to yield, nor did
the Japanese. The President sent Mr. Metcalf, one of
his Cabinet Ministers, to the coast, to investigate. Admiral
Dewey said to me: "The President has serious motives
for doing so. The Japanese are working with extreme
activity at their fleet, trying to put it in condition immediately, as if a break might happen to-morrow."

Questioned by Mr. Roosevelt, the Admiral had answered
that "in ninety days the United States could have fifteen
battleships in the Pacific. Japan could, in the meantime,
capture the Philippines, Honolulu, and be master of the
sea. But," said the Admiral, "then our turn would
come."

He thought that, in any event, the States would have to
keep some battleships permanently on the Pacific coast

[1] Conversation of December 14, 1906.

and have there a fleet somewhat stronger than that of Japan and, on the Atlantic, one somewhat stronger than that of Germany.[1]

The President was to extricate himself by adhering to his own maxim, to speak softly and carry (very visibly) a big stick. In his next message to Congress he spoke more than softly and the music of his words must have delighted not only Japanese ears but Japanese hearts: " During the last fifty years the country (Japan) has been a marvel to mankind, and she now stands as one of the greatest civilized nations; great in the arts of war and in the arts of peace; great in military, in industrial, in artistic achievement. Japanese soldiers and sailors have shown themselves equal in combat to any of whom history makes note."

But in the same message he once more insisted on the necessity for America to possess a powerful army and navy, well trained and ever ready, whatever be the chances: " As yet there is no likelihood of establishing any international power of whatever sort which can effectively check wrong-doing, and in these circumstances it would be both foolish and an evil thing for a great and free nation to deprive itself of the power to protect its own rights, and even, in exceptional cases, to stand up for the rights of others. . . . A just war is in the long run far better for a nation's soul than the most prosperous peace by acquiescence in wrong and injustice. . . . It must always be remembered that even to be defeated in war may be far better than not to have fought at all."

[1] Conversation of November 3, 1906.

CHAPTER XII

MOROCCO
1903–1906

FOR ages we had had special interests in Morocco and Northern Africa, so much so that, by Article VIII of our treaty of 1778 with the new-born United States, we had promised to use our influence " with the King or Emperor of Morocco or Fez " and the neighbouring regencies, to prevent their worrying American citizens, trade and shipping.

Since the overturning by us of the pirates' nest at Algiers in 1830, our interests in Morocco had considerably increased, political, financial and military—military, for rebel tribes used Morocco as a base and renewed therefrom their attacks on pacified Algeria. Our chief concern, however, was, as at Tunis formerly, that no European country, especially no inimical one, should assume there a preponderance to our detriment.

By the beginning of the present century we accordingly made arrangements with several Governments whose special interests elsewhere we were willing to recognize, provided they recognized ours in Morocco: England and her interests in Egypt (April 8, 1904); Italy and hers in Tripoli (December 1900 and November 1902); Spain, who was like ourselves a neighbour, hers in Morocco itself (October 3, 1904). Germany was kept informed. When this was denied later, our Foreign Minister Delcassé reminded M. Bihourd, French Ambassador at Berlin, that: " On the 7th of April, 1904, seventeen days before the signature, I made known to Prince Radolin,[1] which

[1] German Ambassador in France.

310

was more than had been done for several other Powers, the chief clauses of the Anglo-French agreement concerning Morocco, namely: French assistance to the Sultan, especially for the establishing of security, respect of commercial liberty, recognition of the situation and the interests of Spain." " As to the Franco-Spanish agreement that stipulates Spain's adhesion to the Anglo-French one, I made its text known to the German Government," said the Minister, " before it became public." None of these communications " resulted in any protest or request for explanations from Germany." [1]

Bülow declared in fact to the Reichstag (April 12, 1904) that the economic interests of his country being safeguarded, as indeed they were, the Imperial Government could not object. At a later date the Secretary of State Richthofen spoke in the same manner to Bihourd, assuring him that " the German interests in Moroccan affairs were exclusively economic." [2]

---

[1] April 7, 1905, *Livre Jaune, Maroc*, 1901–5, p. 206, concerning those agreements, the editor of Henry White's papers says: " If Jusserand knew of the secret clauses in the Franco-Spanish and Anglo-French treaties, he took good care not to hint anything of the fact to Roosevelt."—Henry White, *Thirty Years of American Diplomacy*, p. 278.

I did not know of any secret clauses and the only text I had was the one published in the Yellow Book of 1904. I doubt, however, that a knowledge of these articles which simply made more explicit, arrangements the general trend of which was public, would have appreciably altered the dispositions of the President. He was in favour of our having, to the largest extent, our way in Morocco, and our ultimate aim was no secret. It was fully explained in a circular of M. Delcassé to the French Ambassadors, printed in 1904, and in which he said: " Morocco being placed under our influence, our empire in Northern Africa is fortified; placed under a foreign influence, it is for the same empire a permanent threat and paralysis."—*Accords entre la France et l'Angleterre, Livre Jaune*, 1904, p. 15. That Spain, having like ourselves possessions in Northern Africa (though much less important), was entitled to certain privileges and the exercise of an influence which, we felt confident, would not be inimical, could not but be recognized by us, and the fact was notified to the foreign powers in a paper stating that an agreement had been reached by France and Spain " as to the extent of the rights and the guarantee of the interests," resulting for both from their possessions on these coasts. October 6, 1904, *Livre Jaune, Maroc*, 1901–5, p. 164.

[2] To Delcassé. Oct. 14, 1904. Same *Livre Jaune*, p. 167.

As Russian defeats succeeded each other and grave symptoms revealed that all was not well in the Tsarist empire, the tone of Germany altered; it seemed to her leaders that the occasion was becoming favourable for the resumption of the sometimes latent, but never abandoned, dream of hegemony; the Triple Entente which balanced the Triple Alliance must be disrupted so that the latter should have no rival. Advances to weakened Russia would have, it was thought, a better chance than before to be well received (and the result was the still-born Bjoerkoe treaty of July 24, 1905, considered by William II as such a triumph that he detected the finger of God in it: " It's God that has willed it "); England—a harder task—should be brought round or brought down, either by direct efforts or with the help of the United States. As for France, who persisted in standing aloof, she should be bullied, humiliated, exhibited to the world in her weakness, and if she did not prove submissive enough, war could be resorted to. As good the occasion offered by Morocco as any other, as good as the assassination of an Austrian Grand Duke was to be, in 1914. What Bülow had considered satisfactory was no longer satisfactory. In the shade in which he chose to live, inconspicuous but influential, Baron von Holstein, the man behind the scenes, formidable even to Bülow, was, as has since become known, for war.

The Kaiser, very apprehensive of the venture, owing to its doubtful results, the difficult landing, the narrow streets, " an Englishman having been almost assassinated yesterday," [1] and (quite excusably given his infirmity) his having to ride an unknown horse, was constrained by his Chancellor to visit Tangier, where he spent some two hours on March 31, 1905, did not even look at the banquet prepared by the Moors for him, but led an uncle of the Sultan to understand that he, the Kaiser, would play at

[1] To Bülow from Lisbon, March 28, 1905; Muret, *Correspondance Secrète*, p. 109.

need, to the benefit of that independent Sovereign, the part of an all-powerful protector.

The effect was not all that Bülow had expected; in America the majority of the papers were unfavourably impressed; they pointed out what there was unchivalrous in the attitude of the Kaiser, who had awaited the discomfiture of Russia to become arrogant, and who, not very wisely, was stirring up the feelings of a proud nation, " the richest in military glories known to the world since the days of Rome "; the conclusion was that Americans could, on this occasion, only sympathize with the French.[1]

King Edward VII refused to be either staggered or coaxed. " The Tangier incident," he wrote to Lord Lansdowne, " was the most mischievous and uncalled-for event which the German Emperor has ever been engaged in since he came to the throne. It was also a political theatrical fiasco, and if he thinks he has done himself good in the eyes of the world he is very much mistaken." [2]

The idea that France should be humiliated was not, however, given up; Russia was helpless; under M. Combes as Prime Minister, General André Minister of War, Pelletan Minister of the Navy, our country was torn by political parties and passions; the bulk of the army, in spite of the repulsive régime of the *fiches* (secret partisan notes on the officers' opinions), and the aftermath of the Dreyfus affair, continued, to be sure, efficient, and American experts seeing it at work were positive in their opinion as to that and sincere in their praise;[3] but armaments, military railroads, and all which goes to make mobilization possible in case of an attack

[1] To M. Delcassé, April 3, 1905.

[2] April 15, 1905. Sidney Lee, *King Edward VII*, II, 340.

[3] Through a misprint or a copyist's error, in the document quoted in *Roosevelt and His Time* by Bishop, I, 480, mention is made of the opinion of *French* experts, which would not have been a very telling argument. The words of Mr. Roosevelt to me were: " The opinion of our experts on your army is not invoked by me simply for the needs of the cause; it is really what they think of it; a German victory is not at all certain." To my Government, June 25, 1905.

had long been neglected.   In the hope that a clash could be avoided, Delcassé, on the demand of Germany, resigned a post which he had filled for seven years to our satisfaction, if not to that of the Kaiser, who reproached him with being " awfully clever and terribly strong." [1] Rouvier, capable of greater, though not limitless, pliancy, replaced him June 6, 1905.

Our opponents thereupon bethought themselves of a conference which, in spite of any enticing assurances, and even engagements, they might favour us with (they took explicit ones on July 8, 1905),[2] would, they hoped, deny us any special position in Morocco as neighbours or otherwise : a neighbourhood consisting in 1,200 kilometres of common frontier.

Bülow was strongly in favour of such a conference, which would have proclaimed to the world that Germany's will was supreme : let the world take note.   With great assurance, but in this case his " prophetic soul " was at fault, he wrote to his master : " In case a conference meets, we are sure of America's help; England will be afraid to oppose America too openly; Austria will be unwilling to fall out with us about Morocco; Italy, I think, will surely act likewise, having a Fortis Cabinet which favours the Triple Alliance."

He added these characteristic, not to say memorable words : " If France refused to take part in the conference, she would place herself in the wrong before the other Powers.   To be right or wrong has, it is true, no importance in the relations between nations, except if the one who breaks loose from right is not powerful enough to rid herself of all scruple.   The France of to-day is not in this case." [3]   To break loose from right is, in other words, a privilege reserved to the strong.

On April 6 I cabled to M. Delcassé that the German

---

[1] To Bülow, Dec. 26, 1904.   *Correspondance Secrète*, p. 87.

[2] *Livre Jaune, Maroc*, 1901–5, p. 251.

[3] To the Kaiser, April 4, 1905.   *Correspondance Secrète*, p. 119.

Ambassador had handed Mr. Taft, Acting Secretary of
State in the absence of Mr. Hay, who was ill, and of Mr.
Roosevelt, who was after the wolves and bears of Colorado,
a memorandum asserting that " his country was as much
for the open door in Morocco as in the Far East,"
and was acting in the interest, " not only of herself but of
all the nations of the world." I had said to Mr. Taft
that we were not disturbed by this statement, for we were
ourselves in favour of such an equality and that it entered
into all our agreements with other Powers: " It was less
the statement itself than the spirit which had inspired it
that deserved attention." We hoped that the United
States, to whom we had rendered some services in Morocco
(of late in the Perdicaris affair), would abstain from what
might increase our difficulties there. " To be sure," Mr.
Taft had answered.

On the request of my Government, asking whether
mention was made in the same memorandum of a conference, I called again on Mr. Taft, who said he did not
remember, but ordered the text to be brought to him
and found that an allusion was made to a conference
which the Sultan might be pleased to convene. There
were added recriminations against us and an intimation
that the Germans were impelled to act as much " by a
sentiment of their dignity " as by the interests of their
commerce. Mr. Taft had answered nothing, but did
not think the States would accept a conference if we did
not.[1]

By dignity all understood what was meant, namely
hegemony. " We," the Kaiser had said in a speech at
Bremen, " are the salt of the earth. . . . God has made
us to civilize the world."—" Rarely has Your Majesty
spoken with more force and profoundness," Bülow had
written him.[2] The French, Italians, English, Spanish,
had taken the liberty of settling between themselves their

---

[1] To my Government, April 14, 1905.
[2] March 27, 1905. *Correspondance Secrète*, p. 101.

own interests. They should not; the Imperial will must be supreme, and those nations were accordingly berated for having ventured so far; they pleaded that they had kept Germany informed: but, the answer was, this had been verbally; it should have been in writing. "At Rome," M. Delcassé cabled me, "the German Government began by casting doubt on the value of the agreements (with us), alleging that the Italians had not formally notified them. The answer was that this notification, an oral one it is true, had been made by Mr. Prinetti and that Berlin had not objected. You will notice that it is exactly the same kind of quarrel as with us on account of the Anglo-French agreement." The treaty of the Triple Alliance forbade Italy, it was also alleged, from taking such liberties. Italy answered that it did not.[1] Remonstrances as severe were made in Madrid.

As I saw Secretary Hay a little later during the few days he spent in Washington on his return from abroad, before leaving the capital for the last time, he told me that he could "give me a still more striking proof of Emperor William's inconceivable state of mind. This sovereign, he said, has just tried to persuade the Americans that their honour and their interests are at stake, as well as his, in the Moroccan business and that the United States should be ready to join him against France in case of a resort to arms.

"This is so astounding, and such suggestions are so preposterous, that their importance is thereby diminished; it cannot be serious, it must be morbid."[2]

On his return from his western hunt, President Roosevelt was plied with letters, notes and visits from the German Ambassador, Speck von Sternburg, who, the Kaiser thought, could "manœuvre" the President at will. Asked, however, about a conference, Mr. Roosevelt answered that "if this idea had been agreeable to France, the United States could have accepted it; but such not

[1] June 21, 1905.　　　　　[2] Cable of June 22, 1905.

being the case, their adhesion was out of the question, being as they were, resolved to give us no trouble in Morocco." [1]

I cabled again on June 14th: " The German Emperor has forwarded to President Roosevelt a note in which he states that France has offered him a zone of influence in Morocco, but that he cannot accept. He insists on a conference, saying that he does not want to defend the interests of Germany alone, but of all the other Powers. He adds that a refusal might cause war.

" He speaks also of a pretended ultimatum which we are supposed to have served on the Sultan and of one he is ready to send us in case the former is acted upon.

" He, moreover, again expresses the thought that the British are even more aroused than we ourselves, and incite us to resist, having no apprehension as to a war in which they would have to play but an insignificant part on land, and would secure (on their own element) easy gains. . . .

" The Emperor's paper deals also with somewhat incoherent hypotheses, such as the danger which would result from a possible alliance between England, France, Russia and Japan.

" William II asks Mr. Roosevelt to intervene in order that England may agree to a conference, which would imply France's assent.

" The President, who, in the course of a long and friendly talk, gave me this information, said that he would not approach the British at all, a move which would be somewhat inamicable to France, a sort of attempt to separate them from us and to diminish us.

" He thought it more loyal and agreeing better with his sentiments toward us to give me these data, which seem to him surprising and difficult to interpret. There is, he thinks, but one chance out of three that William II has really the intentions he says; but there is some chance

[1] Cable of June 6, 1905.

that his threats are serious, and the stake is of such importance that one cannot act with too much prudence.

"There are in the problem," I continued in my telegram, "so many unknown elements that it is difficult to reach a decision. And first of all is it true that a zone of influence which would give us the Germans for neighbours on another point of the globe has been really proposed by us, or is it a vain dream like the ultimatum? . . .

"Struck by the strangeness and incoherence of the hypotheses considered, but also by the gravity of possible consequences, Mr. Roosevelt wonders whether a conference would not be a lesser evil for us than a German zone of influence, supposing such an offer to have been really made. Nothing very important can result, he thinks, from a conference."

In its answer my Government enabled me to state that the offer of a Moroccan zone to Germany was as imaginary as our supposed ultimatum to the Sultan. If, in order to have peace, we found it necessary to make some propitiatory offer to the Germans, it would be in a part of Africa where we had them already as neighbours: we did so later.

President Roosevelt considered this idea wisdom itself; "even if such concessions were of importance, it would be an advantage to make them if by this means the present cloud could be dispelled." In the course of another conversation he said: "Quixotism is forbidden to a chief of State, and I cannot any more than the others indulge in it. Sentiment has, however, a certain legitimate part to play. I hope it would pain you if a catastrophe befell the United States. Well, it would be the same with me if a misfortune happened to France." [1]

He thought the matter over, and at our next meeting he suggested conciliation: "You know," he said, "if I am for submitting to humiliation in the presence of threats. There are, however, many concessions which

[1] Cable of June 16, 1905.

can be honourably made to avoid a conflict; as for me, in the present case, I would not hesitate. Some satisfaction must be granted to the limitless vanity of William II and it would be wise to help him save his face if a war can thereby be avoided."

As symptoms grew worse he was confirmed in his views, and as one of our reasons for refusing was the insistence of the Kaiser for the conference to meet without a programme, which meant that he intended to consider our arrangements with various Powers as valueless, the President " took from his table a bit of paper and tried to find some formula, acceptable for the two countries and saving both William II's pride and our rights." He wrote: " The two Governments consent to go to the conference with no programme and to discuss there all questions in regard to Morocco, save, of course, where either is in honour bound by a previous agreement to another Power."

" I do not pretend," he said, " that this is a perfect formula and an immutable text, but it may supply some ground for an understanding."

" Availing himself," I cabled, " of the system, established on the initiative of William II, of communicating through the German Ambassador, Mr. Roosevelt dictated a letter to the Emperor stating that he had heard of France being disposed to accept a conference, provided, it is true, that there be a programme drawn up beforehand, but this is a rule usual in such cases. The Ambassador is requested to warmly congratulate the Emperor for this success of his diplomacy, a success which the President would not have believed possible, and he earnestly recommends him as a friend, not to risk adventures of a necessarily doubtful issue, and the loss of authority and prestige which a war disapproved by the whole world would unavoidably cause him."

" I do not imagine," the President also remarked, " that I am using an infallible means of success, far from it, but I see no other, and it is not impossible that I should succeed if I act in time. But let not people in France take it amiss if I am found particularly flattering toward the Emperor." [1]

I offered shortly after to the President the thanks of my Government, which considered it could now (though regretfully) accept the idea of a conference. He interrupted me, saying: "What I have done was too natural to deserve any thanks." I replied: "The telegram I received expressed much gratitude, but no surprise." "This is," he replied, "the compliment that really pleases me."

As for the possibility of our going further and allowing in any way our agreements with other Powers to be put in jeopardy, I cabled to my Government what I thought: "It is, I consider, in the interest of all the countries thus ill-treated, to reject in courteous but decisive terms the Germanic pretensions. . . . Such resistance entails maybe some danger, but much less than humble submissiveness would. A personage of the Emperor's temper, who has awaited the defeat of Russia to come forth, would find in excessive yielding but an incitement to new exigencies. He speaks just now as a man who can drive Europe whip in hand. It is indispensable for future peace that he should understand the threatened countries will concede nothing beyond what they can honourably grant, and will not allow themselves to be terrorized. . . .

" Better than any, and without my having had need to insist, Mr. Roosevelt has understood that giving up our treaties would be one of those humiliating acts to which no free nation, and especially not France, could consent. Who would henceforth come to any agreement with us and what would be our discredit? Mr. Roosevelt considers quite justified and wise the limit drawn by you. . . . We may accept a conference, and this is, certainly, a considerable concession, but we cannot go so far as to disown

[1] June 23, 1905.

our previous engagements : as well confess that it is enough to threaten us in order to hold us at mercy.

" You may be assured that the President will support, to the best of his ability, the programme you have adopted. He will not find it amiss that the formula proposed by him be made clearer and if possible more advantageous, but he would not recognize France if, as suggested by a hostile Press, she should disavow her word because it has pleased a neighbour to raise his tone.

" Moreover, one may wonder whether Emperor William really means to go to extremes, and can remember how, after having assumed quite a threatening attitude in the Venezuela business, the very firm remonstrances of his friend, Mr. Roosevelt, caused him to adopt a different one. The risk for the Emperor would, besides, be considerable, now that he has so managed as to cause everybody to mistrust him and that he has collected for himself enmities throughout Europe. It is not at all certain that on such an occasion the chances would not be favourable to right." [1]

During an absence in France I continued to exchange telegrams with Mr. Roosevelt, in one of which he said : " For God's sake, do not have the slightest fear of ruffling my feelings. My only desire is to do what you will think wisest and safest." [2] A formula had been devised by the French Government and accepted by the Germans, on the general lines suggested by the President, but more explicit and comprehensive ; an exchange of letters took place in Paris on July 8, 1905, and the conference was definitively decided upon.

On my return from France and the President's return from Sagamore Hill, I cabled to my Government : " I found Mr. Roosevelt in the same dispositions as when I left. The attentions which the Emperor showers upon American visitors, and especially those whom he believes to have relations with the President, have not modified

---

[1] June 30, 1905. [2] Received in Paris 26th July.

Y

his way of thinking. He continues to show the Emperor the greatest courtesy but not to trust him; it would be imprudent, he thinks, to count on his most solemn assurances. While negotiating with him, he considers it important, on the other hand, not to draw all the advantages possible from his imprudences; we should not bar every outlet to him, but, on the contrary, allow him room for a dignified withdrawal. . . . The President rejoices that, owing to the peace with Japan, Russia reappears in Europe; though greatly weakened, she is still a curb to Germany's ambitions." [1]

The conference met, as is well known, at Algeciras on January 6, 1906. The chief American representative was Henry White, then Ambassador at Rome, who was instructed " to act in favour of the open door system, to see that the special interests of France be respected while the other Powers got what might be necessary for the exercise of their normal rights; he was to show no aggressiveness toward any of the interested parties, but, on the contrary, so to act as to secure an amicable and pacific settlement; lastly, in a general way, to hold himself preferably in contact with the Anglo-French entente." [2]

In other words, said Secretary Root to me, he should side, as much as circumstances allow, with the liberal nations. "You know White, and you can imagine whether he will conform with pleasure to such instructions." He did, with much tact and without wounding any susceptibilities.

He was assisted by Mr. Gummere, American Minister to Morocco, and by a secretary whom I described as " a young man of merit and a distinguished writer," Mr. Lewis Einstein. We were represented by M. Révoil and M. Regnault, both experts in North African affairs, the Germans by the aged Ambassador von Radowitz and fiery Count Tattenbach, who led the fray.

[1] October 2, 1905.   [2] To my Government, January 11, 1906.

In the difficult question of the Moroccan police, in which the President's help would have been even more efficacious if he had been better informed in time of our views, a break was again very near, with new threats of war. On March 2, 1906, I cabled: " Mr. Roosevelt has recently received the visit of a German whom the Emperor sometimes uses for communications of a more personal character than those which pass through Baron Sternburg.

" This German has expressed the Kaiser's regret that the relations between his country and the United States were not more cordial. Mr. Roosevelt answered that they were good and that he thought he had neglected nothing to make them even better. He then spoke of Morocco and expressed his disapproval of Germany's attitude in this affair when ' she has perhaps fourteen times less interests in that country than France.'

" ' We do not admit,' the President's visitor replied, ' that anyone except ourselves be the judge of our interests.'—' Then,' Mr. Roosevelt replied, ' I do not understand this insistence upon having a conference. Why take the opinion of others if only your own counts for you ? '

" The conversation then dealt with the consequences of a possible break. The German asserted that his compatriots were in a better military and moral situation than they had ever been. According to them, not only were they sure of victory on land, but they believed they would be able to beat the English at sea. ' We are certain,' he said, ' that their fleet has lost as much value as their army has shown decrepitude in the Boer war. Our success at sea cannot be doubted; we shall land fifty thousand men in England, and this will be enough for us to have that country at our mercy. The Emperor, Count von Bülow and Admiral Tirpitz are, all three, convinced thereof.'

" Mr. Roosevelt believes that there is in this much bragging; that against an enemy like the Boers other troops than the English would have cut a less brilliant

figure than in a European war; and that it is unlikely
that the naval aptitude of the English, which has ever
existed in the race, has lowered as much as the Germans
fancy. He is, however, struck by the concurrence in these
views of Admiral Tirpitz, whom he considers as a sailor
of the greatest value, and he does not believe, on the
other hand, that his visitor attributed to him an imaginary
opinion." [1]

My Italian colleague, Mayor des Planches, on the other
hand, had repeatedly assured me at the same time, " that,
with the new treaties, in case of war, if France was not the
attacking Power, Italy would not take part in the
struggle." [2]

An Austrian proposal, which was a German one in
disguise, concerning the police, was recommended by the
Kaiser, who stated inaccurately that it had received the
assent of the Russians, Spaniards, Italians, and even
English. Asked to make us yield, Mr. Roosevelt caused
an official answer to be sent, beginning: " We do not
consider the Austrian proposal to be acceptable." He
reminded the Kaiser of his having promised him, in case
the conference met and there were difficulties, to abide
by his judgment, and he offered him his choice: a possibility that the correspondence exchanged be published,
or compliments to him and his people for their success
such as it was. The Kaiser chose the latter. The
President acted accordingly and was not stingy in his
praise. The Kaiser also acted accordingly, and the
conference having peaceably ended its labours on April 7,
1906, he wired to his chief delegate: " Bravo! well
done!" [3] He thanked Austria, though her proposal
had utterly failed; Bülow had been made a Prince in
June 1905.

We had no reason to regret having acted in accordance
with the President's advice, since the conference safe-

[1] March 2, 1906.   [2] March 3, 1906.
[3] Navins, *Henry White*, p. 279.

guarded our special interests, causing them to be even more secure, owing to the solemn assent of all the Powers concerned. The part played by America, disinterested, claiming no advantage or compensation in this important intervention in European affairs, had been decisive.

Some days later I received a letter which filled me with pride and astonishment, so unexpected it was. I kept it to myself, but as it has, of late years, been made public, and since I am writing about " what me befell," I may perhaps be excused if I reproduce it, as nothing befell me which touched me more.

" From the White House, April 25, 1906," President Roosevelt wrote:

" MY DEAR AMBASSADOR,
    " During the past year our relations have been those of peculiar intimacy in dealing with more than one great problem, and particularly in connection with the Morocco conference, and there are certain things which I think I ought to say to you.
    " It is the simple and literal truth to say that in my judgment we owe it to you more than to any other one man that the year which has closed has not seen a war between France and Germany, which, had it begun, would probably have extended to take in a considerable portion of the world. In last May and June the relations between the two countries were so strained that such a war was imminent. Probably the only way it could have been avoided was by an international conference, and such a conference could only have been held on terms compatible with France's honour and dignity. You were the man most instrumental in having just this kind of conference arranged for. I came into the matter most unwillingly, and I could not have come into it at all if I had not possessed entire confidence alike in your unfailing soundness of judgment and in your high integrity of personal conduct. Thanks to the fact that these are the two dominant notes in your personality, my relationship with you has been such as I think has very, very rarely obtained between any Ambassador at any time

and the head of the Government to which that Ambassador was accredited; and certainly no Ambassador and no head of a Government could ever stand to one another on a footing at once more pleasant and more advantageous to their respective countries than has been the case with you and me. If, in these delicate Morocco negotiations, I had not been able to treat you with the absolute frankness and confidence that I did, no good result could possibly have been obtained, and this frankness and confidence were rendered possible only because of the certainty that you would do and advise what was wisest to be done and advised, and that you would treat all that was said and done between us two as a gentleman of the highest honour treats what is said and done in the intimate personal relations of life. If you had been capable of adopting one line of conduct as a private individual and another as a public man I should have been wholly unable to assume any such relations with you; nor, on the other hand, however high your standard of honour, could I have assumed them had I not felt complete confidence in the soundness and quickness of your judgment. The service you rendered was primarily one to France, but it was also a service to the world at large; and in rendering it you bore yourself as the ideal public servant should bear himself; for such a public servant should with trained intelligence know how to render the most effective service to his own country while yet never deviating by so much as a hand's breadth from the code of mutual good faith and scrupulous regard for the rights of others which should obtain between nations no less than between gentlemen. I do not suppose that you will ever gain any personal advantage, and perhaps not even any personal recognition, because of what you have done in the past year, but I desire that you should at least know my appreciation of it.

" With hearty respect and good-will, believe me,
" Very faithfully yours,
" THEODORE ROOSEVELT.

" M. J. J. Jusserand,
The French Ambassador,
Washington, D.C."

I answered the next day, trying to tell the President

of my gratitude: " Only such a heart as yours could dictate such a letter; my life's work, I mean any good that may have been in it, is more than recompensed by the sentiments you expressed."

Some latter-day historians have professed, concerning these events, opinions widely different from those prevalent at the time, going so far as to imply that such success as was reached through the action of President Roosevelt was baneful, not fruitful. It prevented the realization of the Kaiser's dream, and since that dream *had* to be realized, to oppose it was to court war, to become responsible in a way for the Great War. More than ever from that moment the Germans who know what force there is in an oft-repeated word—an oft-repeated word becomes axiomatic—complained of the " encircling " inflicted on them, as if it were possible to have encircled a nation which had access, by her own means, to the Baltic, the North Sea and beyond; through her Allies, to the Adriatic and the Mediterranean; through her influence in Turkey, to Asia Minor and the Persian Gulf; the owner besides, in spite of her having been, by her own choice, a late comer in the colonial field, of important possessions in South-east and South-west Africa, the Pacific and the South Seas.

As for the Kaiser's dream, the opposition of so many countries at Algeciras caused him, it is true, to feel that it could not be fulfilled except by war, a real war, not mere threats as those he had just resorted to. Once more, before the catastrophe of 1914, an attempt was made to bring France into submission, when the *Panther* was sent, in July 1911, to Agadir on the west coast of Morocco with the threat of a seizure of territory. In spite, however, of the British being as much opposed as we ourselves to such a prospect, and of American opinion being in our favour, unwilling to assume the immense risk, we signed in November 1911 an agreement by which Germany expressly recognized our protectorate over Morocco, and received more than 100,000 square miles of our Congo territory, an agreement which many in France considered a humiliating sacrifice, and many in Germany an inadequate one: for the dream remained still but a dream.

And, what was that dream? The Kaiser saw vanishing, writes a recent American authority, speaking of the Algeciras conference, " his dream of a majestic alliance among Germany, Russia, France, Austria and Italy with himself as a new and holier emperor, who would preserve the peace of the world "; [1] a dream in which he was encouraged by such pacifists as Andrew Carnegie, who wanted all armies to be abolished, except a single one under command of the Kaiser, a dream in other words of complete hegemony [2] to the advantage of that country alone which, in its own estimation, was the " salt of the earth." But this was to forget that the time had passed when, as Tacitus said, subject nations would call civilization (*humanitas*), what was servitude.

[1] Pringle, *Theodore Roosevelt*, p. 390.
[2] Writing from Munich to his Government at the time of the Agadir incident, Sir Vincent Corbett said: " Should this (a war) unhappily be the case, domestic differences will be forgotten and the German nation will march as one man to make a final bid for the hegemony of the world." August 20, 1911. *British Documents on the Origins of the War*, VII, 459.

CHAPTER XIII

WALKS WITH ROOSEVELT

AFTER a while, President Roosevelt gave me that unique proof of trust and friendship: he asked me to a " walk." He had once invited the British Ambassador, but the experiment had not proved a success. An excellent rider, polo player, cricket player, a soldier of merit, Sir Mortimer Durand was unprepared for what the President called a walk, a treat which, with his usual sincerity and lack of conceit, he described thus in his journal:

" Since I wrote I have, to my sorrow, seen something more of the President. He invited me to lunch, was very pleasant, and asked me to come back later for a walk. We drove out to Rock Creek, a wooded valley with a stream running through it, and he then plunged down the *Khud* and made me struggle through bushes and over rocks for two hours and a half, at an impossible speed, till I was so done that I could hardly stand. His great delight is rock climbing, which is my weak point. I disgraced myself completely, and my arms and shoulders are still stiff with dragging myself up by roots and ledges. At one place I fairly stuck and could not get over the top till he caught me by the collar and hauled at me. He is certainly a ' strenuous ' man all through. He was dripping with sweat, his clothes frayed by the rocks and bushes and covered with dirt, but he was as happy as a school-boy. We talked chiefly about war and shooting. He greatly admires the Japanese and wants them to win, but not in too crushing a manner. He did almost all the talking, to my great relief, for I had no breath to spare."[1]

[1] May, 1904. *Sir Mortimer Durand: a Biography*, by General Sir Percy Sykes, 1926, p. 275.

The walks were usually in winter, late in the day, when the light was failing and some strenuous rest was held appropriate before the evening meal; mists, rain or snow often added to the President's pleasure, snow sometimes so thick that we had to shake it off our hats to diminish their weight. There were, however, some walks in summer.

My first experience was nearly as bad as that of Sir Mortimer; not knowing the rules of the game, which were never to go around an obstacle, I went around several, unaware that one should walk straight into a river, or a mud-hole and avoid with a feeling of horror paths and bridges. The President was already enough of a friend to condone such a grievous error, and he rarely gave me a better proof of his good-will. But the moment I knew, I stuck to the rule, greatly helped by my youthful climbings in the Forez mountains. "The French Ambassador," the President would say, " is obviously not always pleased with what offers, but he does it."

What offered was of great variety, and we never knew in advance what would be the trouble: mud, rocks, water, brambles or thorns. The President knew apparently every inch of the ground around Washington and could lead us to spots quite near the city which looked as wild as the untrodden parts of Colorado. He was on the look-out for obstacles, and never proposed one that he had not tried, excluding some which he considered fit for himself only, as when he climbed (but he was not yet President) one of the steel trestles supporting the high bridge across Rock Creek valley and slid down the opposite trestle; or when he tried to cross the same creek, using for the purpose, squirrel-like, the branches of two trees that joined over the river. But he weighed two hundred pounds more than an ordinary squirrel, and while he was making the attempt he heard Senator Lodge, who had accompanied him, shouting: " Theodore! Theodore! if you knew how ridiculous you look on the top of that tree, you would come down at once."

The small troop of personal friends honoured with invitations for a walk included, besides any particularly welcome chance visitors, Garfield, Secretary of the Interior, Chief Forester Pinchot, Beekman Winthrop, shortly before Governor of Porto-Rico, Postmaster-General George Von Lengerke Meyer, Assistant Secretary of the Navy Newberry, short and plump, whom we planned to make look "like a wasp," but failed; Mr. Douglas Robinson, who, being a brother-in-law, took liberties, pleading, when so inclined, that " he was not a mountain goat "; Lawrence Murray of the Immigration Service, and with a few more, our shining star, Robert Bacon, Assistant Secretary of State, tall, handsome, who loved his chief with an almost womanly tenderness and would have gone to the stake to spare him even a trifling trouble. Absolutely fearless, he was afflicted—or should not one rather say adorned?—with maidenish sensibility.

Being on a steamer in the Charles River, Boston, he saw a man struggling in the water, and in danger of drowning. Without a moment's hesitation, he jumped overboard all dressed and helped the man to safety. I said to the President: " One of our little group has done something fine; don't you think we should commemorate it by offering him a silver cup? " He highly approved. I was commissioned to buy the cup and have an appropriate inscription engraved, recalling the date of the deed, October 21, 1907; the President asked us all with our wives to lunch at the White House, the Bacons alone being ignorant of the motive. At dessert time our host rose, holding the cup behind his back, revealed the occasion of our meeting and presented the cup. Bacon was so surprised and so moved that he had great difficulty in simply saying: " I thank you," and it was very touching to see so much emotion, caused by gratitude, in a man who had not felt any when it was merely a question of risking his life.

When we, the others, were in the street, after that

lunch, we said: " Now let us look for the next runaway horse, and we distinguish ourselves," but no horse would run away. Shortly after, a fire was announced early one morning in the very house of the Bacons. As if we had passed the word to one another, we were there at once, several of us, in the hope of helping to save Bacon or his wife, or his pretty daughter, but they happened to be already all safe in the street, and Bacon's cup remained a solitary testimonial among us.

The invitations for a walk usually came with the recommendation: " Put on your worst clothes," so often repeated that I had to answer after a while: " But, Mr. President, I have no worst clothes left." Such garments were, on our return, thrown into a bath tub, for the mud to soak, but so much soaking injured them by degrees beyond use. Another notice given by the President was that, should his invitation be declined, he would accept any excuse—except pressure of work. Postmaster-General Meyer having been bold enough once to use work as a pretext for not coming, received from the President and ourselves an indignant letter accompanied by insulting sketches of our composition, and an assurance that the day was not near when he would receive a silver cup like Bacon. He retorted by a cartoon drawn by the clever pencil of Berryman, and showing him at work for the good of the State with a lump of ice on his head, while we were " culling the last rose of summer "—the very last, for our jaunt was of December 3, 1907.

What the President called a walk was a run: no stop, no breathing time, no slacking of speed, but a continuous race, careless of mud, thorns and the rest. Some of the obstacles in Rock Creek Park were so peculiar that we had given them names. There was the chimney: two vertical rocks, very close to one another, and between which one must ascend by an undulating and serpent-like movement. There was the seals' walk, a stone ledge overhanging the river, and which was to be passed stretched on one's stomach and moving along as seals do. Once or twice, as we had begun our "walk" before dark, people on the other side of the river, excusably curious to watch what the chief of the State and his friends were doing, alighted from their carriages and followed us from a distance. The President walked toward them, raised his hat, and politely bowing, asked them to kindly desist, which they all did.

The Rock Creek walk usually ended at the cliff over-hanging the river, near the place in the Zoo where foxes are quartered, or were in my day. When we reached it, darkness·had set in and we climbed in close succession one behind the other, the only feat, thought the President, entailing some little danger, because if one had slipped he would have sent down all those behind him. A walk with no trace of danger would have seemed to the President like food without salt. Nothing, however, happened.

There was once a close call; I had been away in Michigan and I asked what had taken place in my absence. I learned that owing to constant rain and cold, Rock Creek had overflowed its banks, become a deep stream and was carrying ice. Reaching its shore the President walked straight into the water, all dressed, and swam across. "Do not regret not to have been there," said John McIlheny, who had; "to succeed in such cases you must have a good layer of fat under your skin; the cold then does not seize you suddenly. Only the President and I succeeded." Fitzhugh Lee, aide to the President, a brilliant officer and great sport, got a cramp and was with much difficulty helped out.

The cliff we used to climb has been used since as a quarry and its aspect has greatly changed; this was much regretted by Mr. Bryce, who would have liked it to be preserved untouched as a memorial, for future times, of the sportive dispositions of a President long ago.

We were sometimes led to the Potomac islands, now beautiful gardens, full of flowers, but then mud shoals, with thick cane-brakes so high that we had to follow in close formation not to lose the track of our leader, and with unexpected watery holes into which one stumbled knee-deep, by which I really mean up to the knees. We knew that to frown at anything was mere folly, we would be asked to take the obstacle all the same and be viewed with scorn as a punishment. We were once led at dusk, by a drenching rain, to the Potomac. How the President could, so near the White House, discover such muddy ways was a mystery, but he did; we had not walked ten minutes before we were splashing each other with a mud of rarest blackness. Along the bank we came upon a dredge from which emerged an iron drain-pipe reaching a near-by island. The President suggested that we might walk on it and thus reach the island. The pipe was narrow, made slippery by the rain, the turbid waters of the Potomac were uninviting. We never winced, and said: "Let us." We had our recompense; our leader relented, and seeing in the distance a man in a boat, signed to him. The boat was as muddy and leaky as one could wish; we stood in it with our feet in water and were rowed to the island. The President struck an attitude and passing his arm round my neck, said: "Washington and Rochambeau crossing the Delaware."

When we reached the opposite shore there was some embarrassment. We not only wore our "worst clothes," but were careful on such expeditions to leave at home every article of value. One of us having, on a day when there was a swim, kept his watch by mistake, expressed his dismay; the President suggested that he put it in his mouth. In the present case the difficulty was to reward the boatman for his services; none of us had a purse. A strict fumbling in our pockets resulted in the discovery of one single 25-cent piece, and that was all the poor boatman got for having ferried the President, several officers of State and the French Ambassador. Night had come, rain continued, and, running all the time, we had our

fill of tall canes and mud-holes. Reaching the White
House a game of " medicine balls " was offered us for a
rest.

On another occasion, May time, we were driven to the
" Chain Bridge " over the Potomac, crossing to the Virginia side, which is abrupt, lined all along with rocks and
cliffs, some of them worked as quarries, a quantity of
trees and underbrush having grown in the hollows and on
the crest, a beautiful sight, unusual, so near a great city.
No road, but a narrow path along the shore; narrow, but
yet a path; we turned from it with horror. Our little
troop that day included, besides the President, Assistant
Secretary of State Bacon, General Barry in command at
Cuba, two outsiders on a visit to the President and myself.

Our " walk " began with the ascent of a very steep and
slippery rock, luckily used by the quarriers as a short cut
to reach their work; they had tied a rope to a tree on the
top and used it to go up and down. We did the same to
go up, and as it had been thinned by long use, we prudently proceeded to ascend separately, one by one, the
President, as always, leading the way. Then a run, on
the top, in the midst of thorns, stones and rivulets, a
broken, uneven descent toward the Potomac. When a
fine steep cliff was found, it was taken by storm, those
coming last having to pay attention to the stones detached
by the feet of their forerunners.

We were on the shady side of the river but were soon
dripping with perspiration. Standing by the river's
brim, the President suggested that we take a swim. An
excellent notion. As we would have to continue our
" walk " on the same side of the river, there was no need
to carry our garments on our back, and we therefore
dropped them on the shore. A passer-by with a camera
might have taken a picture worth having: the chief of
the State and his friends alined, stark-naked, along the
bank. As we were about to enter the water, the President
shouted: " Eh, Mr. Ambassador, have you not forgotten

your gloves?" I still had them on. We were only too glad when we found thorns in the crevices to use them as a help for climbing, and as my hands had been scratched and bleeding I had put on gloves and forgotten them. I shouted back: "We might meet ladies."

After the swim, having, of course, no towels to dry our dripping bodies, we slipped on our garments, still wet with cooled perspiration, and introduced into our socks feet covered with a layer of greasy mud.

Then some more climbs, indispensable to escape being chilled, the last one too difficult for all of us except the President and Bacon. It was interesting to see Mr. Roosevelt slowly ascending, trying every little protuberance in the cliff, showing the clever patience and composure of a bear. This should not be allowed, one of the visitor friends said, adding that simply to look at the risky performance made him dizzy. But nothing happened. The President reached the top safely, Bacon too, but with the mishap that one leg of his trousers was slit from top to bottom.

In the cool breeze of the evening, dripping with sweat, we were driven back in our open carriages and should have got pneumonia, but did not.

We dined that evening, my wife and I, with the Lodges; the Senator knew of the intended walk and asked me about it. I gave a faithful description, omitting, however, the swim, which I considered confidential. But the President told him afterwards, with roars of laughter, and the Senator teased me for my unwarranted secretiveness.

This was one of our rare walks in summer weather. When it was fine, or sometimes when it was not, and even when it was snowing and difficult to descry the ball among the flakes, we played tennis on the White House court, now built over by the new offices. The President had only a door to open and he was on the court. Intimate friends were asked; on rare occasions a passing visitor. The nucleus of the " Tennis Cabinet," as we were called, included at its dispersion, when Mr. Roosevelt's Presidency came to an end: Robert Bacon, James R. Garfield, George Von Lengerke Meyer, Lawrence O. Murray, William Phillips, Gifford Pinchot, Herbert Knox Smith, Beekman Winthrop.

The President and I played about even, and were for that cause always put in opposite camps. We also played singles. I find in my notes: " October 30, 1908.— Everybody has gone to make speeches for Taft. The President has sent all his Ministers, including Bacon, to help in the campaigning. We remain alone and play singles, which we had not done for a long while. Fate favours me. The President wins first 7 to 5, then I win 6 to 2 and 6 to 4.

" November 2nd.—Eve of the Presidential election. Same solitude. We play singles, with results the reverse of last time; the President wins two sets, and I one; we are quits.

" November 5th.—Tennis again, this time with Bacon and Winthrop. The President's joy at the result of the election is overflowing. He must, it is true, withdraw, from a sense of duty, and it is not a pleasant duty, but his party carries the day; Taft has a considerable majority, at which he rejoices."

A little later we played again, the President then with Garfield, and I with Pinchot. Garfield having hurt his leg, we had a walk over. The winners stood at attention, with their racquets and I shouted in French, addressing the President: " Honneur au courage malheureux! " He instantly retorted, also in French: " A la lanterne! "[1] The President knew French and could remarkably appreciate the value of each word. He would never use a weak one when he felt that there was sure to

---

[1] " Honour to unlucky valour."—" To the lantern " was, as is well known, the shout of the mob during the French Revolution for the hanging of aristocrats from the lamp-posts.

z

be a better one, and he gave chase to that better one, usually succeeding in cornering it.

After tennis, tea was served either in the President's office or in the open, Mrs. Roosevelt often presiding and the wives of the players being now and then invited. When in the office, the moment he had finished his tea, the President began dictating letters, sometimes on very difficult subjects, to his secretary, Mr. Loeb. We, more or less noisily, discussed, meanwhile, the problems of the day. The President remained unperturbed, although he could not help, while dictating, overhearing what we said, and would inject some remark. When, by chance, and that was rare, he lacked that best word he was looking for, he gave us a chance to suggest one; if the word proposed was abstruse, it was rejected with indignation.

When he had been away, he told us of his experiences. After a game with Bacon, Cooley and myself, October 16, 1907, as he was back from the South, he said: " I hold you three, you will not escape my story," and he gave us a lively account of his marches up and down in the cane-brakes along the bayous, of his having killed one bear, twelve squirrels, one deer, one 'possum, and one wild-cat, and having eaten them all (or of them all) except the cat. The welcome in the South, where he used not to be particularly loved, had been enthusiastic. At one place he had had to leave without being able to deliver a speech. After twenty minutes of applause and hurrahs, women and children being in danger of being hurt in the surging crowd, he silently, but gratefully smiling, left the place without a word.

No subject was barred, no restraint was imposed. The greatest compliment paid our little group by the President was that he never asked us to consider anything as confidential, nor recommended us to remain silent about it. He felt that by instinct we would, and nothing, that I know, was ever repeated which ought not to have been.

Years later I was with my wife at Evian, in Savoy, by the shores of Lake Leman, a place described by Topffer in his *Voyages en Zigzag* (1841) as a poor little village, so primitive that it was difficult to get change for a hundred franc note: there is now no longer any such difficulty. We took the boat one day, my wife to go around the lake, I to stop at Meillerie and to return on foot across-country. The place is famous; some of the principal scenes in J. J. Rousseau's *Nouvelle Héloïse* are laid there. Poets, Byron, Lamartine, have sung of Meillerie.

Times have altered, men too. Some incidents in Rousseau brought tears to the eyes of his contemporaries and would now, I am afraid, raise a laugh, as when the heroine shows herself so tender-hearted that she requests all the captured fish to be thrown back into the lake except a trout which had been wounded by a stroke of the oar and would serve for their meal: a very clumsy trout one would think. But Julie was so sensitive that she ate very little of it, and her lover saw that he would ingratiate himself with her if he showed the same moderation. The poor trout had thus at least the consolation of being but partly eaten.

Meillerie is built on a rocky promontory; back of it, steep mountains, covered, in spite of their abruptness, with trees and underbrush; on the summit, dark fir trees; further off, high snow-covered mountains.

To the left, a rocky cliff of considerable height, crowned like all the rest with a green wreath of foliage, forms in the lake a protective little harbour where numerous fishing craft are at rest. The cliff is being, and has long been, used as a quarry. The Geneva pier is built of its stone.

A steep narrow path, along which on the right runs a noisy torrent, leads to the old place and its mediæval church surmounted by a square steeple whose bells have associated themselves for ages with the joys and sorrows of the inhabitants, the graves of whom, in serried ranks, surround the building; the monument, seen on a more recent visit, is to the dead of the Great War, fifty of them, a long list for such a small village; the same names often repeated—Jacquier, nine times—betoken grievous losses in the same families.

A narrow valley at a much higher level opens behind the church, the noisy torrent rushes down the middle of it; both sides of the narrow valley, thickly covered with bright-green verdure, brambles, trees, wild plants and flowers, rise precipitous, and offer so grand a sight that it looks like those often pictured by the romantic brush of Gustave Doré. I had been told that, following a scarcely visible little path along the torrent, I would reach Tollon, and from thence could walk back to Evian, avoiding the commonplace, high-road along the lake.

I followed and followed, jumping from one wet slippery stone to another, in a complete and impressive solitude; several torrents joined mine, small cascades bounding among trees added their watery complement. After a pretty long walk, I found that the principal valley turned to the right, and following it for some while, discovered that it was closed in the distance by a perfectly vertical wall of rock, from the top of which my torrent flowed into the valley. The little path was still dimly visible among the stones, and I was thinking: "What a clever little path! What will it do when it reaches that rocky wall?" I found that it was not so very clever; at the foot of the rock it did nothing, it stopped.

Although to right and left of the bare, abrupt surface, some vegetation had grown in the crevices, the ascent looked uninviting enough. No one knew exactly where I was; the solitude was absolute; if I broke or sprained something, I would remain there helpless. The temptation, I must confess, came to me: to go back. But then a name flashed in my mind: Roosevelt. No! No going back. So I set to my task. With a good deal of trouble, and perhaps a little danger, one leg bleeding, I succeeded, reached the top and saw a real path; after stretching myself at full length on the ground for a rest, I started for Tollon, where the village fair was going on. In company with a merry group of peasants I drank a glass of beer, ate a " brioche," and with wings to my heels, taking all the short cuts I could devise, ran towards Evian, about six or seven miles off, where my delay in appearing must have caused anxiety. It had indeed; but all ended well and my wound was insignificant. I was, however, thoroughly exhausted; and said to my wife: " I shall not take another such walk until I am twenty years younger."

I have kept my word. This will have proved my last " walk."

CHAPTER XIV

UNTIL the end of his presidency, Mr. Roosevelt remained *qualis ab incepto* : same ideal, same means, for better for worse, for reaching such an ideal. That means was to give battle.

His ideal was the improvement of his country in every respect, great things and small ones. It must be powerful, respected; its opinion must count more and more; its morals must be purer; war must be waged at the same time against labourers who violate the law and "malefactors of great wealth" who are just "legally honest," and whose gamblings, watered securities, secret rebates, cause financial crises, to the prejudice of the whole community. The country must be made safer and more pleasant to live in for those who have a particularly heavy burden to carry—farm hands, miners, mothers of families.

From every point of view he wanted improvement, and whatever the occasion, he threw himself into the contest with unrestrained energy, be the question that of a reform of orthography, of the preservation of natural resources, which were thoughtlessly squandered to the detriment of those who would come after us, of pure food, of the coinage of the United States which, he desired, should rival that of the Greeks with the high relief they gave to the images on their coins. A beautiful model was devised by Saint Gaudens. The President gave me once as a specimen a twenty-dollar piece, saying: " I have never offered you any gift; please accept this. People say that such coins do not stack, but for you and

342

me it is certainly a matter of indifference that twenty-dollar pieces should not stack."

The striking of these coins was, however, a matter of great difficulty, the relief was therefore diminished and the resemblance to the Greek coins had to be abandoned.

The Pure Food law rendered great service; serious abuse and fraud had gone on increasing. To react was indispensable. The service was placed in the hands of Dr. Wiley, thoroughly competent, impervious to obloquy, enthusiastic to the verge sometimes of fanaticism. I had great respect and friendship for him and also numerous disputes with him, as when he objected to the entry of some vinegar from Bordeaux because the trade-mark on the label represented vine-leaves and grapes, while the contents were not made from wine. The answer was: " Vinegar can be made from a variety of liquids; if you order some made from wine it will be supplied to you, but the maker cannot, for each kind, change an old-established trade-mark. Note, moreover, that you yourselves call this product vinegar, which means sour wine, though in America it is never made from wine. You should forbid the use of such a misleading word."

The quarrel rose to such a pitch that it had to be referred to the President, and, according to a decision worthy of Solomon, the maker was allowed to preserve the vine-leaves of his trade-mark, but had to remove the grapes.

The questions uppermost in the President's mind and to which he constantly recurred, whatever be the occasion, were the fleet and the relations between employers and employees. He wanted a fleet strong not only on paper or in harbours, but constantly kept in readiness—ships, officers and men, and that the world should know that so it was. Hence the cruise round the world which he ordered for the sixteen battleships of the United States. The news was scarcely given out than enlistments multiplied; as many as possible were accepted, for such a chance for tuition must not be lost; each ship carried at least a hundred men more than the regular number.

Japan was of course included among the countries visited. It was of great importance that it should not be possible to attribute to timidity a " gentleman's agreement " concerning emigration to the United States. *Punch* published a cartoon representing a geisha girl caressing the hooked beak of an American eagle wearing a sailor's cap; the girl says : " It is so kind of you to have come all this way to pay me a visit." The eagle answers : " Yes, I knew you would be pleased."

The cruise was performed without a hitch. Passing near Messina after the earthquake, the ships stopped, made themselves useful and won gratitude. On their return to the United States they took part in the usual target practice as if nothing had happened.

What he expected from the ships, the President expected also from the officers : they must be fit; they should not allow their bodies to become ankylosed. He devised for them a three-day physical endurance test, leaving them the choice of thirty miles to be covered on foot, or ninety miles on horseback, also in three days. And to show that he was not requesting an impossibility he rode more than the ninety miles in one day, in the worst January weather, using chance regimental horses.

On the relations between rich and poor and the obligation for both to observe the law and avoid equally fraud and violence he was inexhaustible. " People say," he told me, " that I repeat the same things. Of course I do, and I have no choice, since I do not change my mind."

The financial crisis of 1907 and the aspirations of individuals who speculate in what they do not possess,[1] had greatly irritated him. We did, in France, all we could to help, and got less gratitude than we deserved.

[1] Special message to Congress, January 31, 1907.

For some unknown cause, part of the gold which was sorely wanted and which we sent, went by way of London. We forwarded preferably American eagles, which could be put to immediate use. The Bank of France discounted as much commercial paper with two signatures as was offered to it. The law did not allow it to do more. I was, however, permitted to propose that, being given the exceptional circumstances, the rule be set aside if the request for help came, not from private banks, but from the American Treasury. The question would have been placed on an entirely different plane. The Treasury, however, declined to interfere, and all I could say to Secretary Root was: " If you cannot ask, we cannot offer."

In all his speeches on the Labour questions the President was extremely careful to show that he had no preference for either party and cared not for any kind of threats or dangers, his desire for parallelisms carrying him sometimes very far. Toward any kind of " malefactors " he was relentless. In an address at Canton, Ohio, before a large crowd, he spoke of wealth, honestly acquired, being necessary to the country. " From the standpoint of our material prosperity there is only one thing as important as the discouragement of a feeling of envy and hostility toward honest business men, toward honest men of means; that is, the discouragement of *dis*honest business men." The latter part of this phrase was enthusiastically applauded, not the first. " Wait a moment, my friends," he said, " I don't want you to applaud this part unless you are willing to applaud also the part I read first, to which you listened in silence . . . I will read a little of it over again," which he did, the crowd laughing and applauding lustily.

His grip on audiences was remarkable; in a few sentences he awoke their interest and captured their good will. At the laying of the corner stone of the Panamerican Building, Secretary Root delivered an excellent speech, full of wisdom, but in a quiet voice, with none of those changes in tone causing the public to think: " Here comes what should be especially noted." The President spoke after him. It did not take him long to secure the eager attention of the audience. Then he said: " The Secretary of State has just said something that you will remember all your lives—all your lives." And turning to Mr. Root he asked: " Have you a text of your address? " The Secretary passed him his notes, which Mr. Roosevelt rapidly turned over, and in his stentorian voice he read a beautiful passage well worthy of remembrance and which had remained unobserved by most people, he being an exception.

This immense popularity he thoroughly enjoyed, not, however, in the same way as Lamartine, who, according to La Gorce, loved it for its own sake. " I love it," said the President, " for the power it gives."

The text of his addresses, as printed, often resembled but imperfectly his real speeches. He had typewritten notes in his hand which he followed to some extent; and then, as the occasion, or some incident, or some disposition he detected in the audience inspired him, he added long and different statements, which newspaper men, counting on the written text, did not reproduce. I have often noticed such differences.

enjoyed not however in the same way as Lamartine did, who, according to La Force, loved it for its own sake. "I love it," said the President, "for the power it gives."

The text of his addresses, as printed, often resembled but imperfectly his real speeches. He had typewritten notes in his hand which he followed to some extent, and then, as the occasion ~~desired him~~, or some incident, or some disposition ~~to~~ be detected in the audience inspired him, he added long and important statements, which newspaper men counting of the written text did not reproduce. I have often noticed such differences.

INDEX

348